Peter Whitney

The History of the County of Worcester, in the Commonwealth of Massachusetts

Peter Whitney

The History of the County of Worcester, in the Commonwealth of Massachusetts

ISBN/EAN: 9783743399655

Manufactured in Europe, USA, Canada, Australia, Japa

Cover: Foto ©ninafisch / pixelio.de

Manufactured and distributed by brebook publishing software (www.brebook.com)

Peter Whitney

The History of the County of Worcester, in the Commonwealth of Massachusetts

John Fiske.

THE HISTORY OF THE COUNTY OF WORCESTER,

IN THE COMMONWEALTH OF MASSACHUSETTS:

WITH A

Particular Account of every Town from its first Settlement to the present Time;

Including its ECCLESIASTICAL STATE,

TOGETHER WITH A

GEOGRAPHICAL DESCRIPTION OF THE SAME.

To which is prefixed,

A MAP OF THE COUNTY, AT LARGE, FROM ACTUAL SURVEY.

―――――

BY PETER WHITNEY, A. M.
Minister of the Gospel in *Northborough*, in said County.

―――――

PRINTED AT *WORCESTER*, MASSACHUSETTS,
BY ISAIAH THOMAS,
Sold by him in WORCESTER, by said THOMAS and ANDREWS, in BOSTON, and by said THOMAS and CARLISLE, in WALPOLE, Newhampshire.

MDCCXCIII.

THE HISTORY of the COUNTY of WORCESTER

IN THE COMMONWEALTH OF MASSACHUSETTS.

WITH A

Particular Account of every Town from its first Settlement to the present Time;

Including its ECCLESIASTICAL STATE,

TOGETHER WITH A

GEOGRAPHICAL DESCRIPTION OF THE SAME, &c.

To which is added

A MAP of the COUNTY, AT LARGE, from actual Survey.

BY PETER WHITNEY, A.M.

Late of [illegible]

Printed at [illegible]
at *Thomas's* [illegible]
M,DCC,LXXXXIII.

TO
JOHN ADAMS, L. L. D.

Vicepresident of the United States,

AND

President of the American Academy of Arts and Sciences, &c. &c.

THIS HISTORY,

INTENDED TO PROMOTE THE KNOWL-
EDGE OF A PART OF HIS NATIVE COM-
MONWEALTH,

IS INSCRIBED,

WITH ALL RESPECT,

BY HIS MOST OBEDIENT,

AND HUMBLE SERVANT,

PETER WHITNEY.

Northborough, July, 1793.

TO

JOHN ADAMS, LL.D.

PRESIDENT OF THE UNITED STATES,

AND

SPEAKER OF THE AMERICAN ACADEMY OF

ARTS AND SCIENCES, &c. &c.

THIS LITTLE

TRIBUTE TO PROMOTE THE NATIVE

GENIUS OF THE AMERICAN COM-

MONWEALTH,

IS INSCRIBED,

WITH ALL THE

ESTEEM OF HIS MOST CLIENT,

AND HUMBLE SERVT.

THE AUTHOR.

PREFACE.

THE Author of the following History would most willingly have been excused from the service, had any other person appeared to have undertaken it. A work of this kind was wanted: The author, however unequal to the task, had advantages herefor above some others, being born in the western part, and having the bounds of his habitation fixed in the eastern part, of the county. Had the writer of these sheets known before he began, what a labour it would have been, he would not have attempted it, but having begun, he was unwilling to desist, and has been urged on by the partiality of his friends. However difficult the collection of materials has been, yet he has derived a satisfaction by no means small, in ransacking records, searching into the antiquities of this part of the country, and in endeavouring to gratify his readers with a history thereof.

The locality of the work may be thought, by some, an objection to it. But to have compleated a history of the Commonwealth, upon this plan, would be a labour too great, and too lengthy for any one, unless he was a person of fortune, and should devote a long life wholly thereunto. If various gentlemen, in different parts of the State, would undertake to write a history of their particular counties or districts, upon this, or a better plan, we might then hope to see a complete history of Massachusetts collected, which would be not merely entertaining, but profitable and instructive from age to age; care being taken to make such alterations in, and additions to the work, as

- time

time would occasion: These would respect the civil and ecclesiastical state of the counties, their population, and their improvements in arts and manufactures.

The greatest care and pains have been taken to ascertain exact dates, where it was possible. Hence towns and churches may know their respective ages, if at any time their records should be unhappily destroyed. The dates, however, are all inserted according to the originals; and, therefore, the reader, in order to know when a century or more has elapsed from the date of any event recorded in this history, will always remember to add eleven days thereto, until he comes down to the 2d of September 1752, when New Style, so called, took place. For instance, if a town was incorporated August 1, 1728, it will not have completed a full century until August 12, 1828.

The author of this work has endeavoured to be impartial, and to do justice to every town in its description and history, and if he has failed hereof, it must be imputed to other causes than any particular local prejudices. He has not omitted any thing worth preserving, which has come to his knowledge.

Many and too great defects will, most likely, be found by discerning readers of this history; but none, however, but such as their candor and ingenuity will readily excuse in this first attempt of the kind; and none but what may be remedied in time, if ever a future edition should be called for. And persons, who find defects or mistakes, or see the necessity of additions or alterations, are requested candidly to point them out to

The AUTHOR.

INDEX TO THE TOWNS, &c.

TOWNS.	Pages.	TOWNS.	Pages.
Ashburnham,	264	Spencer,	212
Athol,	243	Sterling,	298
Barre,	287	Sturbridge,	184
Berlin,	303	Sutton,	89
Bolton,	177	Templeton,	240
Brookfield,	62	Upton,	172
Boylston,	308	Uxbridge,	126
Charlton,	221	Ward,	291
Douglass,	203	Westborough,	120
Dudley,	151	Western,	199
Fitchburg,	252	Westminster,	225
Gardner,	306	Winchendon,	255
Gerry,	315	Worcester,	25
Grafton,	166	Woodstock,	317
Hardwick,	174	The County,	9
Harvard,	154	Courts of Common Pleas,	14
Holden,	188	———— Justices of,	ibid.
Hubbardston,	281	———— Clerks of,	16
Lancaster,	36	Sheriffs of the County,	17
Leicester,	99	Judges of Probate,	ibid.
Leominster,	192	Registers of Probate,	18
Lunenburg,	143	Registers of Deeds,	ibid.
Mendon,	54	General description of the County,	20
Milford,	293	Representatives to Congress,	21
Newbraintree,	207	Senators,	22
Northborough,	272	Rivers,	322
Northbridge,	285	Ministers Settled and Removed,	328
Oakham,	248	Dates of Incorporation of Towns,	ibid.
Oxford,	82	Number of Inhabitants,	ibid.
Paxton,	268	Valuation Lists,	336
Petersham,	215		
Princeton,	232		
Royalston,	261		
Rutland,	109		
Shrewsbury,	134		
Southborough,	130		

The

The following being omitted in its proper place at the end of the book, is here inserted.

THE proportion of Tax, which this County bears to the whole State, will appear by subjoining the following account of what each county pays on the thousand, with its number of polls, agreeably to the last valuation.

Counties.	Polls.	On the thous.			
		£.	s.	d.	q.
Suffolk,	9884	162	12	0	1
Essex,	12376	133	19	7	2
Middlesex,	10109	104	13	4	2
Hampshire,	13912	111	18	0	3
Worcester,	13762	127	15	0	2
Barnstable,	3759	20	15	11	3
Plymouth,	6912	59	9	9	3
Dukes County,	763	5	9	8	2
Nantucket,	1121	6	13	3	1
Bristol,	6547	53	19	6	3
Berkshire,	6265	52	3	3	3
York,	6484	50	1	9	0
Cumberland,	5723	43	6	5	2
Lincoln,	6349	50	13	10	1
Hancock,	1967	13	7	1	0
Washington,	493	3	1	1	0
		£1000	0	0	0

THE

THE HISTORY OF THE COUNTY OF WORCESTER.

THE COUNTY.

IN giving a hiſtory of this county, it is fitting to begin with a recital of the Act of the General Court for forming the ſame, which is as follows:

"An act for erecting, granting, and making a county in the inland parts of this province, to be called The County of Worceſter, and for eſtabliſhing Courts of Juſtice within the ſame,

"Be

"Be it enacted by his Excellency the Governor, Council, and Representatives, in General Court assembled, and by the authority of the same, That the towns and places hereafter named and expressed, that is to say, Worcester, Lancaster, Westborough, Shrewsbury, Southborough, Leicester, Rutland, and Lunenburgh, all in the county of Middlesex; Mendon, Woodstock, Oxford, Sutton, including Hassanamisco, Uxbridge, and the land lately granted to several petitioners of Medfield, all in the county of Suffolk; Brookfield in the county of Hampshire, and the south town laid out to the Narraganset soldiers; and all other lands lying within the said townships, with the inhabitants thereon, shall, from and after the tenth day of July, which will be in the year of our Lord one thousand seven hundred and thirty one, be and remain one entire and distinct county, by the name of Worcester, of which Worcester to be the county, or shire town: And the said county to have, use and enjoy, all such powers, privileges, and immunities, as by law other counties within this province, have and do enjoy.

"And be it enacted by the authority aforesaid, that there shall be held and kept within the said county of Worcester yearly, and in every year, at the times and place in this Act hereafter expressed, a Court of General Sessions of the Peace, and an Inferior Court of Common Pleas, to sit at Worcester, on the second Tuesdays of May and August, and the first Tuesdays of November and February, yearly and in every year, until this Court shall otherwise otherwife order :—Alfo, that there fhall be held and kept at Worcefter, within the faid county of Worcefter, yearly and in every year, until this Court fhall otherwife order, a Superior Court of Judicature, Court of Affize and General Goal Delivery, to fit on the Wednefday immediately preceding the time by law appointed for the holding the faid Superior Court of Judicature, Court of Affize and General Goal Delivery, at Springfield, within and for the county of Hampfhire :—And the Juftices of the faid Court of General Seffions of the Peace, Inferior Court of Common Pleas, and Superior Court of Judicature, Court of Affize and General Goal Delivery refpectively, who are, or fhall be, thereunto lawfully commiffioned and appointed, fhall have, hold, ufe, exercife and enjoy all and fingular the powers which are by law given and granted unto them, within any other counties of the province, where a Court of General Seffions of the Peace, Inferior Court of Common Pleas, and Superior Court of Judicature, Court of Affize and General Goal Delivery, are already eftablifhed.

" Provided, That all writs, fuits, plaints, proceffes, appeals, reviews, recognizances, or any other matters or things which now are or any time before the faid tenth day of July, fhall be depending in the law within any part of the faid county of Worcefter :—And alfo, all matters and things which now are, or at any time before the faid tenth of July, fhall be depending before the Judges of Probate within part of the faid county of Worcefter, shall be heard, tried, proceeded upon and determined in the counties of Suffolk, Middlesex, and Hampshire respectively, where the same are or shall be returnable or depending, and have, or shall have day, or days.

" Provided also, That nothing in this act contained, shall be construed to disannul, defeat, or make void any deeds or conveyances of lands, lying in the said county of Worcester, where the same are, or shall be, before the said tenth of July, recorded in the Regifter's office of the respective counties where such lands do now lie; but that all such deeds or conveyances so recorded shall be held good and valid as they would have been had not this act been made.

" And be it further enacted by the Authority aforesaid, That the Justices of the Court of General Sessions of the Peace, at their first meeting in the said county of Worcester, shall have full power and authority to appoint some meet person, within the said county of Worcester, to be Register of deeds and conveyances within the same, who shall be sworn to the faithful discharge of his trust in the said office, and shall continue to hold and exercise the same according to the directions of the law, until some person be elected by the freeholders of the said county of Worcester, who are hereby empowered to choose such person, on the first Thursday of September next ensuing, by the methods in the law already prescribed, to take upon him that trust. And until such Register shall be so appointed, by the said justices, and sworn,

all

all deeds and conveyances of lands lying within any part of the county of Worcester, which shall be recorded in the Register's office of the respective counties where such lands do now lie, shall be held and deemed good and valid to all intents and purposes as to the recording thereof.

" And be it further enacted by the Authority aforesaid, That the methods, directions and proceedings by law provided, as well for the electing and choosing a Register of deeds and conveyances, as a county Treasurer, which officers shall be appointed in the same manner as is by law already provided, on the first Thursday of September next, and also for the bringing forward and trying any actions, causes, pleas or suits, both civil and criminal in the several counties of this province and Courts of Judicature within the same, and choosing of Jurors to serve at the Courts of Justice, shall extend, and be attended, observed and put in practice within the said county of Worcester, and by the Courts of Justice within the same : Any law, usage or custom to the contrary notwithstanding.

" Provided always, That the inhabitants of the several towns and places herein before enumerated and set off a distinct county, shall pay their proportion to any county rates or taxes already made and granted, in the same manner as they would have done, had not this act been made."

This act passed April 2, 1731.

When the county was thus erected, the following persons were commissioned officers of the Court of Common Pleas, and for the county, viz.

COURTS *of* COMMON PLEAS.

Justices.

Hon. John Chandler, of Woodstock,
Joseph Wilder, of Lancaster,
William Ward, of Southborough,
William Jennison, of Worcester, Esquires,
Judges.

John Chandler, jun. of Worcester, *Clerk,*
Daniel Gookin, of Worcester, *Sheriff.*

And the first Court of General Sessions of the Peace, and Inferior Court of Common Pleas, for the county, was held at Worcester, August 10th, 1731, when the Rev. John Prentice, of Lancaster, preached a sermon before them, which was printed, from 2 Chronicles, Chap. xix. 6th, and 7th verses; " And said to the Judges, Take heed what ye do: For ye judge not for man, but for the Lord, who is with you in the judgment. Wherefore now, let the fear of the Lord be upon you, take heed and do it : For there is no iniquity with the Lord our God, nor respect of persons, nor taking of gifts." This was king Jehoshaphat's charge to the judges of Judah.

The Judges of the Court of Common Pleas, after the first appointment, as there have been vacancies by death, resignation, &c. have been as follow.

When the Hon. John Chandler, of Woodstock, died, Joseph Dwight, Esq; was appointed, and the Hon. Joseph Wilder, of Lancaster, was first.

Upon the death of Judge Jennison, Samuel Willard, Esq; of Lancaster, was appointed a Judge in 1743.

In

In 1745, Nahum Ward, Esq; of Shrewsbury, was commissioned Judge, vice William Ward, Esq.

In 1750, Edward Hartwell, Esq; of Lunenburg, was appointed Judge, in the room of Joseph Dwight, Esq.

In 1753, Jonas Rice, Esq; of Worcester, was constituted Judge, vice Samuel Willard, Esq.

In May, 1754, John Chandler, Esq; of Worcester, who had, from the beginning, been Clerk of the Court, was appointed a Judge of said Court.

In the year 1756, Thomas Steel, Esq; of Liecester, was commissioned Judge of the Court, vice Jonas Rice, Esq; deceased.

In May, 1757, upon the death of Judge Wilder, a new arrangement took place, in the following order:
Hon. John Chandler,
 Edward Hartwell,
 Thomas Steel,
 Timothy Ruggles, Esquires, were commissioned Judges.

Upon the resignation of Judge Chandler, in February, 1762, a commission issued from the Governor and Council, appointing
Hon. Timothy Ruggles, of Hardwick, first Judge,
 Thomas Steel, of Liecester,
 Joseph Wilder, of Lancaster, and
 Artemas Ward, of Shrewsbury, Esquires,
  Judges.

These gentlemen all continued in that office, until the year 1774, when the people, in consequence of the controversy with Greatbritain, put a stop to the exercise of all judicial powers, held

held under the King of England, or the Governor of the province, his reprefentative. In this fituation the whole then province remained, until October 17th, 1775, when a commiffion iffued, from the powers which then were, conftituting and appointing the

Hon. Artemas Ward, of Shrewfbury ;
    Jedidiah Fofter, of Brookfield ;
    Mofes Gill, of Princetown ; and
    Samuel Baker, of Berlin, Efquires, Juftices of the Court of Common Pleas.

In purfuance of which a Court was holden December 5, 1775.

On September 19th, 1776, the Hon. Jofeph Dorr, Efq; of Ward, was appointed a Juftice of this Court, vice the Hon. Jedidiah Fofter, Efq; who was advanced to be one of the Judges of the Supreme Judicial Court of this Commonwealth.

Since the appointment of the Hon. Mr. Dorr, there has been no change or alteration in the Judiciary department ; that is, for more than fixteen years.

CLERKS.

The Clerks of the Court of General Seffions of the Peace, and the Court of Common Pleas, from the beginning, have been as follow :

Hon. John Chandler, jun. of Worcefter, *firſt* Clerk. In November, 1751, the Hon. Timothy Paine, Efq; was appointed joint Clerk with Mr. Chandler ; and after Mr. Chandler's advancement to the bench, in 1754, Mr. Paine continued fole Clerk of faid Courts, to the year 1774. In December, 1775, the Hon. Levi Lincoln, Efq; was
                              appointed

appointed Clerk, who continued in the office but a year, and refigned, when Jofeph Allen, Efq; of Worcefter, was appointed, and ftill continues Clerk.

SHERIFFS *of the* COUNTY *to this time.*

In 1743, Benjamin Flagg, Efq; of Worcefter, was appointed Sheriff, vice Daniel Gookin, Efq; deceafed. Auguft, 1751, John Chandler, jun. Efq; of Worcefter, fucceeded Benjamin Flagg, deceafed. In 1762, Gardner Chandler, Efq; of Worcefter, was conftituted Sheriff, vice, Hon. John Chandler, promoted. Mr. Gardner Chandler continued in the office until the year 1775, when Simeon Dwight, Efq; of Weftern, was commiffioned Sheriff, and continued until his death in 1778, when William Greenleaf, of Lancafter, was appointed, who continued ten years, and was fucceeded by the Hon. John Sprague, Efq; of Lancafter, who refigned the office in 1792, when Dwight Fofter, Efq; of Brookfield, was appointed. Mr. Fofter being chofen a Reprefentative for this diftrict, refigned the office of Sheriff; whereupon William Caldwell, Efq; of Rutland, was appointed in his place, July 9, 1793.

JUDGES *of* PROBATE *from the beginning.*

Hon. John Chandler, of Woodftock; who was
 fucceeded by
 Jofeph Wilder, Efq; of Lancafter; fucceeded by
 John Chandler, Efq; of Worcefter; fucceeded by his fon,
           Hon.

Hon. John Chandler, Esq; of Worcester, in 1762, who continued in office until the Revolution. After that period,

Jedidiah Foster, Esq; of Brookfield, was appointed and continued until his advancement. He was succeeded by

Artemas Ward, Esq; of Shrewsbury; succeeded by

Levi Lincoln, Esq; of Worcester; succeeded by

Joseph Dorr, Esq; of Ward, the present Judge.

REGISTERS of PROBATE.

Hon. John Chandler, jun. Esq; of Worcester, first Register; he was succeeded in the office by

Timothy Paine, Esq; of Worcester. A few years before the Revolution,

Mr. Clarke Chandler, of Worcester, was appointed joint Register with the Hon. Mr. Paine. In 1776,

Joseph Wheeler, Esq; of Worcester, was appointed Register, and continued to his death, Feb. 10, 1793. Upon his decease,

Mr. Theophilus Wheeler was appointed Register.

Probate Courts are held at the Probate Office in Worcester, on the first Tuesday of every month; and, for the accommodation of the inhabitants, on certain other days, in different parts of the county.

REGISTERS of DEEDS.

Hon. John Chandler, Esq; of Worcester, the first, and succeeded by

Timothy Paine, Esq; of Worcester, who continued in the office until the Revolution—when

Mr.

Mr. Nathan Baldwin, of Worcester, was chosen ;— after his death,

Daniel Clap, Esq; of Worcester, was elected, who now fills that station. The office for the registry is kept at Worcester.

The public buildings of the county are good and convenient. The Court House is well situated; is a handsome building, but wants to be enlarged, and in all probability speedily will be.

The Jail is a large, commodious house, lately erected at the expense of the county: it is built with good stones, of a greyish colour, from Millstone Hill, so called, in Worcester; the inhabitants whereof freely gave the stone for this purpose. It is 64 feet in length, and 32 in breadth, and three stories high. The lower story is divided into four arches crosswise, forming four rooms for the safe custody of persons convicted of, or committed for gross crimes. The second is divided, in the same manner, into four rooms, but not arched with stone. These are for the keeping of debtors, who have not the liberty of the yard; and for persons committed for small offences. The upper story has an entry or walk from end to end, and is divided into eight convenient rooms for the use of prisoners for debt who have the liberty of the jail yard. This yard extends so as to include the jailor's house, and the meetinghouse of the second parish. The house built for the keeper of the jail is the property of the county: It is a handsome, well finished building.

The

THE COUNTY.

The Court of Common Pleas, and of the General Sessions of the Peace, have four terms in a year, appointed by Act of the Legislature, for sitting and transacting business—viz. on the fourth Tuesday in March, the second Tuesday in June, the last Tuesday in August, and the first Tuesday in December.

The Supreme Judicial Court of this Commonwealth holds two sessions in this county annually: The times herefor, by law, at present established, are the Tuesday preceding the last Tuesday of April, and the third Tuesday of September.

Since the establishment of this county, sixty two years ago, twelve persons have been tried and executed for the following crimes:

  For Murders,   5
  For Burglaries,   5
  For Rapes,   2

A GENERAL DESCRIPTION OF THE COUNTY.

THE County of Worcester, however small in its beginning,* consisting of but fifteen or sixteen towns, the greater part of which were infant plantations, with but few inhabitants, has flourished

---

* The late Governor Hutchinson, who was then a member of the General Court, strenuously opposed, as it is said, its being erected into a county; urging the utter improbability of its ever making any figure. He lived to see that he was greatly mistaken in his conjectures. This is an instance which may show us we have no certain rules to proceed upon in calculating the growth and population of new settlements; they, generally, exceed the most raised expectations of people, and, often, all rational probability.

THE COUNTY.

flourished and increased in the most rapid and surprising manner. It has risen to eminence and distinction among the counties of the Commonwealth; for while it is but the tenth in age, it is the third in wealth, paying a larger proportion of a state tax, than any of the other counties, except Suffolk and Essex, and falling but a little short of these two.

It is large in extent; being bounded on the south, almost equally, by the States of Connecticut and Rhodeisland; and on the north by the state of Newhampshire. On the east it is bounded, *mainly*, by the county of Middlesex, just touching at its south east angle upon the county of Suffolk; and on the west by the county of Hampshire. It is about 48 miles in length from north to south, and about 35 miles in width from east to west. It contains forty nine towns, the most of which are large in extent of lands, and number of inhabitants.

According to a late census, taken by an act of Congress, in order to a just apportionment of the number of Representatives among the several States, it contains 56807 souls.

REPRESENTATIVES to CONGRESS.

IN the first and second Congress, under the present Constitution, this county was entitled to an eighth part in the representation of this Commonwealth. The Hon. Jonathan Grout, Esq; of Peterham, was elected Representative for this county in the first Congress. The Hon. Artemas Ward, Esq;

Esq; of Shrewsbury, was chosen to represent this county in the second Congress, whose term expired on the fourth of March, 1793. And whereas by an enumeration of all the inhabitants of the United States lately made, the number of Representatives for this Commonwealth, according to Constitution, is increased to fourteen; so the Legislature by a late Act, joined the counties of Worcester, Hampshire and Berkshire, in one district, for the choice of four Representatives for the third Congress; one of whom was to be chosen in each county, and the fourth in either of the three. At the late election, in this district, the Hon. Artemas Ward, Esq; was chosen Representative for this county, by a large majority of the votes of the three counties. The Representative chosen for the district, in whose election this county gives its voice, is the Hon. Dwight Foster, Esq; of Brookfield, the late Sheriff of the county of Worcester.

Besides that this county may have its full share of representation in Congress, it gives in its suffrages, with a number of other counties, for one Representative for the State at large, who is chosen, viz. the Hon. David Cobb, Esq; of Taunton, in the county of Bristol.

The county of Worcester, also, chooses annually, an eighth part, five, of the Senators in the Legislature of the Commonwealth.

SENATORS.

THE following is a list of the gentlemen who have been chosen Senators for this county, from

the

the commencement of our new conſtitution, on the 25th of October, 1780, to the preſent time.

1780, Hon. Moſes Gill, of Princeton; Samuel Baker, of Berlin; Joſeph Dorr, of Ward, Iſrael Nichols, of Leominſter; and Seth Waſhburn, of Leiceſter, Eſqrs.

1781, Hon. Moſes Gill, Samuel Baker, Joſeph Dorr, Iſrael Nichols, Jonathan Warner, of Hardwick, Eſqrs.

1782, Hon. Moſes Gill, Samuel Baker, Joſeph Dorr, Iſrael Nichols, Jonathan Warner, Eſqrs.

1783, Hon. Moſes Gill, Samuel Baker, Iſrael Nichols, Seth Waſhburn, Jonathan Warner, Eſqrs.

1784, Hon. Moſes Gill, Samuel Baker, Iſrael Nichols, Seth Waſhburn, Jonathan Warner, Eſqrs.

1785, Hon. Moſes Gill, Samuel Baker, Iſrael Nichols, Seth Waſhburn, John Sprague, Eſqrs.

1786, Hon. Moſes Gill, Samuel Baker, Seth Waſhburn, Abel Wilder, of Winchendon; Iſrael Nichols, Eſqrs.

1787, Hon. Seth Waſhburn, Abel Wilder, Amos Singletary, of Sutton; John Feſſenden, of Rutland; Joſeph Stone, of Harvard, Eſqrs.

This year, 1787, Hon. Peter Penniman, Eſq; of Mendon, was choſen Counſellor.

1788, Hon. Samuel Baker, Abel Wilder, Amos Singletary, John Feſſenden, Jonathan Grout, of Peterſham, Eſqrs.

This year the Hon. Artemas Ward, Eſq; was choſen Counſellor.

1789,

1789, Hon. Moses Gill, Abel Wilder, Amos Singletary; John Fessenden, and Peter Penniman, of Mendon, Esqrs.

1790, Hon. Moses Gill, Samuel Baker, Abel Wilder, Amos Singletary, John Fessenden, Esqrs.

1791, Hon. Moses Gill, Samuel Baker, Jonathan Warner, Abel Wilder, Timothy Newell, Esqrs.

1792, Hon. Moses Gill, Samuel Baker, Abel Wilder, Jonathan Warner, Timothy Newell, Esqrs.

In the fall of 1792, the Legislature, according to Constitution, chose the Hon. Josiah Stearns, Esq; of Lunenburg, to fill the vacancy occasioned by the death of the Hon. Mr. Wilder.

1793, Hon. Moses Gill, Samuel Baker, Jonathan Warner, Timothy Newell, Josiah Stearns, Esqrs.

The Hon. Moses Gill, Esq; has uniformly been elected a Counsellor for this county, from the commencement of the Constitution, in 1780, to this time, 1793, except only in the years 1787 and 1788.

As by the Constitution of the Commonwealth, every town in the state, having 150 rateable polls, may send one Representative to the State Legislature: And every town, having 375, may send two, and so on in the same ratio; so every town in the county can send one, except Gardner: Divers of them are entitled to two, and some of them to three.

WORCESTER.

WORCESTER.

AS this is the shire town of the county of Worcester, we will first give an account and description of this place, and then proceed to the other towns in the county according to their respective ages, reckoning from the dates of the acts of incorporation.

Worcester is *part* of a tract of land called by the aboriginals, *Quinsigamond;* which territory was by them esteemed to bound easterly, partly on Quinsigamond pond, and partly on Hassanamisco, now Grafton; southerly, on the Nipnet, or Nipmug country, where Oxford and some adjacent towns now are; westerly, on Quaboag, now Brookfield, and lands in that vicinity; and northerly, on Nashawogg, now Lancaster, Sterling, &c. &c. On October 24th, 1668, a township of land of rather more than eight miles square, to be bounded, easterly on Quinsigamond pond, was granted by the General Court, to Daniel Gookin, Daniel Henchman, Thomas Prentice, and their associates. But war, at that time, and for several succeeding years, prevailing with the Indians, the settlement of the place was prevented until the year 1685: At which time, the natives appearing peaceably disposed, and behaving in a friendly manner to the English, the above named persons, together with John Wing, George Danson, Peter Goulding, Dickery Sargeant, Isaac Bull and Jacob Leonard, ventured to begin the plantation.

WORCESTER.

The town was incorporated the preceding year October 15, 1684, and the name of Worcester given to it. But the first town meeting ever held in the place, was on the last Wednesday of September, 1722. A special order of the General Court passed directing Judge Fulham of Weston, to call said meeting.*

In the year following several other men, with their families, moved into the place. And the settlement thereof went on prosperously until the year 1701, when the Indians began again to attack the frontier towns in Massachusetts. In the year 1702, the Indians killed the wife of Dickery Sargeant, and two of his children, and carried three of his children into captivity.† In this town also, Mr. Elisha Ward was supposed to be killed, for he was known to be shot at, and never after seen, or heard of. The war raged with such fury at this time, that Worcester was entirely depopulated. But peace being concluded with the Indians, in the beginning of the year 1713. Some of the proprietors of the township applied to the General Court for encouragement and direction towards its resettlement.

In

---

* Here we must observe, by the way, that the method of the Government was very different in former times, from what it has been since.—In those earlier days, plantations were named, and said to be incorporated, when there were few, or no inhabitants in them; and when a sufficient number of people had settled in them, a special resolve of Court passed to empower them too meet, and choose their town Officers: But for 60 years past, they have been *incorporated, named,* and empowered to hold town meetings, by the same act.

† These children, two sons and a daughter, chose to dwell among the Indians.—However, in 1726, they accompanied Miss Williams, taken from Deerfield, on a visit to their friends in Newengland.

In consequence of this application the Court appointed a committee to ascertain the claims of the grantees; and conduct the resettlement of the place. On the 21st of October, 1713, Jonas Rice, with his family, moved into the place and remained there, without any other inhabitants, until the spring of the Year 1715, when a considerable number of persons joined him. The number of settlers was augmented by Emigrants from Ireland in 1718: Since which time it has flourished and increased exceedingly, and become large, populous and wealthy. In the year 1740, Holden was set off from Worcester, and became a distinct town; and in 1778, 2200 acres, with the inhabitants thereon, were taken from this town to aid in forming the town of Ward;—Yet still Worcester is large in its dimensions, being about six miles square: And bounded, northerly, on Holden; easterly on Shrewsbury, Boylston and Long Pond; southerly, on Ward and Sutton, and westerly, on Leicester, and Holden. It is become very populous, containing two thousand one hundred inhabitants, according to the census taken in the year 1791: And it will no doubt, still greatly increase for many years. It is also wealthy and opulent, being the third town in the county, in the proportion which it pays in a state tax; and would be the first, most certainly, in the list, did not the other two, Brookfield, and Sutton, greatly exceed it in extent and dimensions; and also in the number of souls.

The inhabitants, in the outer parts of this town, subsist by husbandry. But in the centre, in the compafs of one mile, and moftly on one ftreet, are collected the county officers, a number of merchants and fhop keepers, profeffional men, and mechanicks of various forts. A very great trade is here carried on, in European and Weftindia goods; and the adjacent country is fupplied from this town: Here are large apothecary ftores, and ftores of all kinds of hardware.

A printing prefs was here fet up in 1775, by Mr. Ifaiah Thomas, who is thought to do far more bufinefs than any other in the ftate, or in the United States of America.* The houfes in the ftreet, are very compact, many of them large and elegant, as alfo the ftores and fhops. And here they have a number of large inns, not only for the accommodation of the people of the county, at the times for

* In the time of the political controverfy between Great Britain, and thefe States, previous to the war, near the clofe of the year 1774, feveral gentlemen applied in Bofton, to Ifaiah Thomas, printer of the Maffachufetts Spy, (a Newfpaper famed for its oppofition to the Britifh government, and which was no fmall fpoke in the wheel of the American Revolution) to fet up a printing prefs in Worcefter: He confented, and iffued propofals for that purpofe, and for printing a newfpaper weekly, in the town of Worcefter: But, foon after, the politicks of that time wearing a more ferious afpect, and Mr. Thomas being one of a lift of perfons, who, it was thought, would firft feel the weight of Britifh vengence, fecretly withdrew himfelf, and his printing materials, from Bofton. His printing apparatus he fent off for Worcefter, about three days before the battle of Lexington, and he himfelf followed the day after that battle. On the 3d of May, 1775, he, at Worcefter, recommenced the publication of the Maffachufetts Spy, which was the firft printing performed in the county. This newfpaper is ftill printed at Worcefter, and is the oldeft in the State, the Bofton Gazette excepted.

When the war ceafed, Mr. Thomas extended his bufinefs, and in the year 1788, reeftablifhed a printing office in Bofton, he himfelf refiding in Worcefter, where he ftill carries on the printing bufinefs on a very larger fcale, as he does alfo in Bofton. Among other large works which have

for holding the courts, but for travellers, and it is a place of great resort. On the street has lately been erected a large and handsome schoolhouse, of about 60, by 30 feet, and two stories high. On the lower floor are two apartments, one designed for a grammar school, and the other for a writing school. In the upper story there is one large apartment, with a fire place at each end: This is used by the scholars on their exhibition days. On the top there is a cupola with a bell. The street is wide, straight, and very pleasant, and adorned on either side with trees. And upon the whole, this town is one of the most populous, lively, flourishing, agreeable inland places in the state. There are two congregational religious societies in this town, called the first and second parishes. These have no parochial boundaries, but are called poll parishes; each inhabitant having a right by law, to pay and to connect himself to which parish he pleases, only signifying his choice, by leaving his name

have issued from his presses in Worcester, are three editions of the Bible, viz. a large Folio, with 50 copper plates; a large Royal Quarto, with Concordance, &c. and one in Octavo;—they are all the first of the kind ever printed in America:—And; upon examination, his editions are found the most correct of any now extant, He is now preparing to print two other editions of the Bible; viz. a small Quarto; and one in Duodecimo, or the common school Bible: For this last, all the types will be kept standing for the whole work, as is the method in the King's printing houses in England and Scotland. Mr. Thomas has also carried on the Bookbinding business very extensively; and is now engaged in building, in Worcester, as large a Paper Mill as is in this State. His Bookstore in Worcester is kept well filled with a large assortment of books in all branches of Literature, which is a great accommodation to purchasers, in the town and county. His manufactures employ and support a large number of people; and it may justly be said, that the business of no one person, has added more to the consequence and advantage of the town and county of Worcester, than his.

name at any time for that purpofe, with the town clerk. They have accordingly two large and elegant meetinghoufes, about three quarters of a mile apart; one ftanding near the fouth end, and the other the north end of the ftreet, by which the inhabitants are happily accommodated.

In the year 1719, the firft meetinghoufe was erected, and here a church was gathered, and the Rev. Andrew Gardner, the firft minifter was ordained in the autumn of that fame year 1719, but the month and day cannot be afcertained. He was difmiffed from Worcefter on the laft Wednefday of October 1722, and was afterwards fettled at Lunenburgh. Mr. Gardner was fucceeded in the facred office by the Rev. Ifaac Burr, who was ordained their fecond paftor, on the 25th of October 1725. He, likewife, after a few years, was difmiffed from his work, viz. on November, 1744.

After his removal the Rev. Thaddeus Maccarty, for a fhort fpace Minifter of Kingfton, in the county of Plymouth, where he was ordained November 3d, 1742, was inftalled paftor, the third in fucceffion, of the church and people of Worcefter, on the 10th of June 1747. He continued in office until his death, which was on July 20, 1784.

After the Rev. Mr. Maccarty's death, a fecond church was formed here on December 1ft, 1785, and the Rev. Aaron Bancroft was ordained to the paftoral care thereof, February 1, 1786. This fecond religious fociety was incorporated, as a diftinct Parifh November 13, 1787.

To

To the Rev. Mr. Maccarty succeeded, as pastor of the first church and society in Worcester, the Rev. Samuel Austin, who was installed here on the 29th of September, 1790. This gentleman had been for a short space, minister of the fourth congregational society in Newhaven, in Connecticut.

In Worcester, a Social Library company has lately been established; their stock already amounts to 90l. and as the institution is founded on a large and liberal plan, it will doubtless be greatly increased.

In this town, a number of gentlemen, requesting the same, received a charter in April, 1793, from the Massachusetts Grand Lodge for holding a LODGE of FREE MASONS, by the name of the MORNING STAR LODGE, and Isaiah Thomas, was unanimously elected Master. And on the 11th of June, the Grand Lodge, of Massachusetts, meeting at Worcester for the purpose, he was installed by the most worshipful Grand Master, John Cutler, and the Lodge consecrated. The stated meetings of the Morning Star Lodge are on the third Tuesday of every month.

We shall now present our readers with a geographical description of the town of Worcester.

The town is full of round gradual rising hills, and of dales: There are few craggy precipices, and few extensive plains. The middle, or most thick settled part, is in a valley, surrounded by pleasant hills, and from the hill as we enter the town from the east, it makes an agreeable appearance. Tatnuck and Boggachoag hills are remarkable for having formerly had Indian towns on them. They are

are neither of them very high. Millstone hill, about a mile from the courthouse, to the east, is the common property of the inhabitants, who procure from thence stones, some of which they split out, and hew for underpinning to their houses, for door stones and steps. The stones are hard grained, and peculiarly fit for Millstones. It must be a singular advantage to such a town as Worcester, to have such an inexhaustible quarry of building stone, which can be worked into any shape, where there are, and will be so many gentlemen who wish to build with elegance, as well as for convenience.

The natural growth of wood is oak, walnut and chesnut, on the higher lands, some pine on the small plains and valleys, and in the swamps and low lands, ash, birch and maple. The town is well supplied with wood. And as every farmer has his own plat of woodland upon his homestead, so the face of the town appears more woody from the hills, than it is in fact. The interspersion of hills and dales, fields and woods, affords an agreeable and variegated prospect, extending about six or seven miles from the observer's eye. And a more enlarged view is not to be had from the greatest eminence in the town.—The soil is pretty good, warm, more inclined to sand than clay, however it cannot be called sandy; is is friendly to the growth of Indian corn. Some of the farmers have lately turned their attention to raising wheat and flax, and with considerable success. Rye is raised here in great quantities. The rising grounds are very good for pastures and orchards; and the lower not indifferent

ferent for hay. Indeed, there is foil of almoſt every kind in Worceſter, and almoſt on every farm. It is not eaſy to deſcribe its general properties; for it is productive, in a degree, of almoſt all kinds of country produce, and not noticeable for any particular one.

How far this town affords mines and minerals, has never yet been fully aſcertained. About the year 1754, a broad flat vein, about a foot thick, of lead and ſilver ore, in the proportion of $2\frac{1}{2}$ pennyweights of ſilver to one pound of lead, was diſcovered, running flauntwiſe down into a rock. Some perſons purchaſed it, and procured a miner, who followed it a little way into a rock, on a hill; and then adviſed to meet it by digging away before it. In this undertaking conſiderable money was expended, but they never met the vein. After a while, they left off diſcouraged. However, in digging to meet this vein, they found ſeveral pieces of ore, about the ſize of a peck, or half buſhel.

Worceſter has really but one pond within its limits, this is called *North Pond*, and is of an oval form; covering about 30 acres of ground, and is ſurrounded partly by woods and partly by a ſwamp and meadow. Though not an agreeable pond, yet it is well ſupplied with the uſual ſorts of common pond fiſh, as pickerel, perch, ſhiners, breams, eels, and pouts. Theſe fiſh, however, are not of the beſt quality, as the water is rather ſtagnant, and the bottom muddy. As to Quinſigamond, or Long Pond, or what is ſometimes called Worceſter Pond, the facts are theſe, that all the water of that pond

which

which lies within the line of the town of Worcester, does not cover more than one acre of land, being two or three small coves: The rest of the pond lies within the bounds of Shrewsbury, and will be particularly described when we come to speak of that town.

Worcester is very well watered by rivers, brooks and rivulets. Bimilick, or Mill brook has its source in North Pond ; and running southerly, it crosses the great road a little north of the Courthouse, and empties into Blackstone river. It is not more than ten feet wide and one foot deep ; but a fine stream. Turkeybrook, which is about the same size, originates in Holden. Tatnuck, or Halfway River, in the southwesterly part of the town, runs also from Holden, empties perhaps ten times as much water, and is about two rods wide. This passes on through Sutton, to the southward. Boggachoag river, which runs northwardly, through a corner of Ward, is nearly as large as Halfway River. These three streams unite in French River, so called.

Upon these streams there are, within the town of Worcester, a very large paper mill, four grist mills, four saw mills, two fulling mills, and two trip hammers. The fulling mills are the property of Messrs. Stowell, father and sons, by whom the clothier's business, in all its branches, is carried on to as great perfection as any where in the state. They dye fine scarlet, and deep blue colours, in the best manner.

Besides the above mentioned, there are two or three works for the making of Potash, in which Pearlash is also made: Also a distillery for gin.

There

There is a Poſt office in this town ; the Poſtmaſter is Iſaiah Thomas.

The great poſt road, from Boſton to Springfield is very good in that part of it which goes through Worceſter. As this is the ſhire town, roads from all parts of the county, and in every direction, centre here. There is now a Poſt road eſtabliſhed, from Worceſter to Providence, which paſſes through Mendon.

Worceſter is ſituated 47 miles from Boſton, a little to the ſouth of weſt.

Having ſaid what may be thought ſufficient, in deſcribing the town of Worceſter, we cannot take our leave of it, without mentioning with reſpect, the name of Chandler. The town of Worceſter, in particular, and the county of Worceſter at large, were originally greatly indebted to the Hon. John Chandler, Eſq; of Woodſtock, the firſt Judge in the county, and his ſon, the firſt Col. John Chandler of Worceſter, who, in procefs of time ſucceeded his father in all his offices, titles and honours, for their addreſs, activity and enterpriſe. And their names ought to be held in grateful remembrance.

LANCASTER,

LANCASTER.

THIS is, by several years, the eldest town in the county of Worcester, and, originally, one of the largest, as will appear in the sequel of this history, when we come to mention the several large towns which have been set off from it. So early as in the year 1645, *Sholan*, alias *Shaumauw*, proprietor of *Nashawogg*, and Sachem of the *Nashaways*, who lived at *Waushacum*, (which is in Sterling) informed Mr. Thomas King of Watertown, with whom he traded, and for whom he had a respect, of this tract of land as well accommodated for a plantation, desiring the English would come and set down by him. Accordingly, Mr. King, Mr. John Prescot, Harmon Garret, Thomas Skidmore, Mr. Day, Mr. Symonds, with others, procured of said *Sholan*, a deed of Nashawogg, ten miles in lengh, and eight in breadth, under these restrictions, that the English should not molest the Indians in their hunting, fishing, or usual planting places.—And the General Court confirmed the deed. And here we ought to observe, the fidelity of *Sholan* who conveyed this tract of land to the English, that he always behaved in a peaceable, friendly manner towards them. As did also *Matthew*, his nephew, and successor as Sachem; but *Sagamore Sam*, nephew to Matthew, and succeeded him, was of a different temper and character; and, joining with Philip in his rebellion, was taken by the English, and executed as a rebel. They of the tribe

LANCASTER. 37

tribe who survived this war of Philip's divided; one part moving to Albany, and the other to Pennicook, with which tribe they incorporated.

Let us return from this digression. Mr. King sold all his interest in this grant to his associates, who having given lots of land to Richard Linton, Lawrence Waters, and John Ball, sent them up to perform divers things at the common expense of the proprietors: And these were the first inhabitants. For the space of seven years little was done to forward the settlement of the plantation; nevertheless, there being nine families in the place, they petitioned the General Court to be incorporated as a town, which was granted on the 18th of May, 1653, and the name of Lancaster was given to it.

The town was in peace and prosperity for the space of twenty two years, from its incorporation— and the Indians were very serviceable to the inhabitants, by supplying them, on reasonable terms, with such corn and wild meat as they needed.

But on the 24th of June, 1675, Philip, Sachem of Pocanoket, commonly called *King Philip*, rebelled against the English, and commenced a most bloody and destructive war.—And on the 22d of August following, eight persons, viz. George Bennet, William Fagg, Jacob Farrar, Joseph Wheeler, Mordecai MacLoad, with his wife and two of their children, were killed in different parts of the town. The Narraganset Indians, joining Philip in his rebellion, marched into the country, and persuaded the Nipnets and Nashaways to take up arms also against the English.

Philip

Philip at the head of about 1500 Indians, marched for Lancaster, in which there were then above fifty families. And on the the 10th of February, 1676, very early in the morning, assaulted the town in five distinct bodies and places, burning most of the unfortified houses, and killing several persons, viz. Jonas Fairbank, Joshua Fairbank, Richard Wheeler, Ephraim Sawyer, Henry Farrar, and Mr. Ball and wife. However, they destroyed no garrison, but that round the Rev. Mr. Rowlandson's house; in which there were soldiers and inhabitants to the amount of forty two.

The enemy soon set fire to the house, which reduced the English to the sad necessity of surrendering to the Indians, rather than to perish by the flames. The men, except Ephraim Roper, who made his escape, were immediately slain, or reserved for torture: Their names were, Mr. Divol, Abraham Joslin, Daniel Gains, Thomas Rowlandson, William and Josiah Kerley, John MacLoad, John Kettle and his two sons, Josiah Divol, &c. &c.

Two of the women, one the wife of Capt. Kerley, the other the wife of Ephraim Roper, were killed in attempting to escape; the other women, with the children, about twenty in number, were carried into captivity; among whom was the consort of the Rev. Mr. Rowlandson, with three children, the youngest of which died on the 18th of the same month of its wounds in the wilderness, at an Indian place called Wenimesset, or Meminimesset, north of Quaboag, aged about six years and a half. This place, was included in the original grant of Lambstown, or Hardwick, but is now

within

within the limits of Newbraintree. In the fame place alfo, the wife of Abraham Joflin, being unable to travel by reafon of her pregnancy, the Indians firft knocked her in the head, with her child about two years old, made a large fire, ftripped them naked, and then threw them both thereinto. The other women and children, or the moft of them, foon after returned. Mrs. Rowlandfon, with her two furviving children, returned in about three months. We muft in this place, obferve the reafon of Mr. Rowlandfon's not falling into the hands of the enemy with the garrifon, was, that he was then at Bofton, foliciting the Governour and Council for more foldiers for the protection of the town; and met the heavy tidings, before related, on his return. Capt. Wadfworth, then at Marlborough, hearing of the affault of Lancafter, with forty brave men, marched immediately for its relief, and, entering the town undifcovered, forced the enemy, at that time, to quit it. He quartered his men in various parts of the town, and tarried feveral days, but before his departure, had one of his men, George Harrington, killed by the Indians.

This is that famous Capt. Wadfworth, who afterwards with Capt. Brocklebank, and the much greater part of their men, glorioufly fell, in the caufe of their country, in a fight with the enemy at Sudbury.

About fix weeks after the above affault of the town, it being judged untenable under the then prefent circumftances both of that and the country, the remainder of the inhabitants, except John Roper, who was killed by the enemy that fame day

day, drew off under a guard of horfe and foot. And immediately on this defertion of the place, all the buildings, fave two, were reduced to afhes. In this ftate of defolation, the town continued about four years; during which time the Rev. Mr. Rowlandfon preached at Wethersfield in Connecticut, and there he died, before the refettlement of the town. From 1680 to the year 1692, they were not molefted in the refettlement of the town. But the French king efpoufing the caufe of James the fecond in 1688, who had abdicated the Britifh throne, involved the nation in a war with France, and Newengland in a war with the Canadians, both French and Indians: In the calamities of which this town had a large fhare. For, on the 18th of July 1692, the Indians affaulted the houfe of Peter Joflin, who was at his labour in the field; and knew nothing thereof, until, entering the houfe, he found his wife and three children, with a widow Whitcomb, who lived in his family, barbaroufly butchered with their hatchets, and weltering in their blood. His wife's fifter, with another of his children, were carried into captivity—fhe returned; but that child was murdered in the wildernefs.—In 1695, on a Lord's day morning, Mr. Abraham Wheeler, was mortally wounded.—On the 11th of September, 1697, when the inhabitants, not fufpicious of any enemy, were gone out to their labour, the Indians came, in feveral companies, into the town, and were near furprifing Thomas Sawyer's garrifon, both the gates being left open; but Jabez Fairbank, who was at his own houfe half a

mile's

mile's diſtance, and, deſigning to bring his little ſon from ſaid garriſon, mounted his horſe, (which came running to him in a fright) and rode, full ſpeed, into the gate, but yet nothing ſuſpicious of an enemy: However, this was a mean of ſaving the garriſon; for the enemy, who were juſt ready to ruſh into it, ſuppoſing they were diſcovered, gave over that deſign, and fired at ſuch as were in the fields.—At this time, the Rev. John Whiting being, on ſome occaſion, at a diſtance from his garriſon, they ſurpriſed and killed him—they, indeed, offered him quarter; but he choſe rather to fight to the laſt, than reſign himſelf to them whoſe tender mercies are cruelty. At the ſame time they killed twenty others, viz. Daniel Hudſon and his wife and two of their daughters, Ephraim Roper, and wife and daughter, John Skait and wife, Joſeph Rugg and wife and three children, widow Rugg, Jonathan Fairbank, and two of his children, and two of the children of Nathaniel Hudſon: They wounded two, but not mortally; and captivated Jonathan Fairbank's wife, widow Wheeler, Ephraim Roper's ſon, John Skait's ſon, Joſeph Rugg's ſon, and Mary Glaſier: Five of theſe returned.

In 1704, a large army of French and Indians came from Canada, with a deſign to deſtroy Northampton, but, finding they were prepared to receive them, they turned their courſe towards Lancaſter; and on the 31ſt of July, early in the morning, they fell furiouſly upon the town; and in their firſt onſet killed Lieut. Nathaniel Wilder, near the gate

gate of his own garrifon; and on the fame day three others, viz. Abraham How, John Spaulding, and Benjamin Hutchins, near the fame garrifon.

The enemy were uncommonly brave, and therefore, though Capt. Tyng, who commanded the foldiers, of the garrifon, and Capt. How, with a company from Marlborough, who marched immediately to their affiftance, together with the inhabitants of the town, maintained a warm conflict with them, for fome time, yet being much inferior in number were obliged to retreat into the garrifon. Upon this the enemy burned the meetinghoufe, and fix other buildings, and deftroyed much of the live ftock of the town. Before night there came fuch numbers to the relief of the town, that the enemy retreated; and though purfued, were not overtaken.

What number of the enemy were killed at the above time is uncertain; but it was fuppofed to be confiderable:—A French officer, of fome diftinction, was mortally wounded, which greatly exafperated them.

On the 26th of October, the fame year, 1704, a party of the enemy having been difcovered at Still River, the foldiers and inhabitants belonging to Mr. Gardiner's garrifon, with divers others, went in queft of them, and returned in the evening much fatigued with the fervice of the day—Mr. Gardner, (who had been preaching feveral years with the people of Lancafter, and was now their Paftor elect) in compaffion to the foldiery, took the watch that night upon himfelf; and coming

out

out of the box, late in the night upon some occasion, was heard by one Samuel Prescott in the house, between sleeping and waking, who, supposing him an enemy, seized the first gun which came to hand, and shot him through the body in the parade. But the fatal mistake immediately appeared; and he, being carried into the house, forgave the person who shot him, and in an hour or two expired, to the great grief, not only of his consort, but of his people, who had an high esteem of him.

On the 15th of October, 1705, Mr. Thomas Sawyer, with his son, Elias Sawyer, and John Biglow, were captivated at his garrisoned house, about the dawn of day. Mr. Sawyer's youngest son, about fourteen years of age, escaped through a back window of the house.

The Indians treated Mr. Sawyer with much cruelty, but at length they arrived at Montreal. There Mr. Sawyer observed to the French Governor, that on the River Chamblee there was a fine seat for mills; and that he would build a sawmill for him, provided he would procure a ransom for himself, his son, and Biglow. The Governor readily closed with the proposal, as, at that time, there was no sawmill in all Canada, nor artificer capable of building one. He accordingly applied to the Indians, and obtained the ransom of young Sawyer and Biglow, without the least difficulty; but no sum would purchase Mr. Sawyer's redemption: Him, (being distinguished for his bravery, which had proved fatal to a number of their brethren)

ren) they were determined to immolate.—The victim was accordingly led forth and actually fastened to the stake, environed with materials, so disposed as to effect a lingering death.—The savages, surrounding the unfortunate prisoner, began to anticipate the horrid pleasure of beholding their captive writhing in tortures amidst the rising flames, and of rending the air with their dismal yells.—On a sudden a Friar appeared, and, with great solemnity, held forth what he declared to be the key to the gates of Purgatory; and told them unless they immediately released their prisoner, he would instantly unlock those gates, and send them headlong thereinto. Superstition prevailed, and wrought the deliverance of Mr. Sawyer: For they, at once, unbound him, and gave him up to the Governor. In one year he compleated a mill, when he and Biglow were discharged. They detained his son Elias one year longer, to instruct them in the art of sawing and keeping the mill in order; when he was amply rewarded, and sent home to his friends; where his father and he both lived to a good old age, and were gathered to their graves in peace.

On the 16th of July, 1707, Mr. Jonathan White was killed by the Indians. And on the 18th of August in this same year, 1707, twenty four stout Indians, who, according to their own account, had all been captains, came to Marlborough, and, besides other mischief they did there,* captivated Mr. Jonathan Wilder, a native of Lancaster: The next day, they were pursued by about thirty people from Marlborough

* See mention of this same company, in the account of Northborough.

Marlborough and Lancaster, and overtaken in what is now Sterling. The front of our men came upon them before they had the least apprehension of a pursuit.—Their packs were all flung, and, it being a misty day, their cases were on their guns:—And, therefore, had our men all run down upon them, they might probably have destroyed, or taken them all, and saved the life of the captive.—The enemy, at the first appearance of our men, had determined to resign themselves to their mercy—But observing only ten of the thirty, to come towards them, they took courage, unflung their packs, and fought like men, having first dispatched their captive Mr. Wilder.—In this action the enemy lost nine of their number, and all their packs: And on our part two men, Mr. John Farrar and Mr. Richard Singletary, were killed, and two, Mr. Ephraim Wilder and Mr. Samuel Stevens, were wounded, but not mortally.

On August 5th, 1710, a party of the enemy coming by advantage of the bushes very near to Mr. Nathaniel and Mr. Oliver Wilder, and an Indian servant at their labour in the field, the servant was killed, but the men escaped to the garrison.—And this was the *last mischief* done by the enemy, in Lancaster.—After that period they were a peaceable, prosperous, happy people; they grew and flourished, multiplied and increased, they spread and extended their branches far and wide: So that, with the greatest propriety, the people of this place may adopt the words of the psalmist, in reference to Israel, and say,—" Many a time have they

they afflicted me from my youth—many a time have they afflicted me from my youth, yet they have not prevailed againſt me."———I would here obſerve, the account given above of the deſolations, and calamities which befel the town of Lancaſter, is, *chiefly* in the words of the Rev. Mr. Harrington, in a century ſermon he preached there on the 28th of May, 1753.

I will now proceed to give ſome particular account of the Eccleſiaſtical ſtate of this town, from its beginning.—It was incorporated, as we have ſaid, in 1653. The following year, Mr. Joſeph Rowlandſon preached among the people, and continued ſo doing, until April 14th, 1658, when they invited him to ſettle with them in the work of the miniſtry; their invitation he accepted, and probably was ordained the ſame year, at which time, no doubt the Church of Chriſt was gathered here: Although of theſe things we cannot ſpeak with certainty, ſince the records of the Church, in Mr. Rowlandſon's time, were, in all probability, conſumed in his garriſon. As the town was wholly broken up and deſtroyed, as above related, in 1676, ſo the Rev. Mr. Rowlandſon continued with the people from the firſt but about 22 years, and died before the reſettlement of the town.—The place lay in ruins about four years. In 1680, they began to reſettle: And divers gentlemen preached with them. In February, 1688, Mr. John Whiting was invited to preach with them on probation; and continued preaching until November, 1690, when he was invited to take the overſight of them

in

in the Lord; and he, accepting their invitation was, probably, foon after ordained.

But we cannot be certain of the precife day, as no records of the time of his miniftry have ever been found.—He continued but a fhort fpace, in the facred office, being cut off, by the enemy, as before mentioned, on the 11th of September, 1697.

In May, 1701, Mr. Andrew Gardner, began to preach at Lancafter, and in September following the people gave him a call to fettle with them in the work of the gofpel miniftry. This invitation he accepted, and his ordination was appointed; but before the day came a fudden and furprifing death arrefted him: Being unfortunately, but mortally wounded in the houfe of his friends, in his own garrifon, in the night following the 26th of October, 1704; the particulars of which have been related above.

In May, 1705, Mr. John Prentice came to preach among this people, and fupplied the defk until February, 1707, when he received an invitation to fettle among them, which he accepted; and he was accordingly, folemnly feparated unto this facred employment on the 29th of March, 1708. In his day there was peace, and the town grew and flourifhed exceedingly: For during his miniftry, from his diocefe were formed the towns of Harvard, Bolton, Leominfter, and the fecond precinct, which is now called Sterling. He was a good and faithful fervant of Jefus Chrift, continuing in his office almoft forty years, living much beloved; and died greatly lamented, on the 6th of January, 1748.

The breach made upon the Church and town was happily repaired the enfuing fall, in the inftallment of the Rev. Timothy Harrington, to the paftoral office among them, November 16th, 1748; who ftill continues, in an advanced age.

The Rev. Mr. Harrington, through age and bodily infirmities, being taken off from his publick labours, the people of Lancafter have invited Mr. Nathaniel Thayer, to fettle with them in the work of the gofpel miniftry, as colleague with the venerable Mr. Harrington, who, having accepted their invitation, is, by the leave of Providence, to be folemnly feparated unto the fame October 9th, 1793.

We muft here obferve, that although this place was greatly frowned upon, in their early days, in the fhort lives, and premature deaths of their firft minifters, yet fince that time, the people have been as fignally fmiled upon, and bleffed in the long and ufeful lives of two eminent minifters in fucceffion, whofe courfes together make up the long fpace of 84 years.

The Rev. Mr. Harrington, was firft fettled in the miniftry at a place then called, *Lower Afhuelot, now Swanzey*, in the ftate of Newhampfhire : Here he was ordained November 16th, 1741. This place was totally deftroyed by the Indians on the 2d of April, 1747, from whence he was driven with his family and flock. The people of Lancafter having invited Mr. Harrington to fettle with them, and there being no profpect of the return of his former Church and flock to Afhuelot, he firft obtained a regular difmiffion from them, and there-

upon

LANCASTER. 49

upon generoufly refigned to them his whole intereft there, and all arrearages due to him, and accepted the invitation to take the overfight of the Church and flock of God in Lancafter.

Let us return; the town of Lancafter has all the appearances of age. A number of gentlemen have built very elegant feats here: And there are a confiderable number of ftores and fhops in the town: And as there are large roads, and much travel through the place, of courfe much bufinefs is done here in the way of trade. The pleafantnefs of the place has invited many perfons of education and fortune hither. And here they have a large focial library, under good regulations and confifting of a fine collection of good and ufeful books.

In this town there is eftablifhed a Lodge of Free Mafons, the hiftory whereof is as follows. Upon the petition of a number of gentlemen to the ancient Grand Lodge of free and accepted Mafons, a charter was granted January 31, 1778, to the petitioners, and their fucceffors, for holding a Lodge in Lancafter, by the name of *Trinity Lodge*. This is held on the firft Tuefday evenings in each month. From the date of the charter to this time, there have been initiated 166 perfons, from this and other towns in the vicinity: Of thefe 135 have received the degree of Fellow Crafts; and 125 have been raifed to Mafter Mafons. From its commencement the Lodge has been governed by the following mafters, viz.

In the year 1778, Michael Newhall was elected Mafter. 1779, Edmund Heard, do. 1780,

1780, do. do. 1781, do. do. 1782, do. do. 1783, Isaiah Thomas, do. 1784, Timothy Whiting, jun. do. 1785, do. do. 1786, Ephraim Carter, do. 1787, Timothy Whiting, jun. do. 1788, Abijah Wyman, do. 1789, Edmund Heard, do. 1790, do. do. 1791, do. do. 1792, do. do. 1793, do. was again chosen master, but soon after leaving the government was succeeded by Timothy Whiting, jun.

We proceed to a Geographical, and Topographical description of Lancaster. It is about nine miles in length from north to south, and four in width from east to west : Bounded by Lunenburgh and Leominster on the north and north west ; by Shirley in the county of Middlesex, on the northeast ; by Harvard, Bolton and Berlin, on the east ; by Boylston on the south, and by Sterling on the west. The body of the town is situated on low and level lands near the intervals ; and so as to afford an agreeable prospect of a considerable part of it. There are two main branches of the River Nashaway. The north branch originates from a Pond in Westminster, and, running through Fitchburgh and Leominster, enters Lancaster in the North west part of the town ; and pursues a southeast course into the middle of it, within a few rods of the meetinghouse. The south branch springs up from the foot of Watchusett, in Princeton, and running through Sterling and Boylston, enters at the southwest angle of the town ; then running northeasterly, meets the north branch about half a mile below the meetinghouse ; and then, keeping a northeastern course, enters Shirley. On both branches and within

within the town of Lancaster they have corn and saw mills. There are nine large bridges within the town: Two on the north branch, three on the south, and four after their junction. None are less than five rods in length; and the first after the confluence of these waters is planked ten rods. On the two branches, and after they unite, there is a vast body of exceeding rich interval land, of a great depth of soil, and which is most excellent for grass, and produces in abundance the best of hay. This interval is also good for raising flax and hemp: It is also good for Indian corn; and a steam of fog from the waters preserves the corn in the intervals, when at the distance of ten or fifteen rods, the corn will be destroyed by frosts. The river Nashaway overflows the whole interval, of nearly 3000 acres, twice in a year, in the spring, and in autumn, and in some places two miles in width. Sometimes it has overflowed the interval lands in summer; and then it has generally done vast damage, by carrying off fences, great quantities of hay and flax, &c. and destroyed large fields of Indian corn. In 1787, by a freshet, a saw mill, on the north branch, about two miles from the meetinghouse, was swept off, and about three acres of good rich interval land washed away to the depth of 12 feet, leaving only a bed of cobble stones, entirely useless. The lands rising from the interval are, mostly, plain and level, on which the buildings, in the middle of the town, stand; and these lands are good for all kinds of grain: Wheat and hemp are raised upon them in great plenty. The higher lands are good for wood and pasturage.

George

George hill, so called, lays all along on the westerly side of the town, on which there are a number of very excellent farms; it rises, gradually, high, but is not too rocky: It is a moist soil, abounding with springs, and clay: And in this town are annually made many hundreds of thousands of brick. There is a great plenty and rich variety of fruits on the high hilly lands, west of the town; large and good orchards: But there are very few apple trees in the middle of the town.

The growth of wood, on the higher lands is oak of the various sorts, chesnut and walnut. The intervals abound with elm, buttonwood, butternut, and shagbark. In the north and south and east parts of the town there are extensive plains covered with pitch pine. Here are works for making pearl and pot ash. And the late Col. Caleb Wilder, was the person who first discovered the method of making potash in kettles.

In the northeasterly part of Lancaster is the fine and valuable, and, perhaps, inexhaustible, slate pit, furnishing slates and tile for the roofs of houses; and most excellent stones, for tombs and graves.*

Lancaster has a number of ponds within its limits. Cumberry Pond lies in the north part of the town, towards Lunenburgh, not far from the slate pit. It is not large; but what is very noticeable is, the water in this pond is observed to rise as much as two feet just before a storm. Not far from

---

* This was first discovered by a Mr. Flagg. The slates have been in use about 40 years. The quarry is now owned by Mr. Joseph Wales. No slates equal to these have yet been discovered on the Continent. Great numbers are used in Boston, every season. They are also exported to Virginia, to Newyork, to Hartford in Connecticut, &c. &c. &c.

from this, and about five miles from the meeting-house, is situated Turner Pond; there is a small outlet from hence to Spectacle Pond, in form of a bow, whence they take the name, Spectacle Pond. Near these is another, called *Fort Pond*, whence issues a stream on which there are mills in Shirley. From Spectacle Pond a stream runs sufficient to carry a saw mill, and a fulling mill, and then falls into the north branch of Nashaway River. In the southwest part of the town there is a small pond, called *Sandy Pond*, from the border of which between high and low water marks, they gather a fine white sand. At the southeast angle of the town lays, *Clamshell Pond*, near to Berlin, from whence issues *Northbrook*, as mentioned in the description of Berlin.

On the west of the stream which carries Prescott's mills, which runs from Little Pond in Sterling, is situated Mossy Pond, opposite to, and about the size of *Sandy Pond*. This last mentioned pond always rises in a dry time.

We have now to observe, that the town of Lancaster is at great expense in building and repairing bridges and causeways: And the General Court, in consideration hereof, granted a Lottery, a few years past, whereby they might raise a certain sum of money for these purposes. Nevertheless, although their rivers occasion the people much cost, and sometimes great loss and damage by the freshets, yet the bounteous Author of Nature, seemed to consider these things, and made them great, if not full compensation, by some singular natural advantages in the town; and in particular,

lar, by the richness and fertility of their large intervals; and the ease with which their lands are cultivated, and made productive. And upon the whole, notwithstanding it has been curtailed on every side, this is still a very large and wealthy town; peaceable and happy; prosperous and flourishing; and the people are industrious and good.

In this town when the general census was taken, in the year 1791, there were 214 houses, and 1460 inhabitants. The town is just about 40 miles from Boston, very little to the north of west, and 14 miles from the Courthouse in Worcester a little to the northeast.

MENDON.

THIS is a very ancient town indeed, the second in age in the county. It was an original grant to certain persons, of eight miles square, made by the General Court, at an early period, we cannot say exactly when; it was called Quanshipauge by the natives. It was incorporated by an Act of the Legislature, on the 15th of May, 1667, and the name of Mendon given to it. It was located, a plan drawn, and return made to the General Court, by a Mr. Joshua Fisher. After the Province line was settled, it was again surveyed, and a plan of it drawn by a Mr. William Rider,

Rider, in the year 1725; according to which plan its boundaries and extent were as follow, beginning at southwest corner it ran east seven and an half miles on the line between Massachusetts and Rhodeisland; then north four miles and 40 rods; then east, one mile by a river; then north again, three miles and 280 rods; then west, eight and an half miles; then south eight miles, to the first bounds. But this measure must be very large, since all Uxbridge, almost the whole of Northbridge, and a large part of Upton were taken from Mendon, together with Milford; and still there remain two parishes in the town. Its present boundaries by actual survey, are south, by Rhodeisland State, six miles and a quarter; on the west, by Uxbridge and Northbridge, seven miles and 140 rods to Upton line; northwest, by Upton, two miles; northeast, by Milford, four miles and a quarter; east, by Bellingham in the county of Suffolk, four miles and three quarters. When they held their first town meeting, or first acted as a corporate body, does not appear, nor when the Church was gathered and the first minister was settled. Here, as in some other instances we may meet with, we have to lament the entire want of ancient records. If ever any records were kept in those early days, of these matters, they were lost when the town was broken up in the time of the Indian wars, or in some other way. We have also to regret the obscurity and defects attending such records as are to be found.

In little more than eight years from the incorporation of Mendon, commenced the Narraganset, or King Philip's war. And all that I can find in "Hubbard's history of the Indian wars," or in "Governor Hutchinson's history of Massachusetts," or by any other way, is this; viz. "On the 14th of July, 1675, the Nipnet or Nipmuck Indians, killed four or five people at Mendon." And this was the first mischief ever done by the Indians within the ancient limits of the Massachusetts. For it must be remembered, that the colony of Plymouth was not annexed to Massachusetts until the charter from William and Mary in 1691. I cannot find that ever any other mischief was done by the Indians in Mendon, except the abovementioned. However the people then here were in such fear and danger, as that the town was entirely broken up for some time, and most or all of them moved off. How long the place remained desolate, we are unable to say with certainty. It could not be long, as will appear by the following account of the ecclesiastical state of Mendon.

All we can find on record is simply this—"The Rev. Joseph Emerson was the first Pastor of the Church in Mendon. He lived here before the war, known by the stile of King Philip's Indian war." I add, in this war the town and church were broken up, and Mr. Emerson never returned to officiate with them in the pastoral office. Tradition says, he was minister here about eight years, this will carry back the date of his ordination, and the gathering of the Church, to the year 1667, that is, to about the time when the town was incorporated.—The records go on to say—

" The

MENDON. 57

"The Rev. Grindall Rawson was the second Paſtor of the Church in this town. He was ordained in the 20th year of his age. He died February the 6th, 1715, in the 57th year of his age, and 37th of his miniſtry." But here we muſt obſerve, his tombſtone ſays, "he died in the 35th year of his miniſtry:" And this is the more probable for ſeveral reaſons. According to the town record, he muſt have been ſettled in the year 1678, which is carrying it back too near the time when the town was broken up: And conſidering the then ſtate of the country, in conſtant fear, and great danger from the Indians, it is not at all likely they ſhould reſettle ſo ſoon; but in the year 1680 they probably might.

The records further ſay, "The Rev. Joſeph Dorr was the third Paſtor of this Church. He died March 9th, 1768, in the 79th year of his age, and the 52d year of his miniſtry." This will carry back the time of the Rev. Mr. Dorr's ordination to the year, 1716. The Rev. Joſeph Willard ſucceeded Mr. Dorr in the work of the goſpel miniſtry in Mendon, whereunto he was ſolemnly conſecrated on the 19th of April, 1769. He was diſmiſſed from his paſtoral relation to this Church and people, on the 4th of December, 1782, in the 13th year of his miniſtry. This diſmiſſion of Mr. Willard was occaſioned by the coldneſs and inattention of the people. The Rev. Mr. Willard was inſtalled Paſtor of the Church and flock of God in Boxborough, in the county of Middleſex, on the 2d of November, 1785, where he lives in

E   peace

peace and harmony with his people. The Rev. Caleb Alexander succeeded Mr. Willard as Pastor of the first Church and congregation in Mendon, (the fifth in succession) where he was installed the 12th of April, 1786, in the 31st year of his age, and where he continues in his sacred employment. This gentleman had been previously settled at Newmarlborough in the county of Berkshire for a short space.

There is a second parish in this town, which was incorporated as a distinct precinct for ministerial purposes, by the appellation of " The south parish in Mendon," in the year 1766. In this same year the congregational inhabitants of this parish began to build them a meetinghouse for the publick worship of God, and accomplished the work in a short time. And in the year 1768, the Church of Christ, in this south parish was imbodied, and the Rev. Benjamin Balch was ordained their Pastor. And on Saturday morning March 27th, 1772, before daylight, Mr. Balch left the parish, without knowledge or consent of the people of his charge. Mr. Balch was, a few years since, installed at Barrington in Newhampshire. About one half of the people of this south parish have been Anabaptists and Quakers, ever since that part of the town was first settled, which was about 90 years ago. And from the time when Mr. Balch left this parish, the congregational interest therein has been in a declining state. They seldom have any preaching; nor is there any present prospect of their

MENDON.

their ever having another minifter fettled among them.

As to the religious ftate of both parifhes in Mendon, let it fuffice to fay, there are, in general, three denominations, Congregationalifts, Anabaptifts, and Friends. There is another clafs without a name. A fmall fociety of Friends are very punctual in attending their form of worfhip; and they have a very decent meetinghoufe for the purpofe. Some who are, politically, Friends, do not intereft themfelves much in any form. There is not in the town any incorporated fociety of Anabaptifts. They who are of this perfuafion, go fometimes on the fabbath to other towns, to attend publick worfhip, in their way.

Having faid what will be thought fufficient, refpecting the religious ftate and ecclefiaftical polity of Mendon, fome Geographical Defcription of the town fhall now be prefented to the reader.

The land, in general, is good, though there is fome which is rough and hard: The foil is rich and very productive. It is moftly high, hilly land, yet not very uneven: And there is a fufficiency of ftones to fence their farms. The old parifh abounds principally in mowing and pafture land. The fouth parifh is better adapted to grain. The town is excellent for orcharding, and all kinds of fruit trees. There are three high hills in this place, from either of which the four Newengland States, may be feen, in a fair day. They are known by the following names, *Caleb*'s *Hill*, this is near the centre of the town; *Wigwam Hill*, is fituated a little

tle to the south west, from Caleb's Hill; and *Miskee* or Misqueo Hill, this lies in the northwest corner of the town, and part of it falls within the limits of Upton.

The groves of wood here are, in general, very thrifty and tall, consisting for the most part of walnut and oak. There are fine forests of most excellent chesnut, suitable for buildings or for fences.

The town of Mendon, like almost all other high, hilly, rocky places, is moist, rich, strong land, well watered with numerous springs and rivulets: But there are no streams of note, except two: The first is Charles River, which touches on the eastern part of this town. This River takes its rise from a marshy place in the southwest part of Hopkinton, in the county of Middlesex, and runs south, through Milford in this county, and the easterly part of Mendon; and then passes on to Bellingham, in the county of Suffolk. The second is Mill River, which also originates in the southwestern part of Hopkinton, and, running through the western part of Milford, passes through the easterly side of Mendon, and crossing the road to Providence, joins Blackstone River, near Winsooket Falls, in the town of Cumberland, in the State of Rhodeisland. There is but one Pond in this town, situated in the western part of it, and called *Taft's Pond*; it is large, and affords great plenty of the usual sorts of hook fish. There is no visible stream which runs into this pond; but a stream issues from it sufficient to carry a grist mill. On these

these rivers and streams, within the town, there are five grist mills, two saw mills, two clothiers' works, and one forge. There is some good interval lands upon these streams, and some bodies of excellent meadows, and industry might make more.

The people subsist chiefly by farming; they have indeed the common mechanicks, and one or two dealers in European, East and Westindia goods: And here they have both pot and pearl ash works.

The place derives great benefit from the publick roads which pass through it in various directions. The road from the northerly part of Connecticut, passes through Mendon to Boston. The post road from Worcester to Providence also goes through this town; as also a road, of much travel, from Vermont and Newhampshire, and the north part of the county of Worcester into the State of Rhodeisland. Mendon is situated quite at the southeast angle of the county; and is 37 miles from Boston, to the southwest, and 18 miles from the Courthouse in Worcester. When the late enumeration was made there were 222 dwelling houses, and 1555 inhabitants, in the place. It has stood as the twelfth among the towns, in the proportion it pays to a state tax.

BROOKFIELD.

THIS is the third town in age, and the firſt as to its wealth and number, in the county, containing, when the cenſus was taken, 438 dwelling houſes, and 3100 inhabitants. A number of inhabitants of Ipſwich, in the county of Eſſex, petitioned the General Court for a tract of land, and obtained their requeſt, in the words following, " At a great and general Court of election held at Boſton the 20th of May, 1660. In anſwer to a petition of ſeveral inhabitants of Ipſwich, this court judgeth it meet to grant the petitioners ſix miles ſquare, or ſo much land as ſhall be contained in ſuch a compaſs, in a place near Quaboag pond." The grantees, that they might have a juſt and equitable, as well as a legal, right to the land, purchaſed it of the natives, who claimed and poſſeſſed it, and it was conveyed to them by deed. Notwithſtanding the great diſadvantages under which they then laboured, in the infancy of our country; in the midſt of the Indian enemy, and no Engliſh ſettlements nearer than Marlborough on the eaſt, and Springfield on the weſt, the inhabitants ſo increaſed and flouriſhed, as that upon application to the General Court, they were incorporated into a townſhip, by the name of Brookfield, by an act which bears date, October 15th, 1673. But the court appointed and continued a committee of three gentlemen, belonging to other places, to direct,

rect, regulate and ratify all affairs relative to settling and building up the town. A committee, appointed as aforesaid, petitioned the General Court to be released from such services, and prayed that the inhabitants might be left to conduct and manage their own affairs, which was granted November 12th, 1718. The inhabitants, not satisfied with their first grant, petitioned the Court for more land, when an act passed December 3, 1719, making the town eight miles square.

In the year 1675, not two years after its incorporation, Brookfield was utterly destroyed by the Indians, when the inhabitants consisted of about twenty families; they had then a house for publick worship, and preaching, but no settled minister. The circumstances of its desolation are of importance to be transmitted to posterity, and I shall relate them, as I have collected and laid them together from the late Governor Hutchinson's history of Massachusetts, the Rev. Mr. Hubbard's history of the Indian war, and Capt. Thomas Wheeler's narrative thereof. " The Nipnet or Nipmuck[*] Indians, having on the 14th of July, 1675, killed four or five people at Mendon, the governor and council, in hopes of reclaiming them, sent Capt. Edward Hutchinson, of Boston, to Quaboag, Brookfield, near which place there was to be a great rendezvous of those Indians, to treat with several Sachems, in order to the publick peace: and ordered Capt. Thomas Wheeler, of Concord, with a part of his troop, about 20 men, to accompany

[*] " These were seated upon less rivers and lakes, or large ponds, where Oxford now is, and towns near it." Hutchinson's history.

pany him for security and assistance. They arrived on the Lord's day, August the 1st, and sent a message to the Indians, desiring to treat with them. Three of the chief Sachems promised to meet them next morning about eight o'clock, August 2d, upon a plain at the head of Wickaboug Pond, two or three miles west of the meetinghouse. Captains Hutchinson and Wheeler, with their company, and three of the principal inhabitants of Brookfield, Capt. John Ayres, John Coye, and Joseph Pritchard, resorted thither at the appointed time, but found not the Indians there. They then rode forward about four or five miles towards the Nipnet's chief town. When they came to a place called Mominimisset, a narrow passage, between a steep hill and a thick swamp, they were ambushed by two or three hundred Indians, who shot down eight of the company, viz. Zechariah Phillips of Boston, Timothy Farley of Billerica, Edward Colburn of Chelmsford, Samuel Smedley of Concord, Sydrach Hapgood of Sudbury, and Capt. Ayres, John Coye and Joseph Pritchard of Brookfield, named above, and mortally wounded Capt. Hutchinson. The rest escaped, through a bye path, to Brookfield. The Indians flocked into the town; but the inhabitants, being alarmed, had all got together in the principal house, on an eminence, a little to the southeast of where the west parish meetinghouse now stands. They had the mortification to see all their dwelling houses, about 20, with all their barns and outhouses burnt. The house where they had assembled, was then surrounded, and a variety of

attempts

attempts were made for two days and nights to set fire to it, but did not succeed. "At length, August 4th, at evening, the Indians filled a cart with hemp, and other combuftible matter, which they kindled, and endeavoured to thruft to the houfe in order to fire it; but this attempt was defeated, partly by a fhower of rain which fell and wet the materials, as Capt. Wheeler fays in his narrative, who was on the fpot, and partly by aid arriving: For Major Willard, who had been fent after fome other Indians weftward of Lancafter and Groton, hearing of the diftrefs of Brookfield, when he was about four or five miles from Lancafter, altered his courfe, and the fame night reached Brookfield, with Capt. Parker, and 46 men about an hour after it was dark, after a tedious march of 30 miles. And though the Indian fcouts difcovered him and fired their alarm guns, yet the main body, from their high joy, always accompanied with a horrid noife, heard them not. Willard joined the befieged, and the Indians immediately poured in all the fhot they could, but without execution, and then burning all the buildings, except this garrifon, and deftroying all the horfes and cattle they could find, withdrew to their dens. They were not purfued being much fuperiour in number.

It is fitting to add to the above, the very particular account, which the Rev. Dr. Fifke of Brookfield, has given in a marginal note, annexed to an hiftorical difcourfe concerning the fettlement of this town, and its diftreffes during the Indian wars,

preached

preached December 31ft, 1775, and immediately publifhed. The account is as follows, viz. "That three of the men killed in the ambufhment, belonged to Brookfield, as above named: That when the Indians purfued the party into the town, they fet fire to all the buildings except a few in the neighbourhood of the houfe in which the inhabitants had taken fhelter: That they endeavoured to intercept five or fix men who had gone to a neighbouring houfe to fecure fome things there: But they all got fafe to the place of refuge, except a young man, Samuel Pritchard, who was ftopped fhort by a fatal bullet: That the houfe in which they were befieged was unfortified, except by a few logs haftily tumbled up on the outfide, after the alarm, and by a few feather beds hung up on the infide. And though the fiege continued from Monday in the afternoon, until early on Thurfday morning, Auguft 5th, in which time innumerable balls entered the houfe, only one man, Henry Young, who was in the chamber, was killed. The Indians fhot many fire arrows to burn the houfe, but without effect.—When the troop which relieved Brookfield, got into the town, which was late at night, they were joined by great numbers of cattle, which had collected together in their fright at the conflagration of the buildings, and the firing and war whoops of the Indians; and for protection thefe poor animals followed the troop till they arrived at the befieged houfe. The Indians deceived hereby, and thinking there was a much larger number of horfemen than there really was, immediately fet fire to

the

the barn belonging to the besieged, house, and to Joseph Pritchard's house and barn, and the meetinghouse, which were the only buildings left unburnt, and went off. A garrison was maintained at this house till winter, when the court ordered the people away, soon after which the Indians came and burnt this house also."

Having mentioned Major Willard, Capt. Hutchinson and Capt. Wheeler, it will be proper to say something further respecting each of them.—Captains Hutchinson and Wheeler, tarried at Brookfield until August 13th, and then, with most of their men, set off for their homes; they arrived at Marlborough the next day, where Capt. Hutchinson, fatigued with his journey and his wound growing worse, died August 19th, and was there buried the next day, August 20th, 1675.

Captain Wheeler, who accompanied Capt. Hutchinson, and saw him buried, the next day, August 21st, arrived safe at Concord, where he and they who returned with him, kept October 21st, 1675, as a day of praise and thanksgiving to God for their remarkable deliverance and safe return, when the Rev. Mr. Bulkley of Concord preached a sermon to them from those words in Psalm cxvi. 12, ¿ " What shall I render unto the Lord for all his benefits towards me?" which was printed.

Major Willard tarried at Brookfield, and at Hadley and the adjacent towns, for several weeks, and then returned to Groton, where the safety of that and some neighbouring towns required his presence. He was soon after displaced for going to Brookfield without orders, or while under orders to march another way. The Rev. Dr. Fiske's observations hereupon in a note, are well worthy insertion in this place. "Major Willard's conduct in altering his course and coming to the relief of Brookfield, being dictated by humanity and executed with bravery and success, has gained him the applause of people in general. But as it was beside his orders, he was censured by the court and cashiered, which disgusted his friends, and broke his heart. And though the punishment may seem too rigorous, yet it is to be remembered, that if commanders of parties, sent upon particular expeditions, may take liberty to vary from their express orders, nothing effectual could be accomplished, and only confusion, disappointment, loss, and in many cases ruin, would be likely to ensue."

To return to Brookfield. The town, totally destroyed by the Indians in August 1675, lay in ruins several years, and the inhabitants were dispersed. "But, says the Rev. Dr. Fiske, in the sermon above referred to, peace being settled with the Indians, some of the dispersed, after a while, returned to the place of their former habitation, and in conjunction with others, gradually resettled the town, so that in the year 1692, they had a committee appointed by the court, as formerly, to direct and regulate the settlement of said plantation and the affairs thereof. But it being still in the midst of a wilderness, and always exposed to the blood thirsty savages, whenever they should

BROOKFIELD. 69

should take it into their heads to molest the English, its increase and improvements were flow."

In the war which is commonly denominated Queen Anne's war, which broke out not long after the resettlement of the town, and continued several years, Brookfield, as well as many other towns, was greatly harassed and annoyed; the Indians frequently making sudden inroads, killing and scalping, or captivating one and another of the inhabitants. During this war, a number of men, women and children were killed, several taken prisoners, and some were wounded. The particulars are as follow, as related by the Rev. Dr. Fiske, in the sermon above referred to. " The first mischief was in the latter end of July or beginning of August 1692. A party of Indians came into the town and broke up two or three families. Joseph Woolcot being at work at a little distance from his house, his wife, being fearful, took her children and went out to him. When they returned to the house at noon, they found the Indians had been there, for his gun and several other things were missing. And looking out at a window he saw an Indian, at some distance, coming towards the house. He immediately sent out his wife and his two little daughters to hide themselves in the bushes; and he taking his little son under his arm and his broad ax in his hand, went out with his dog in sight of the Indian. The dog being large and fierce, attacked the Indian so furiously, that he was obliged to discharge his gun at the dog to rid himself of him; immediately upon which Woolcot

sat

sat down the child and pursued the Indian till he heard the bullet roll down his gun, the Indian charging as he ran; he then turned back, snatched up his child and made his escape, through the swamps, to a fort. His wife being greatly terrified, discovered by her shrieks where she was; and the Indian soon found and dispatched both her and her children. Others of the party about the same time, came into the house of one Mason while the family were at dinner. They killed Mason and one or two children, and took his wife and an infant which they had wounded, and carried them off. They also took two brothers, Thomas and Daniel Lawrence; they soon dispatched Thomas, pretending he had misinformed them about the number of men which were in the town. John Lawrence, their brother, rode with all haste to Springfield for assistance. A company, under Capt. Colton, came with the greatest speed and pursued the Indians. They found Mrs. Mason's child, which the savages had knocked on the head and thrown away in the bushes; and continuing their pursuit, they came upon the Indians' encampment, which was a sort of brush hedge, which they deridingly called "Englishmen's fort." The party waited till break of day, and then came so near as to put their guns through this brush and fire upon the Indians, fourteen or fifteen of whom were killed, the rest fled with such precipitation as to leave several of their arms, blankets, powderhorns, &c. and their prisoners, Daniel Lawrence and Mrs. Mason, whom our men conducted back. This same John Lawrence, who

who rode exprefs and procured the company which refcued the abovementioned prifoners, was afterwards going in company with one Samuel Owen, in fearch of a man who was miffing; the Indians came upon them, killed Lawrence, but Owen efcaped. Mary MacIntofh was fired upon and killed as fhe was milking her cows. Robert Grainger and John Clary were paffing along the road, on a certain day, and being fired upon by the favages, Grainger was killed on the fpot; Clary attempted to efcape, but had not fled far before he alfo was fhot down. At another time, Thomas Battis of Brookfield, riding exprefs to Hadley, was killed in the wildernefs, in a place now called Belchertown. Early one morning John Woolcot, a lad about twelve or fourteen years old, was riding in fearch of the cows, when the Indians fired at him, killed his horfe from under him and took him prifoner. The people at Jennings's garrifon hearing the firing, and concluding the people at another garrifon were befet, fix men fet out for their affiftance, but were waylayed by the Indians. The Englifh faw not their danger, till they faw there was no efcaping it. And therefore, knowing that an Indian could not look an Englifhman in the face, and take a right aim, they ftood their ground, prefenting their pieces wherever they faw an Indian, without difcharging them, excepting Abijah Bartlet, who turned to flee and was fhot dead. The Indians kept firing at the reft and wounded three of them, Jofeph Jennings in two places; one ball grazed the top of his head, by which

which he was struck blind for a moment; another ball passed through his shoulder, wounding his collar bone; yet by neither did he fall, nor was he mortally wounded. Benjamin Jennings was wounded in the leg, and John Green in the wrist. They were preserved at last by the following stratagem. A large dog, hearing the firing, came to our men; one of whom, to encourage his brethren and intimidate the Indians, called out, "Capt. Williams is come to our assistance, for here is his dog." The Indians, seeing the dog, and knowing Williams to be a famous warrior, immediately fled, and our men escaped. John Woolcot the lad abovementioned, was carried to Canada, where he remained six or seven years, during which time, by conversing wholly with Indians, he not only lost his native language, but became so naturalized to the savages, as to be unwilling, for a while, to return to his native country. Some years afterwards, viz. in March, 1728, in a time of peace, he and another man having been hunting, and coming down Connecticut River with a freight of skins and fur, they were hailed by some Indians; but not being willing to go to them, they steered for another shore. The Indians landed at a little distance from them; several shots were exchanged, at length Woolcot was killed.

The last mischief which was done by the savages, in Brookfield, was about the 20th of July, 1710. Six men, viz. Ebenezer Hayward, John White, Stephen and Benjamin Jennings, John Grosvenor and Joseph Kellog, were making hay in the meadows,

dows, when the Indians, who had been watching an opportunity to furprife them, fprung fuddenly upon them, difpatched five of them, and took the other, John White, prifoner. White fpying a fmall company of our people at fome diftance, jumped from the Indian who held him, and ran to join his friends; but the Indian fired after him, and wounded him in the thigh, by which he fell; but foon recovering and running again, he was again fired at and received his death wound."

   Great indeed were the difficulties, difcouragements and hardfhips, under which this then infant plantation laboured, fo that it was more than forty years from the breaking up of the town, and burning the firft meetinghoufe, before they erected another. A church was gathered, and the Rev. Thomas Cheney was ordained their firft Paftor, the third Wednefday of October, 1717. He continued their minifter a little more than 30 years, as he died December 11th, 1747, aged 57 years. To him fucceeded, in the work of the miniftry, the Rev. Elifha Harding, who was folemnly feparated hereunto September 13th, 1749. So rapidly did the town increafe and flourifh, after the fettlement of their firft minifter, that on March 29th, 1750, a fecond parifh was incorporated in the northerly part of the town. Here a church was gathered May 28th, 1752, and the Rev. Eli Forbes was ordained their firft minifter on the third of June the fame year. Mr. Harding continued the minifter of the firft precinct until the people fell into a moft unhappy controverfy about erecting a

F   new

new meetinghouse. The contention was so sharp, and the opposite parties so uncomplying that they parted, and formed two distinct religious societies. The act for dividing the first parish, and incorporating the third precinct passed November 8th, 1754. In consequence hereof, Mr. Harding requested a dismission, which was granted by the church and confirmed by a mutual ecclesiastical council, May 8th, 1755. After his dismission the Rev. Joseph Parsons was ordained Pastor of the first church and precinct, on the 23d of November, 1757. A church was gathered in the third parish, or east precinct, April 15th, 1756, and on the 24th of May, 1758, the Rev. Nathan Fiske, D. D. was ordained their spiritual overseer, and still continues. Mr. Parsons continued Pastor of the first church upwards of thirteen years, being released from the sickness and pains of this mortal state January 17th, 1771, in the fourteenth year of his ministry, and 38th of his age. In about nine months after his decease, viz. on October 23d, 1771, the Rev. Ephraim Ward was separated to the pastoral office, the fourth in succession in the first church and precinct.

The Rev. Mr. Forbes continued in the faithful discharge of the ministerial work among the people of the second precinct almost 23 years; and on the 1st of March, 1775, the pastoral relation was dissolved by mutual consent, under the conduct of an ecclesiastical council, each party in charity with, and heartily recommending the other. To him succeeded, as second Pastor of the second precinct, the Rev. Joseph Appleton, who was solemnly

BROOKFIELD. 75

emnly separated to the work of the gospel ministry, October 30th, 1776.

The Rev. Mr. Forbes was, June 5th, 1776, installed Pastor of the first church in Gloucester, Cape Anne, where he continues, faithfully serving God in the gospel of his Son. It is fitting farther to observe, that Mr. Forbes, while minister in Brookfield, went repeatedly Chaplain to provincial regiments, in the last French war, to the westward, which qualified him the better to endure the hardships and fatigues of a mission to the western tribes of Indians, which he was requested by the board of Commissioners at Boston to undertake. His people were at first averse to his going; but were at length prevailed upon by a committee of that board to consent, May 30th, 1762, that he might go for a few months. He accordingly set out the first of June, with Mr. Rice, now minister of Westminster and Mr. Elisha Gunn of Montague, for an interpreter: They followed Mohawk River about 70 miles, then turned southward to lake Ostiego near *Cherry Valley*, (this lake makes the head of one of the main branches of Susquehannah River) crossed the lake, went down that river 120 miles to a town called *Onoquagie*, pleasantly situated on the eastern bank of the Susquehannah, then containing 30 houses, 40 families, and 300 inhabitants, besides upwards of 20 warriors. Here they arrived June 21st, 1762. Near this place were two small towns of Tuscaroras. Here he preached; opened two schools, one for adults, and another for children; gathered a church; administered

ministered special ordinances to them; and left them September 1st, 1762, under the care of Mr. Rice. During his stay there, he baptized great numbers; some brought their children 60 and 70 miles to receive Christian baptism: They were mostly infants, whose parents had been baptized by former missionaries, or in the Dutch or English churches in the vicinity of Albany.

Having gone through with the ecclesiastical history of Brookfield, a Geographical Description thereof shall now be presented.

Brookfield is distant from the Statehouse in Boston between sixty and seventy miles. The great post road from Boston to Newyork, runs through it; and the sixty one mile stone stands near the eastern boundary, and the seventy milestone near the western line. This town is bounded on the east by Spencer; on the south by Sturbridge and Western; on the west, by Western and Ware; and on the north, by Newbraintree and Oakham. It is a township of most excellent land in general. The face of the town is pretty uneven and stony, though there are three or four plains of considerable extent within it, one especially in the first parish, extensive, excellent for raising grain, and beautiful for building spots, and large tracts of meadow and interval upon Quaboag River, which runs in a westerly direction through the town. The main branch of this river comes from Rutland, another branch issues from North Pond, so called, in Leicester, and, running through Spencer, falls into Quaboag River in the easterly part of Brookfield.

The

BROOKFIELD.

The land is generally fertile, and richly repays the cultivator for his labour and pains; and there is such a variety of soils, as to be suited to tillage, grazing, mowing and fruit. All kinds of grain are raised here to advantage; and farmers here, as well as elsewhere are making great improvements in husbandry.

There is so little descent in Quaboag river for five miles, that the current is very sluggish, the waters almost stagnant, and the extensive meadows on each side are of small value in their present state, being so liable to be overflowed. This evil has been growing for many years, through increasing obstructions in so torpid a stream; so that the grass, from being large and of good quality, is now so poor, and the making it into hay so uncertain, as to be very generally rejected. By much labour and expense in clearing the channel of obstructions, this evil may be cured. A trial was made last year by the proprietors of the meadows, whereof they reaped, sensibly, good effects; and hence are encouraged to a determined perseverance. Besides this flat meadow, there are large tracts of swaley or swampy land, which yield considerable quantities of fowlmeadow and other valuable grasses, to the amount of two tons on an acre when made into hay.

There is one large pond in the south precinct of the extent of a mile square, called by the Indians Quaboag Pond; but now more generally denominated Podunk Pond, from a tract of meadow adjoining, which the Indians called Podunk.

Quaboag river advances directly to the very bank of this pond; then turns, almoſt at right angles, and runs parallel with the edge about twenty rods, leaving a narrow beach or ridge; then diverges ſo as to form a ſmall iſland, upon which ſhrubs, alders and buſhes are growing; then bends its courſe and opens a channel into the pond, at the northeaſt, running nearly through the middle of it, and paſſes off in an outlet at the weſterly edge. Cloſe to the ſide of the pond where the river enters, is a large bridge, there being a county road along the beach of this pond, for more than half a mile; and travellers paſs about twenty rods on a narrow ridge, between the river and pond, which, though very moderately ſloping on the ſide next the pond, is perpendicular on the ſide of the river, and is generally overflowed in the ſpring and fall, to the hazard and ſometimes ſuſpenſion of travelling. This beach had formerly a row of large pines and ſwamp white oaks growing upon it. But the floods, agitated by the winds, have ſo waſhed away the ſoil, that the moſt of them are dead and blown down, and the beach is gradually wearing away.

On the ſouth of this pond, and about a quarter of a mile diſtant, is another pond, of not more than half the amplitude of the former, known by the name of the South Pond. This communicates with, and empties its redundant waters into the larger pond, by a creek or brook, except in the time of a freſhet, when the waters flow ſo much faſter

faster into the great pond as to reverse the current of the brook, and replenish the lesser.

There is another considerable pond in the west precinct, called Wickoboag Pond, from whence quantities of iron ore are annually collected. This pond is supplied by several rivulets, and has one large outlet into the river, about twenty or thirty rods in length, called Lashaway. These ponds and rivers, and the other smaller streams, by which the land is intersected, are plentifully furnished with pickerel, perch, and divers other kinds of fish.

On the rivers and streams in the town, there are seven grist mills, six saw mills, and three fulling mills. Mr. Jenks, besides his mills, prosecutes the blacksmiths' business largely, and has two trip hammers, and a grindstone carried by water.

One of the clothiers' works above referred to, is in the first parish; a very convenient situation indeed for carrying on the clothiers' business in all its branches. Ellis and company are the proprietors hereof. About 5000 yards of cloth are annually dressed at these works. These men have obtained the art of coloring scarlet, which competent judges pronounce equal to any which is imported; an art which few in this Commonwealth have attained unto.

In a considerable part of the low lands, the clay lies near the surface. There is much clay adjoining the south pond, and clay forms the bed of the river. No mines have, as yet, been discovered, although search therefor has been made at no small

small expense. There is some iron ore, a bed of yellow ocre nearly exhausted, and large quantities, both of mud and stone, which yield copperas, and contain a strong vitriolic quality. Many of the wells, both on high and low grounds, have what is called hard water. There are also stones which contain sulphur; but how to extract it has not yet been discovered.

There are two large hills, principally in the first parish. One is called Coye's Hill, and supposed to take its name from one Coye, a proprietor of, and an early inhabitant in Brookfield. This hill extends into Western. The other is called *Ragged Hill*, probably from its extreme rough and rocky appearance. Both these hills are excellent for mowing, for pasturing, and for orcharding; and there are several very good farms upon them. Partly between these two hills there is a large ledge of rocks, which in all probability was rent asunder ages ago, by an earthquake: The rock on one side is shelving over, and the opening made is sufficient to contain an hundred men; and the appearance indicates that it was formerly a place of rendezvous for Indians. This place is called by the people of Brookfield, *The Stone House*.

The rivers, ponds and meadows, in this town, occasion heavy fogs, which, in some seasons, have produced putrid fevers, &c. But observation clearly teaches that the inhabitants here are as healthy as in other places; and they who live in the low lands, as they who live on the high. This place has been famed for the longevity, and

fruitfulness

fruitfulness of some of its inhabitants. In 1782, a Mr. Green, then above ninety, followed his fifth child, a woman in her sixty second year, to the grave, above four miles, riding erect and steady, on a lively horse. He died not long since, in the vicinity of Hanover in Newhampshire, aged upwards of an 100 years. Also in 1782, died the widow Elizabeth Olds in her 92d year. Her posterity were as follow; ten children, seventy three grand children, two hundred and one great grand children, and two of the fifth generation; two of her granddaughters being grandmothers. Total, two hundred and eighty six. Of these, two hundred and thirty two were living at her decease. In 1788, died Mr. Cyprian Rice, in the ninety eighth year of his age; and in a few months after died Mr. Elisha Rice, his brother, in the ninety ninth year of his age. They were born at Marlborough. They left not a numerous issue. There is now living in Brookfield a Mr. Thomas Ainsworth, who supposes he is the last surviving soldier who was in the famous Lovell's fight.

It is so long since the aboriginals quitted these grounds, that their monuments are almost effaced. Once in a while a point of an arrow, or some stone is found which bears the mark of Indian labour and dexterity. And there is still to be distinguished the spot on which they had a fort, and a cemetery where they buried their dead.

The growth of wood is principally chesnut, white oak, red oak, and some walnut. The

swamps

swamps and swales yield maple, black birch, ash, and some hemlock.

The inhabitants of Brookfield are chiefly farmers, though there is a proportion of mechanics, traders, and professional gentlemen. And the general appearance of the farms, buildings, roads, and manners of the people, makes a favourable impression, and denotes a good degree of cultivation, taste and improvement.

Brookfield is distant from the Courthouse in Worcester, about twenty miles to the southwest.

OXFORD.

THIS was a grant made by the government in the year 1682, to Joseph Dudley, Esq; Governor, to William Stoughton, Esq; Lieutenant-governor of Massachusetts, to Major Robert Thompson, Messrs. Cox and Blackwell, and their associates. It was stiled, A tract of land lying in the Nipnet or Nipmug country. The grant expressed eight miles square; but as surveyed and located, it must be near twelve miles in length from east to west, and about nine in width, from north to south, comprehending all Charlton, a part of Dudley, and a part of Ward. It was originally bounded west, on Newmedfield, (now Sturbridge) north, on a tract of land called the Country Gore,

and

and Leicester; east, on Sutton; and south, by a gore of land and Dudley. It was surveyed by Mr. Gore of Roxbury, and a return thereof being made to the court, they accepted the same, and on the 16th of May, 1683, they granted the plantation, and gave it the name of Oxford.

The original proprietors of Oxford, in the year 1686, let on about thirty families of French protestants, who were driven out of France, in consequence of the repeal of the edict of Nantz, by Lewis XIV, in the year 1684. These unhappy French people, being seated at the easterly part, or end of Oxford, were grievously annoyed and distressed by the Indians, and were soon destroyed, or driven away and dispersed by them. Tradition says, one Johnson (whether a Frenchman or Englishman is uncertain) was here killed, and one or two of his children, while his wife escaped unperceived out of the house, at evening, with a child in her arms, and walked to Woodstock, about fifteen miles, that night, to a garrison there. At what time this was we cannot precisely say. But in the year 1693, a particular act passed, empowering Oxford to send a representative to the General Court; as appears by the records in the Secretary's office of this Commonwealth.

As Oxford was then in the county of Suffolk, its first and earlier records were kept in Boston, and are said to have been burnt in the Statehouse there.

A deed was given by the original proprietors, or their heirs and executors, to such as were there, or

others,

others, of a part of the original grant, dated July 8th, 1713, that they might settle and build up the town. The first town meeting held in Oxford for the choice of town officers was on the 22d of July, 1713. The people inhabiting this territory were in continual fears from the natives; in consequence of which, the settlement of the town went on but slowly for many years. Except what has been related above, I cannot find that any persons were killed by the Indians in Oxford. But Governor Hutchinson gives a piece of history, which must not be omitted in this work. It is in these words. " On the sixth of August, 1724, four Indians came upon a small house in Oxford, which was built under a hill. They made a breach in the roof, and as one of them was attempting to enter, he received a shot in his belly from a courageous woman, the only person in the house, who had two muskets and two pistols charged, and was prepared for all four, but they thought fit to retreat, carrying off the dead, or wounded man." It is pity the name of this heroine has not been preserved, that it might be handed down to latest posterity.

The first settlers in Oxford, considering the then state of the country, took early care for the enjoyment and support of a preached gospel, and the institutions of Christianity among them: Accordingly the first church of Christ in this place was gathered January 18th, 1721, and the Rev. John Campbell was ordained the first minister, that same year, viz. March 11th, 1721. This gentleman

man came from the north of Scotland; was educated at Edinburgh, and received the honours of that Univerſity. He came into America in the year 1717. He continued the worthy and faithful paſtor of the church and flock here, until May 25th, 1761, when he died in the 71ſt year of his age, and in the 42d of his miniſtry.

The Rev. Mr. Campbell was ſucceeded in the ſacred office by the Rev. Joſeph Bowman, who was inſtalled here November 14th, 1764. (This Mr. Bowman was firſt ordained at Boſton, Auguſt 31ſt, 1762, to the work of the goſpel miniſtry, more eſpecially, among the Mohawk Indians on the weſtern borders of Newengland. He went to Onohoquague, an Indian town on the Suſquehannah, in October following. He returned the laſt of May, 1763; but hoſtilities commencing between the Indians tribes in June, he did not go back to them; and the war continuing, he was, by the board of commiſſioners, diſmiſſed from his miſſion in June, 1764.)—Mr. Bowman lived in great harmony with the people of Oxford until 1775, when the then ſtate of the country, as to the controverſy and war with Greatbritain, occaſioned differences among the people; theſe led a number to profeſs themſelves Quakers, and then they declared themſelves to be of the ſect, called Univerſaliſts, which finally ended in Mr. Bowman's diſmiſſion, at his deſire, with advice of council, Auguſt 28th, 1782. After his removal from Oxford, the Rev. Mr. Bowman was inſtalled at Bernard, in the State of Vermont, September 22, 1784, where he ſtill continues, enjoying

joying the affection of the people, in a growing, flourishing town, and bleſſed with peace and proſperity in his latter days.

The Rev. Elias Dudley was ordained ſucceſſor to Mr. Bowman at Oxford, April 13th, 1791.

In the town of Oxford there is a ſociety of them who are denominated Univerſaliſts, (about a fifth of the inhabitants :) Theſe, with ſome families from ſeveral neighbouring towns, make a reſpectable ſociety : And they have erected a large elegant meetinghouſe, towards the ſouth end of Oxford plain, where the road from Connecticut interſects the road from Worceſter to Dudley. This houſe is conſtructed upon the moſt modern plan, with a tower and bell. This ſociety have not, as yet, any ſettled miniſter. There is alſo a number in Oxford of the Anabaptiſt perſuaſion; they are deſtitute of any ſtated teacher.

We will now give ſome Geographical Deſcription of this town. Oxford, though very extenſive at firſt, has been much curtailed, neverthelefs, it is ſtill a large and reſpectable town, being about ſeven miles in length from north to ſouth, and about five miles in width from eaſt to weſt. The preſent boundaries of Oxford are as follow ; north, it is bounded on Leiceſter, Ward, and a country gore of land : Eaſt, by Sutton ; ſouth, by a gore of land, and Dudley ; and weſt, by Charlton. When the late cenſus was taken there were 150 houſes, and 1000 inhabitants in the town. The town of Oxford is not very hilly and uneven : In the centre thereof there is a large and fine plain of

OXFORD. 87

a mile and a half in length, and about a mile in width: This plain is almoſt wholly under cultivation, and is pretty level. On this plain, the road from Worceſter to the eaſterly part of Connecticut, and to Rhodeiſland, runs from the north to the ſouth: Near the north end of it ſtands the congregational meetinghouſe; and about a mile ſouth of this is the meetinghouſe of the ſociety of Univerſaliſts: Theſe houſes are both large and elegant: On either ſide of the ſtreet there are many good buildings; and almoſt the whole plain is under the eye of the traveller at once. From the plain the lands riſe on all ſides, eſpecially on the eaſt and on the weſt; but not very high. The ſoil on the plain is good for grain of all kinds; but not ſo for paſturage or mowing. But the higher lands are very good for mowing, paſturing and orcharding, the ſoil is ſtrong and fertile. Dudley hills, ſo called, on the ſouth, which are pretty high, fall partly within the limits of Oxford. About three quarters of a mile weſt of the great road on the plain, runs French River from the north to the ſouth, which falls into the river Quinebaug in the town of Thompſon in the State of Connecticut. This river derived its name from the French proteſtants who firſt ſettled in Oxford. On this river are ſome very good meadows of ſeveral hundreds of acres. On the eaſt ſide of the plain there is a fine ſtream, which heads in Great Meadow, ſo called, in the northerly part of the town, containing 100 acres, or more. By the ſides of this ſtream there are ſome pretty good meadows. This brook empties into French River.

River. Potash Brook, so called, which is never dry, is a fine rivulet, and falls into the above mentioned brook. Upon the river, and on these streams, there are within Oxford limits, three grist mills; six saw mills; and two clothiers' works. There are also, in the town, potash works. There are two very pretty ponds in the town: One in the westerly part, called Augootsback: The other a little north of the first meetinghouse on the Worcester road, known by the name of *Oxford Pond*. There are some small cedar swamps, in this town, which yield cedar for shingles, and other valuable uses. The town is in general well wooded: On the higher lands are oaks of all kinds, walnut and chesnut: On the lower, grow ash, birch, maple, &c. There is some pitch pine in the town: But not much white pine, at this day, that being chiefly taken off. On the plain, there are two or three stores of European and India goods: And in the town there are all the common artificers, tradesmen and mechanics; but the body of the people are farmers. The roads of travel through Oxford are an advantage to the town—the largest road is that which comes from Connecticut through Charlton, Oxford, to Sutton, and so on to Boston, falling into the post road in Weston: The next, is the road from Worcester, through Oxford, to Dudley, &c. &c. Oxford is situated to the southwest from Boston, at the distance of 54 miles; and from Worcester courthouse it is 10 miles, nearly south.

SUTTON.

SUTTON.

THIS tract of land was originally purchased by a number of gentlemen, of Sachem John Wampus, and his company, Indians who claimed it. Wampus first reserved four miles square, for his countrymen the Indians, which they called *Haſſanamiſco*; this is now Grafton. It was to begin at a certain bound, which he fixed upon; and then the purchasers above referred to, were to have as much land, as eight miles square would amount to, situated in the Nipmug country, between the towns of Mendon, Marlborough, Worcester, Oxford, and New Sherburne (now Douglass) and this was confirmed to the purchasers, May 15th, 1704, and formed into a township and called Sutton, by an act of the General Court, dated June 21st, 1715. That part of the original purchase, which fell to the eastward of Haſſanamiſco, or Grafton, was, part of it, many years ago annexed to the town of Westborough, and the other part, with some from Mendon and Hopkinton, taken to form the town of Upton. So that what now is properly Sutton does not lie in a bad form. A few families were annexed to Northbridge, some years ago: And a few also, at the northwest angle of the town, were annexed to Ward. The general boundaries of Sutton, are at present, as follow: North, by Worcester; east and north, by Grafton; east,

east, by Northbridge and Uxbridge; south, by Douglass; west, by Oxford; and northwest, by Ward. Oxford line is S. 1° W. Douglass, E. 60° N. Mendon, N. 8° E. Worcester, W. 22° S.

The settling and peopling of the town was retarded for some time, by reason of wars with the Indians. However, in the year 1716, three families had got seated in the place, and wintered there in the winter of 1716 and 1717, when the great snow fell, as our fathers have told us. This snow fell on some of the last days of February, old stile, and came so deep, that it wholly covered over the hut in which one of the families lived. The man being from home, the family might have perished had not an Indian, who knew the circumstances, come to their relief. He found the hut only by the hole which the smoke from the fire place had made through the snow.

In September 1717, the fall after the great snow, the first child was born in the town, named Abigail Marsh, daughter of Mr. Benjamin Marsh, who was afterwards an anabaptist elder in the town. This woman is now living, has had four husbands, and is, at this time, a widow; her name is Chase.

The inhabitants of Sutton first acted as a body corporate, or held their first town meeting on the 2d day of December, 1718, at the dwelling house of Mr. John Stockwell. Their business was to organize themselves, and to choose a committee to join the proprietors' committee in order to procure preaching. Consequently they must have been incorporated a little before by an act of the Legislature

SUTTON.

ture, and vested with full town powers and privileges: And this was previous to the incorporation of Leicester or Rutland.

The exact day when the first congregational church in Sutton was imbodied cannot be ascertained. The record says, "In the fall of the year 1720." The first minister, the Rev. John MacKinstry, was ordained November 9th, 1720. He was a gentleman of good abilities and had his education in Scotland. Observe, by the way, the early care and pains this people took to have the gospel preached, and a minister settled among them. In about four years from their beginning the settlement of the place, they had a minister ordained.

Mr. MacKinstry differed so much from the people in his notions of church government, that they parted: And he was dismissed from his pastoral relation to them, September 2d, 1728. This gentleman was afterwards resettled in Connecticut.

The second minister of the town, the Rev. David Hall, was ordained October 15th, 1729. He received the honourary degree of *Doctor of Divinity*, at Dartmouth college, in the year 1777. After a life of piety and usefulness, he died May 8th, 1789, in the 85th year of his age, and the 60th year of his ministry.

Dr. Hall was succeeded in the sacred office by the Rev. Edmund Mills, who was separated thereunto June 23d, 1790. The people of the first congregational church and society have lately repaired their meetinghouse, and built a tower to it: And Mr. Ebenezer Warters, a man of large property

erty in the town, has given them a bell weighing about 750 ℔. and which cost upwards of 80*l.* And Mr. Gardner Warters, deceased, gave 30*l.* towards a clock for the meetinghouse.

The second parish in Sutton was incorporated by an act of Court, October 28th, 1743. This is about three miles wide, and six and one half miles in length ; so that the old parish is much larger. The first meeting of the second parish was held December 26th, 1743. The second congregational church in the town, was formed by a covenant, dated September 10th, 1747. The Rev. James Welman was consecrated Pastor of the second church October 7th, 1747, and was dismissed from office July 22d, 1760. The Rev. Mr. Welman was, in 1768, resettled at Cornish, in the county of Cheshire, in the State of Newhampshire.

Mr. Welman was succeeded in the pastoral office, in the second church in Sutton, by the Rev. Ebenezer Chaplain, who was ordained November 14th, 1764.

There is no record to be found when the first Anabaptist society was collected in Sutton, nor when Mr. Benjamin Marsh, their first elder, was ordained. Tradition says, it was about the year 1735. They built a small meetinghouse about a mile westerly from the first parish meetinghouse. After some years part of Elder Marsh's congregation left him, and joining with new ones, in the year 1767 introduced Mr. Jeremiah Barstow, as their Elder, and built another Anabaptist meetinghouse about a mile further westerly, on the road towards

towards Oxford. In 1772, the major part of Elder Barſtow's ſociety became diſſatisfied with him; he then, with his adherents, aſked a diſmiſſion from the reſt, and adjoined to Elder Marſh and the remainder of his ſociety. In January 1775, Elder Marſh died in the 89th year of his age. Mr. Barſtow kept up a ſociety in town, until 1782, when he moved away. In 1783, they introduced Mr. Ebenezer Lamſon as their teacher, and who, continuing with them until the firſt of April, 1788, was then ordained their elder. In the ſoutheaſt part of the town the people have for ſeveral years heard one Mr. William Batcheldor, who lived among them, and in October, 1792, he was ordained their elder.

About ten years paſt, the Shakers made conſiderable appearance in the ſecond pariſh, in this town, but have ſome time ſince, wholly ſubſided.

There have alſo, for ten or twelve years paſt, been a number of the ſect called Univerſaliſts, in Sutton; the moſt of them congregate at Oxford; a few at Grafton. There is one family in town, who profeſs to be Quakers. The number of theſe ſeveral denominations cannot be aſcertained, as many of them are unſtable.

We will now preſent our readers with ſome Topographical Deſcription of the town of Sutton.

The general face of it is hilly land, of a deep loam, pretty rocky, good for orcharding, and for Indian corn and graſs; but indifferent for all other ſorts of grain, and for flax. There are ſeveral meadows and ſwamps, but none very extenſive, or any way remarkable. There is a confiderable body of poor land in the fouth part of the town; and there is a fmall quantity of poor, broken land in the northeaft corner of the fecond parifh. There is fome good, both high and low interval land, on Blackftone River, fo called. As this river has its fource in Sutton, and is fingular in its formation and courfe, we fhall attempt a particular defcription of it. The reputed head of this river is a pond of about 70 acres, called Ramfhorn Pond, becaufe of the crookednefs of the ftream which iffues from it. The pond is fituated about two miles fouthweft from the fecond parifh meetinghoufe. It has a fmall inlet at the fouthweft part; the outlet is at the northeaft; and the ftream runs northeaft until it comes within about half a mile weft of faid meetinghoufe; then bears away northweft, and runs through Ward, within about half a mile of Ward meetinghoufe; takes in feveral ftreams in that town, which have mills on them, particularly one coming from Leicefter, called Kettle Brook; paffes on to Worcefter; and about a mile foutherly from the fouth meetinghoufe, receives Bimilick or Mill Brook, which comes from the North Pond in Worcefter, then turns back, running foutheafterly, and comes within half a mile eaft of Sutton fecond parifh meetinghoufe; paffes on and takes in the Mill Brook, fo called, the outlet of a large pond, called Crooked Pond, lying a little weft of the line between the two meetinghoufes in Sutton; and which is about a mile eaft of the little or Ramfhorn Pond firft mentioned. The inlet of this pond is on the fouthweft, southwest, the outlet is northeast, has a grist mill (in the north parish near the pond) with two runners, which, according to the original grant, has the sole command of the water. This pond is supposed to be fed chiefly by springs, and is little affected by droughts. Many people from the neighbouring towns bring their grain to this mill, in dry seasons. On this same brook, about half a mile below, is Messrs. Burbanks' paper mill. A few rods below, is an oil mill. A few rods below the oil mill, is a fulling mill. A few rods below the fulling mill, in the late war, powder mills were erected, but are since discontinued. A little further down, in the year 1776, a gun manufactory was erected, but is since converted into a manufactory for scythes, axes and mill irons; and here they have trip hammers, bellows, and grindstones, carried by water. Having described this brook, issuing from the pond, and the water works upon it, we return to the river. The river, after it has received this brook, bears away, and runs northeast, and east; and takes in a brook from a pond in the northeast part of the second parish in Sutton, called *Dorrett's Pond*; having an inlet on the northwest; the outlet is at the southeast. Said river then runs easterly into Grafton, and there receives the stream which issues from Quinsigamond, or Shrewsbury Long Pond. The river then bears away, and runs southerly through Northbridge and Uxbridge; and, about a mile southeast from Uxbridge meetinghouse, takes in a stream which issues from a pond chiefly in Sutton, near the

southwest

southwest corner of the town, called Manchaug Pond. This pond has an inlet on the northwest; the outlet is to the southeast, and both in Sutton. This outlet runs along near the south line of Sutton, until it comes to Uxbridge.

Having mentioned the river, and the streams, we would just observe, this town is famed for its manufactures, its mills, and water works. Here are, one paper mill, one oil mill, ten grist mills, six saw mills, three fulling mills, seven trip hammers, five scythe and ax makers, one hoe maker; several who work at nail making; and six works for making of potash. But here are no mines, no forge, furnace, pearlshery, nor fish of any consequence.

There are two or three natural curiosities worthy of particular notice.

As first, In the west part of Sutton, within sixty rods of the rise of the inlet of Ramshorn Pond, which is the head of Blackstone River running to Providence and falling into the sea at Bristol, is a brook so large as to carry a saw mill in Sutton, then bears away into Oxford, joins French River, which unites with the river Quinebaug, and enters the sea at Newlondon.

Secondly, A few rods west of the second parish meetinghouse, there is a swamp, having two outlets; one at the southwest; the other at the northeast: Both these outlets enter Blackstone River, above described, at about one mile's distance from each other: But the river is estimated to run ten or twelve miles, after the entrance of that on the

westerly

westerly side, before it returns and takes in that on the east.

Thirdly, In the southeasterly part of the town is a cavern in the earth or rocks, commonly called *Purgatory*. The rocks on each side of the chasm evidently appear to have been rent asunder. People may enter some rods under the ground or rocks, and there are cracks down which they drop pebbles, and after these strike the sides alternately several times, they are heard to fall into the water; and a brook issues out at the bottom of the hill.

It may be acceptable to give a more particular description of this place, called Purgatory.

It is the side of a hill, which consists of vast ledges of rocks: Where the natural descent begins, a chasm has been formed of perhaps thirty, and in some places, forty feet in width, in these ledges, by some violent concussion, which left this body of stones of all shapes and sizes, to fall in: Above, it is all open to the heavens; and the ledges, on either side, are from five to ten, and so on to twenty, and even forty feet in height. This chasm is, perhaps, near eighty rods in length; and the descent is gradual, and not very difficult. Where the greatest depth is, water issues from crevices in the rocks, and hangs in icicles, and even in solid bodies of ice, not only in May, as I have seen, but in June, although the descent is to the south. Some small caverns were formed by the falling of these rocks, through which persons have descended, and come out several rods below. This is a most stupendous place,

and

and fills the mind of the beholder with most exalted ideas of the infinite power of the great Creator of all things, "who removeth the mountains, and they know not; who shaketh the earth out of its place, and the pillars thereof tremble." After all, no description given of this place, by another, will enable persons to form just and adequate conceptions of it.

The growth of wood in Sutton, is oak of all sorts, and what they call the oak chesnut, the bark whereof is like the common gray oak, but the leaves resemble, almost exactly, those of the chesnut tree; walnut of all kinds; great plenty of chesnut; considerable of butternut; but little of buttonwood. In the low lands the wood is ash, beech, birch, elm of all sorts, maple, white and pitch pine. They have also sassafras, sarsaparilla, and alders. Here are to be found ginseng, and the cohush root, of special medicinal qualities.

There is much travelling through this town. The principal roads are—one coming from Connecticut, through Oxford, and passing from west to east, through the town. About three miles west of the first parish meetinghouse this road parts; the left hand road passes by the meetinghouse, and so on through Grafton, Westborough, and Southborough, and leads to Boston, falling into the post road in Weston. The right hand road, at said parting, passes on about two miles south of said meetinghouse, and enters what is called the middle road in Uxbridge, and so goes on, through Mendon, to Boston. Another principal road, is a county ty road from Worcester, passing from north to south through the town, by both meetinghouses : At the south meetinghouse it parts, and, by various partings, leads to Douglass and the west part of Uxbridge.

There is another county road, which leads from Uxbridge to Worcester, through the east part of Sutton. This was lately in contemplation to be made the post road from Worcester to Providence.

The town of Sutton is distant from the Statehouse in Boston 46 miles to the southwest. And from Worcester courthouse, it is six miles to the north parish meetinghouse ; and to the south parish meetinghouse, to the south nine miles.

This is a large and flourishing town, the second in wealth in the county; and when the census was taken in 1791, there were 2642 inhabitants therein.

LEICESTER.

THE township of Leicester was granted by the General Court, on the tenth of February, 1713, to Col. Joshua Lamb, of Roxbury, and others, his associates ; and on the fifteenth day of the same month and year, the Court, by a particular resolve or act, gave this tract of land the name of Leicester. The natives called the place *Towtaid;* and

and by the English it was usually called *Strawberry Hill.* The place was not incorporated, and vested with town powers and privileges, until the close of the year 1720, or the beginning of the year 1721: For the first town meeting held in Leicester was on the sixth of March, 1721. A survey of this grant being ordered, and a return thereof made, the General Court established the lines and boundaries of it by a special act, on the 19th of January, 1714. The tract was to be eight miles square; and was granted on these conditions, that the proprietors should reserve a sufficient quantity of land for the use of the ministry and schools, and see that fifty families were settled thereon in seven years. The proprietors accordingly, at a meeting in Boston, on the 23d of February, 1713, voted to give one half of the township to fifty families who should settle thereon, in that space of time. That number of families having removed to, and settled at Leicester, the proprietors, at a meeting held at Boston, on the 23d of July, 1722, chose a committee, consisting of William Dudley and Joshua Lamb, Esqrs; Mr. Nathaniel Kenny, Mr. Samuel Tyler, and Mr. Samuel Green, to make and execute a deed of the easterly half of Leicester, lying west of and adjoining to Worcester; east of Brookfield, south of Rutland, and north of a gore of land lying between Oxford and Leicester, to Mr. John Stebbins, and others; which deed bears date January 8th, 1724; and was recorded November 26th, 1729, Libro 29th, page 329 of the records of the county of Middlesex.

sex. This grant was intended to be eight miles square : But the measure was large, and included the whole of what is now Spencer: And at the north end, two miles in width and four in length were taken off to help form the town of Paxton, in 1765: And at the southeast part of the town, about 2500 acres were taken off to aid in making up the town of Ward, in 1778. Leicester is still a very considerable town, and contained when the enumeration was made, nearly 1100 inhabitants.—It is bounded on the north by Paxton ; on the east by Worcester and Ward ; on the south by Oxford ; and on the west by Spencer.

The first settlers of Leicester, like the people in general, of that day, paid early attention to religion, to the support of the gospel, and the institutions of Christ among them. When the congregational church in this place was gathered, cannot now be exactly ascertained, as there were no church records kept or preserved, till within about 40 years. But the probability is this, that the church was formed at the time of the first minister's being settled with them, who was the Rev. David Parsons. This Mr. Parsons was ordained at Malden, near Boston, but soon removed with a considerable part of his people, to Leicester, where he was installed, by the best account to be now had, September 15th, 1721. He did not continue long in the ministry at Leicester, but was dismissed from his pastoral relation to that flock, and died in about two years after. He was succeeded in the sacred office, at Leicester, by the Rev. David Goddard,

who

who was solemnly conseciated thereto June 30th, 1736. He was not suffered to continue long with this people, by reason of death; for being on a journey, at Framingham, he was there seized with a fever which put a period to his days January 19th, 1754, in the 48th year of his age, and the 13th of his ministry.

The Rev. Joseph Roberts succeeded Mr. Goddard in the ministry at Leicester, whereunto he was ordained October 23d, 1754, and he was dismissed therefrom December 15th, 1762. To him succeeded in the work of the gospel ministry, the Rev. Benjamin Conklin, who was separated thereunto on the 23d of November, 1763, and still continues in office.

There is a considerable society of Anabaptists in Leicester, and which has been of long standing. Their first teacher was Mr. Thomas Green, a physician. After his death, the Rev. Benjamin Foster, A. M. was ordained among them; but for want of support he removed, and has been resettled in the city of Newyork; where he is a worthy minister, and has lately received the degree of Doctor of Divinity. The Anabaptist society in Leicester, have for their present teacher Mr. Nathan Dana. Their house of worship is in the south part of the town.

Also, there is in Leicester, a number of the people called Friends, or Quakers, who have a very good house for their way of worship, erected in the north part of the town in the year 1791.

Notwithstanding

LEICESTER.

Notwithstanding the difference of sentiment, in religious matters, between the various denominations of the people of Leicester, the greatest liberality and cordiality prevail, both in their town meetings, and family connexions and intercourse.

[There is an Academy established in this town, and called *Leicester Academy*, for the purposes of promoting true piety and virtue, and for the education of youth in the English, Latin, Greek, and French languages ; together with writing, arithmetick, and the art of speaking ; also practical geometry, logick, philosophy, and such other of the liberal arts and sciences or languages, as opportunity may hereafter permit. Ebenezer Crafts, Esq; of Sturbridge, and Jacob Davis, Esq; of Charlton, in the county of Worcester, generously gave a large and commodious mansion house, lands and appurtenances, in Leicester, for an Academy. This Academy was incorporated by an act of the Legislature, March 23d, 1784, and trustees were appointed ; their number is never to be more than fifteen, nor less than eight.]

The principal instructor, ex officio, is always to be one.

The first trustees, appointed by the Court, were, Ebenezer Crafts, Esq; of Sturbridge ; Jacob Davis, Esq; of Charlton ; Hon. Moses Gill, Esq; of Princeton ; Hon. Samuel Baker, Esq; of Berlin ; Hon. Levi Lincoln and Joseph Allen, Esqrs. of Worcester; Hon. Seth Washburn, Esq; and Rev. Benjamin Conklin, of Leicester ; Rufus Putman, Esq; of Rutland ; Rev. Joshua Paine, of Sturbridge ; Rev. Joseph

seph Sumner, of Shrewsbury; Rev. Archibald Campbell, of Charlton; Rev. Joseph Pope, of Spencer; Hon. Timothy Danielson, Esq; of Brimfield.

Whenever any vacancy happens in the board of trustees, the remainder are to elect some person to fill the place.

The Hon. Moses Gill, Esq; was elected President, the Rev. Benjamin Conklin, Vicepresident; the Rev. Joseph Pope, Secretary; Joseph Allen, Esq; Treasurer.

PRECEPTORS. Benjamin Stone, A. M. was the first Preceptor, Thomas Payson, A. B. assistant Preceptor; Amos Crosby, A. M: Samuel Sumner, A. M. David Smith, A. B. Ebenezer Adams, A. B. the present Preceptor; John Pierce, present assistant Preceptor.

The present Trustees of Leicester Academy, are, The Hon. Moses Gill, Esq; President; Hon. Samuel Baker, Esq; Hon. Seth Washburn, Esq; Hon. Levi Lincoln, Esq; Joseph Allen, Esq; Treasurer; Rev. Benjamin Conklin, Vicepresident; Rev. Joshua Paine; Rev. Joseph Sumner; Rev. Joseph Pope, Secretary; Rev. Archibald Campbell; Rev. Daniel Grosvenor; Capt. Thomas Newell, Leicester; Deacon Jonas Howe, Rutland; Hon. Dwight Foster, Esq; and the Hon. Timothy Newell, Esq.

Besides the buildings and lands given by Ebenezer Crafts and Jacob Davis, Esqrs; the town of
Leicester gave,	£ 500
Hon. Moses Gill, Esq; - -	150
Rufus Putnam, Esq; - -	100

Capt.

Capt. Thomas Newhall,	—	£ 100
Col. Thomas Denny,	— —	100
Jeduthun Baldwin, Efq;	—	100
Mr. Reuben Swan,	— —	50
Mr. John Southgate,	— —	80
Col. Samuel Denny,	— —	80
Jofeph Allen, Efq;	— —	30
Ifaiah Thomas, Efq;	— —	20
Caleb Ammidown, Efq;	— —	18
Hon. Timothy Paine, Efq;	— —	15
Capt. Samuel Green,	— —	15
Capt. William Watfon,	— —	12
Mr. Samuel Green, jun.	— —	10
Mr. Samuel Watfon,	— —	10
Mr. Peter Taft,	— — —	10
Mr. Phinehas Jones,	— —	10
Mr. John Peirce,	— — —	10

Befides the above funds for the fupport of Inftructors for this academy, the General Court granted in 1792, a townfhip of land, in the diftrict of of Maine, of fix miles fquare to the ufe of this academy. Alfo the Hon. Judge Gill has given a number of well chofen books, which coft 30l. fterling in England, to the academy, for the ufe of the inftructors, and alfo for the ufe of the ftudents, under certain regulations.

Some Topographical Defcription of this town fhall now be attempted.

Leicefter is fituated upon the height of land between the Atlantick Ocean, eaft and fouth, and Connecticut River on the weft. The town is very hilly and uneven; it is indeed famed for its hills;

hills, but thefe are moift, fpringy and rocky yet not exceedingly fo. The foil is pretty good, deep and ftrong, but rather cold clayey and wet, not fo well adapted to grain as to grafs and pafturage: It is pretty good for orcharding and fruit trees of all kinds.

There are divers hills of note and fame in the town; the firft we fhall mention, and the moft confiderable, is Strawberry Hill, fo called by the Englifh when they firft came there, in confequence of the exuberant growth of thofe berries. On this hill ftands their elegant new meetinghoufe, on the northweft fide of the common which is level, facing to the foutheaft, erected in 1784. At the northeaft angle of the fquare ftands the academy buildings; the other fides of the fquare are lined with large handfome dwelling houfes. This hill is high and rather fteep, but not large and extenfive. A fecond hill is called *Indian Hill*, or *Bald Hill*, on account of its being cleared and planted with corn by the Indians, a long time before the white people went up fo far to live. A third is called *Moofe Hill*, becaufe of the great number of thofe quadrupeds which were wont to harbour there. Another is called *Cary's Hill*, from one of that name who went thither and digged a cave in the fide of this hill, and lived there as an hermit many years, while that part of the country was in its wildernefs ftate. A fifth is known by the name of *Grafs Hill*.

Although there is no river running through the town, yet it is well watered by fprings and rivulets, and

and by several large brooks upon which there are three corn and five saw mills; here also are clothiers' works, where that business is carried on in all its branches. Two of the brooks above referred to, run from north to south, and are emptied, one into Providence river, the other into the Sound or sea, at Newlondon, in Connecticut. The first of these is called Kettle Brook, and has its source in that part of Paxton which was formerly Leicester; is a very considerable stream, and running through the easterly part of the town, passes into Ward, and there falls into Blackstone River. The other rises from a large meadow in the westerly part of the town, of upwards of an hundred acres, part of which is in Spencer; this stream connects itself with the outlet of a pond which is situated a little easterly of the centre of the town of about forty or fifty acres: These two are the sources of French River, which runs through Oxford, and falls into the sea at Newlondon.

There is another pond in the northwesterly part of the town, containing about one hundred acres, whence issues a stream which runs westerly, and forms a branch of the River Chicabee, and falls into Connecticut River at Springfield. On this stream or outlet from the pond there is a grist mill, and by a drain and dam the pond may be raised or lowered ten feet, which is of singular advantage to the inhabitants of the vicinity, on account of grinding in the summer season.

In the easterly part of the town there is a place where the water, running from the northerly side of the post road, goes to Providence, while that on the south side goes to Newlondon. In the westerly part of the town there is also a place where the water, from the north side of the road, runs to Connecticut River; and that on the south side goes to Newlondon.

There is in this town a great variety of timber and wood, being a good proportion of almost every kind which is known to grow in this part of the country, except pitch and yellow pine.

The principal roads of travel, are, first, the post road from Boston to Springfield, through the middle of the town: Secondly, about one hundred rods west from the meetinghouse is the county road to Sturbridge, which turns to the left hand: Thirdly, through the north part of the town is a county road from Worcester to Newbraintree and Hardwick: Fourthly, from Rutland, and the northern part of the county, there is a large road through the town, leading through Charlton, Dudley, Pomfret, &c. to Norwich.

The inhabitants of Leicester mostly live by the cultivation of the soil; and here are many very fine farms, and the buildings are in general good, and indicate a very considerable degree of wealth. There are several persons here who deal in foreign and domestick articles of trade; and they have besides the usual mechanicks and tradesmen, a famous gunsmith, Mr. Thomas Earle, who is supposed to equal any workman in the United States, in that branch of business.

Here

Here also there are established manufactories of cotton and wool cards, and the work is carried on in all its branches to the greatest perfection. In this business are constantly employed fifteen or twenty men, exclusive of a great number of women and children. And they vend, annually, from twelve to fifteen thousand pair.

Leicester is a growing flourishing town; and is situated upon the post road from Boston to Hartford, Newyork and Philadelphia : It is six miles from the courthouse in Worcester, a little to the southwest ; and from Boston, it is fifty three miles, several degrees to the south of west.

RUTLAND.

WE are happy in being able to say, that the records respecting Rutland, have been kept very correct and perfect, and in fine order from the first.

From them we find, that on the 22d of December 1686, Joseph Trask, alias Puagaftion, of Pennicook; Job, alias Pompamamay, of Natick; Simon Piticom, alias Wananapan, of Wamaffick; Saffawannow, of Natick, and James Wifer, alias Qualipunit, of Natick, (Indians who claimed to be lords of the soil) gave and executed a deed to Henry Willard, Joseph Rowlandson, Joseph Foster, Benjamin Willard, and Cyprian Stevens, for 23l. of the then currency, of a certain tract of land containing twelve miles square, according to the buts and bounds following, viz. "The name in general being *Naquag*, the south corner butting upon Muscopauge Pond, and running north to Quanitick and to Wanchatopick, and so running upon great Watchusett, which is the north corner; so running northwest to Wallamanumpscooke, and so to Quaquanimawick, a little pond, and so to Asnaconcomick Pond which is the northwest corner; and so running south and so to Musshauge a great swamp, and so to Saffakatassick, which is the south corner; and so running east to Pascatickquage, and so to Ahumpatunshauge, a little pond, and so to Sumpauge Pond, and so to Muscopauge, which is the east corner." This Indian deed, signed and acknowledged by the above named Indians, was received April 14th, 1714, and entered with the records of deeds, for the county of Middlesex, libro 16, page 511, by Samuel Phips, register. Of this tract of land thus purchased of the Indians we hear nothing for upwards of 26 years. But upon the petition of the sons and grandsons of Major Simon Willard,* of Lancaster, deceased, and others, for approbation and confirmation of their title to the above tract of land, the General Court, on the 23d of February, 1713, passed this order, " That the lands in the Indian deed, and according to their buts and bounds, be confirmed to the children of the said Simon Willard, deceased, or to their legal representatives, and to the other petitioners, or their legal representatives,

and

---

* This was the famous Major Willard who went to relieve Brookfield, when beset by the Indians. See Brookfield.

and associates, provided that within seven years time there be 60 families settled thereon and sufficient lands reserved for the use of a gospel ministry and schools, except what part thereof the Hon. Samuel Sewall, Esq; hath already purchased, and that this grant shall not encroach upon any former grant or grants, nor exceed the quantity of twelve miles square. The town to be called Rutland, and to lye to the county of Middlesex." But this order, resolve or act of court was not considered as an act of incorporation, as will presently appear. This tract of land contained 93160 acres including 1000 acres for the Hon. Mr. Sewall; and was surveyed by William Ward, in October 1715. The names of the original proprietors of Rutland as named in the associate deed, and their shares, are Joseph Foster had two shares, the rest had one share each. Cyprian Stevens's wife, Mary Willard's heirs, Joseph Rowlandson's heirs, Simon Willard, John Willard, Benjamin Willard, Joseph Willard, Josiah Willard's heirs, Rev. Samuel Willard's heirs, Henry Willard's heirs, Daniel Willard's heirs, Jonathan Willard's heirs, Thomas Brintnal, Nathaniel Howard's heirs, Robert Blood's heirs, Joshua Edmund's heirs; and Col. William Taylor, Penn Townsend, Paul Dudley, Adington Davenport, Col. Adam Winthrop, Capt. Thomas Hutchinson, Major Thomas Fitch, Thomas How, John Chandler, Col. William Dudley, Esqrs. Mr. John White, John Farnsworth, Col. Buckley's heirs, Moses Parker, and Jacob Stevens. In all 33 shares.

The proprietors, at a meeting at Boston, December 14th, 1715, voted that the contents of six miles square be surveyed, and set off for the settlement of 62 families in order to the performance of the condition of the grant. The six miles square, granted to men who would go on and settle, was that part which is now called Rutland. The settlers on the 11th of August 1720, entered into a written agreement with the proprietors, and bound themselves by certain articles, signed and witnessed. And on the 26th of June 1721, this six miles square was confirmed to the settlers by the proprietors, as a sure estate of inheritance to them, their heirs and assigns forever, and recorded. On the 12th of July 1721, the inhabitants of Rutland were assembled, by order of the committee of the proprietors, to choose a minister, when the Rev. Joseph Willard was chosen, by a great majority of the voters. At a meeting of the freeholders and inhabitants of this six miles square, or Rutland, October 9th, 1721, Samuel Wright moderator, "Voted, that the town will prefer a petition to the General Court, to give their sanction, and establish them as a town, to have and enjoy all the privileges other towns enjoy."

A petition was accordingly presented to the General Court, and they sometime in their session, which was begun at Boston upon Wednesday the 30th of May 1722, passed an act of incorporation, entitled,

" An act for further establishing the town of Rutland, and empowering them to choose all proper er officers, and for the empowering them to raise and collect money for the defraying of the necessary charges of the said town. Forasmuch as it appears that the proprietors of the township of Rutland, have performed the conditions of the grant made thereof by the Great and General Assembly, of this Province in 1713, Be it enacted by his Excellency the Governor, the Council, and House of Representatives in General Court assembled, and by the authority of the same, That the inhabitants and freeholders of the said town of Rutland be invested with, and forever hereafter enjoy all the powers, privileges and immunities, which other towns within this Province, by law, have and usually enjoy ; and that they be, and hereby are enabled, to levy, assess and collect three pence per acre, per annum, for the space of two years and a half from the first day of July last past (the time that the minister began to officiate as a minister there) on all the lands both improved and unimproved, whether divided or undivided, contained within the lines of the contents of six miles square, as is already laid out, and within which the present inhabitants settled ; and that the said land be subjected and made liable to the payment of the same, to defray the charge of building the meeting-house, and paying the minister's settlement and salary, excepting only the present minister's lot, and ministry lot, with their divisions, also the school lot ; and also one thousand acres of land appertaining to Samuel Sewall, Esq; (the committee of Rutland having agreed, for certain considerations with

the

the said Samuel Sewall, Esq;) and five hundred acres of land appertaining to the Artillery Company of this Province, and eighty acres of land on and near Buck Brook, and one hundred and forty acres of land about Mill Brook (being part of Benjamin Willard's nine hundred acres laid out there to promote a mill) which said lands shall be free from said tax or assessment, any law, usage or custom to the contrary notwithstanding.

" Passed in the house of representatives, and in council, and consented to by the Governor.

" A true copy examined,
            per Josiah Willard, Secretary."

From the foregoing statement, it appears that the whole grant of 12 miles square was named Rutland, in 1713 ; but that only the six miles square granted by the proprietors to the settlers, was called Rutland, and incorporated as a town ; and that this was not done until the session of the General Court which was begun May 30, 1722. And in consequence of the above recited act, an order of the General Court passed July 6th, 1722, authorizing and empowering Capt. Samuel Wright to call a meeting of the freeholders and other inhabitants of the town of Rutland, on the last Monday of July current, then to choose town officers to serve until the general meeting in March next. The town was notified and met accordingly ; and this was the first legal town meeting ever held in Rutland.

After the settlers had performed their conditions, and the six miles square was incorporated, we find the proprietors of the township of Rutland, in all
                                          future

future meetings, had nothing to do with said six miles square, which is now the town of Rutland; but concerned themselves only with the other parts of their original grant, we shall therefore leave them, and confine ourselves to the account of Rutland.

We have said, the settlers of the six miles square, on the 12th of July 1721, invited the Rev. Joseph Willard to settle with them in the work of the ministry, which invitation he accepted. This Mr. Willard had been ordained a minister of Sunderland in the county of Hampshire, but continued a very little time with them before he was dismissed. After he had accepted the invitation to settle with the people of Rutland, he met with many and great discouragements, and particularly by reason of the fears and dangers arising from the Indians; so that an appointment of his installation was deferred. However, at length a day was fixed upon for his solemn separation to the work of the ministry in that place, in the fall of the year 1723; but he lived not to see the day, being cut off by the enemy, as shall be now related. As Deacon Joseph Stevens and four of his sons were making hay in a meadow, at Rutland, a little north of the place where the meetinghouse now stands, August 14th, 1723, they were surprised by five Indians. The father escaped in the bushes; two of his sons were then and there slain; the other two, (Phinehas the eldest, and Isaac the youngest) were made prisoners. Two of the five Indians waylaid a Mr. Davis and son, who that afternoon were making hay in a meadow not far off, but weary of waiting they were returning to the others, and met Mr. Willard in their way, who was armed: One of the Indians' guns missed fire, the others did no execution. Mr. Willard returned the fire, and wounded one of them, it is said mortally, the other closed in with Mr. Willard; but he would have been more than a match for him, had not the other three come to his assistance: And it was some considerable time before they killed Mr. Willard. This account Phinehas Stevens gave upon his return from captivity, who was a spectator of some part of the tragedy. The Indians having killed and scalped Mr. Willard, and taken some of his clothes, went off to Canada with the two captives above named. They were redeemed in about a year. Phinehas Stevens was a famous warrior, a captain, and a principal man in building up and defending the then young plantation No. 4, now Charlestown, in Newhampshire state. Isaac Stevens lived at Rutland. They have both been dead many years. On the 3d of August 1724, the Indians came again upon Rutland, killed three persons, wounded one, and made another prisoner. This is as I find it related in Governor Hutchinson's history. Others speak of but two killed: But the names of the killed, wounded, or prisoner, cannot now be ascertained. This was the last mischief done at Rutland by the Indians, so far as we can learn.

The Ecclesiastical History of Rutland is brief and as here follows. The church of Christ in the town was gathered November 1st, 1727, and on the

the same day the Rev. Thomas Frink was ordained their first Pastor. Mr. Frink continued but a little time as their minister, being dismissed from his office September 8th, 1740. (Mr. Frink was installed Pastor of the third church in Plymouth, November 7th, 1743, where he continued minister but a short space; being dismissed from thence, he was installed at Barre on the last Wednesday in October 1753; from whence also he was dismissed July 17th, 1766.) The Rev. Joseph Buckminster succeeded Mr. Frink, as a minister of the gospel of Christ, at Rutland; whereunto he was ordained September 15th, 1742. Mr. Buckminster continued the able faithful and worthy minister of Rutland until November 3d, 1792, when he died in the 73d year of his age, and the 51st of his ministry. He was succeeded in about eight months, by the Rev. Hezekiah Goodrich, who was separated to the pastoral office in Rutland, on the 19th of June 1793.

In this town upwards of forty persons have lately united, and established a social Library, of the value of nearly 30*l.* and containing about 70 volumes at present.

Some Geographical Description of Rutland shall now be attempted.

The town is situated on the height of land between the sea and Connecticut River: It is hilly and very uneven. The hill on which the meetinghouse stands is high: And the meetinghouse may be seen in many of the adjacent towns, and even at a great distance to the west and northwest; but

as

as the town abounds with hills it affords no extenfive and commanding prospect of itself. East of the meetinghouse is a hill called Muschapauge hill or Rice's hill, containing two or three hundred acres, this is very good land, and has some fine farms upon it. Part of Turkey Hill, so called, on the south falls within Rutland, the rest is in Paxton. This is high, but most excellent land.

Other hills there are many, but none particularly noticeable. The land in general is very good, and the soil is rich and strong: It is not extraordinary for raising of grain, though a sufficiency is produced for the inhabitants; it is very well adapted to grass and grazing, and most excellent for orcharding: Here are large and fine orchards, and much cyder is made in the town.

Rutland, being the height of land, has no large rivers running through it. Piss River, so called, which originates on the west side of Watchusett Hill, runs through Hubbardston, and passes across the northwest angle of this town, and so falls into Ware river. On this river are one corn mill, two saw mills, one fulling mill, and one trip hammer, within the limits of Rutland; and the meadows on this river are confiderable. There is a large stream, called Long Meadow Brook, running through the town, in the westerly part thereof, on which are large meadows, and two corn mills and two saw mills within the bounds of this town. About half a mile east of the meetinghouse is a famous spring, the waters whereof soon divide; part runs to Merimack, and part to Connecticut River;

River: And it is to be obferved that all the waters of Rutland run to thefe two great rivers. There are divers ponds in the town; Mufcopauge Pond, mentioned in the Indian deed; this is large, covering about 100 acres. In this pond two perfons have been drowned. Evans's Pond, fo called, of about 60 or 70 acres, in the fouthwefterly part of the town. Alfo, Gregory's or Long Pond, which is long and narrow, in the fouthwefterly quarter. Thefe are all well ftored with fifh. Browning's Pond is large, this is fituated in the foutherly part, and is partly in Rutland, partly in Spencer; but the largeft part is in Oakham. The growth of wood in Rutland is, oak of all forts, chefnut, walnut, pine of all forts, afh, maple, birch, beach, poplar, elm, faffafras, hemlock, hackmatack, &c. &c. In the wefterly and northwefterly part of the town is an extenfive plain, a great part of which is ftill covered with pitch pine. This is rather light land. The people of Rutland are principally farmers, except a few traders in European, Eaft and Weftindia goods, the ufual mechanicks, and thofe employed in the card making bufinefs, which is newly fet up here: And they are a peaceable, happy, flourifhing people. In this town, pot and pearl afh making is carried on very largely. When the cenfus was taken about two years ago there were 1072 fouls in the town.

Rutland is bounded, on the north by Hubbardfton; on the northeaft, by Princeton; on the eaft, by Holden; on the fouth, by Paxton; on the weft, by Oakham; and on the northweft, by Barre.

re. This town is situated about west from Boston, at the distance of 56 miles; and from the court-house in Worcester, it is northwest, at the distance of fourteen miles.

WESTBOROUGH.

THIS town was taken from Marlborough, and lying the whole length of that town on the west side, thence was called Westborough when incorporated by act of the General Court on the 18th of November 1717. This before used to be called *Chauncey* Village at the west end of Marlborough. Here a Church was gathered on the 28th of October 1724, and on the same day the Rev. Ebenezer Parkman, their first Pastor, was ordained. Having obtained help of God, he continued to minister to the people in holy things until within about six weeks of his death, which was on the 9th of December 1782, in the 80th year of his age, and 59th of his ministry. The town remained destitute of a settled minister until January 14th, 1789, when the Rev. John Robinson was consecrated their second pastor. This town increased so fast that on October 20th, 1744, the north part was made a separate parish; the particulars whereof will be related when we come to give an account of the town of Northborough.

This westerly part of Marlborough, being then a frontier, having no town between it and Brookfield

field on the weft, about 40 miles diftant, did not fettle fo faft: Neverthelefs, towards the clofe of the feventeenth century feveral families had here feated themfelves; and among others, Meffrs. Thomas and Edmund Rice had families, and were fixed down but a little weft of where the prefent meetinghoufe in Weftborough ftands. On Auguft 8th, 1704, as feveral perfons were bufy in fpreading flax, on a plain about eighty rods from the houfe of Mr. Thomas Rice (the firft fettler in Weftborough, and feveral years reprefentative of the town of Marlborough, in the General Court) and a number of boys with them, feven, fome fay ten, Indians fuddenly rufhed down a woody hill near by, and, knocking the leaft of the boys on the head (Nahor, about five years old, fon of Mr. Edmund Rice, and the firft Englifh perfon ever buried in Weftborough) they feized two, Afher and Adonijah, fons of Mr. Thomas Rice, the oldeft about ten, and the other about eight years of age, and two others, Silas and Timothy, fons of Mr. Edmund Rice abovenamed, of about nine and feven years of age, and carried them away to Canada. The perfons who were fpreading flax, efcaped fafely to the houfe. Afher, in about four years, returned, being redeemed by his father. This was effected by the kind mediation of the Rev. Mr. Lydius, then minifter of Albany. And here, by the way, it fhould be noted, that when the old Indian Sachem *Ountaffogo*, the chief of the Cagnawagas, at the conference with Governor Belcher at Deerfield, made a vifit to Bofton, he ftopped awhile in Weftborough;

borough ; the beforementioned Asher Rice saw and knew him to be one of the Indians who rushed down the hill, as above related, when he was taken by them. This Mr. Asher Rice married, had a family, and was living but a few years past in Spencer. His brother Adonijah, grew up in Canada, and married there, first a French, afterwards a Dutch woman, and followed the business of husbandry on some land a little way off from *Montreal*, on the north side of the great river St. Lawrence, and had a good farm there, as we have been certified. The Indian name whereby he was called was *Assaunaugooton*.

As to the other two, Silas and Timothy, they mixed with the Indians ; lost their mother tongue; had Indian wives, and children by them ; and lived at *Cagnawaga*. The name by which Silas was distinguished among the Indians was *Tookanowras*.

Timothy, the youngest, however, was much the most noticeable person. The accounts received from thence, have uniformly represented him as the third of the six chiefs of the *Cagnawagas*. This advancement was in consequence of the death of his foster father, or master, who had adopted him for a son, instead of a son which he, the former chief, had lost. " However,) said the Rev. Mr. Parkman, who had the best means of information). Timothy had much recommended himself to the Indians, by his own superior talents, his penetration, courage, strength, and warlike spirit, for which he was much celebrated, as was evident to me from conversation with the late Sachem Hendrick,

drick, and Mr. Kellogg, when they were in the Maſſachuſetts; and his name among them the ſame as we had ever heard, viz. *Oughtſorongoughton*."

The venerable Mr. Parkman, in a manuſcript account of theſe perſons found among his papers ſince his death, adds, with reſpect to this Timothy, in theſe words: " He himſelf, in proceſs of time, came to ſee us. By the interpoſition of Col. Lydius, and the captive Tarbell, who was carried away from Groton, a letter was ſent me, bearing date July 23d, 1740, certifying that if one of their brethren here would go up to Albany, and be there at a time ſpecified, they would meet him there; and that one of them, at leaſt, would come hither to viſit their friends in Newengland. This propoſal was readily complied with, and it ſucceeded.

The chief aboveſaid came, and the ſaid Mr. Tarbell with him as interpreter and companion. They arrived here September 15th. They viewed the houſe where Mr. Rice dwelt, and the place from whence the children were captivated; of both which he retained a clear remembrance; as he did likewiſe of ſeveral elderly perſons who were then living; though he had forgot our language. His Excellency Governor Belcher ſent for them, who, accordingly, waited on him at Boſton. They alſo viſited Tarbell's relations at Groton; then returned to us in their way back to Albany and Canada. Col. Lydius, when at Boſton, not long ſince, * ſaid this Rice was the Chief who made the

ſpeech

* This account was written in 1769.

speech to General Gage, which we had in our public prints, in behalf of the Cagnawagas, soon after the reduction of *Montreal*," Thus far the Rev. Mr. Parkman.

To the above account I would add, there are at this present time, 1793, a brother and sister of the abovenamed Silas and Timothy, living in Northborough, in a very advanced age, though not born when their brethren were captivated, who have heard that these men were living in Canada, in the summer of 1790.

Let us proceed to some Geographical Description of Westborough. The town is pretty large, and very generally settled, containing, when the census was taken in 1791, houses 118, and inhabitants 934. It is about 34 miles from Boston, a little to the south of west, and 13 miles east from Worcester. The middle of the town is level, but the lands rise, at about a mile's distance from the meetinghouse into higher, especially to the east, south and west. The soil is in general good, the farms are large, and the inhabitants industrious and wealthy, as any one must naturally suppose from the appearance of their places and buildings. The growth of wood here is similar to that in the neighbouring towns : The higher lands bear plenty of oak and chesnut, some walnut; in the swamps and low lands grow ash, birch and maple : Here also they have large and excellent cedar swamps, which afford the people much cedar for shingles and other important and necessary uses : There is, at this day, but little white pine, but considerable pitch pine.

pine. There is very little broken poor land in the town; neither is it very rocky; but bears all kinds of grain in plenty; it is good for orcharding, grafs and pafturing: It is very well watered by fmall ftreams and rivulets, on which they have mills; and on thefe they have confiderable bodies of good meadow land. The river Affabet, running through the northweft angle of the town, has upon its banks a very large body of very excellent meadow or interval.

Ponds there are feveral in the town, as Great Chauncy in the northeafterly part, into which a rivulet enters at the fouth end from fwamps and low lands; this is a fine pond, and here is a plenty of fifh. A fmall ftream iffues from the north end of this pond and empties into Little Chauncy, which is in Northborough.

About a mile fouth of Great Chauncy, there is a fmall pond, near the road from Weftborough to Bofton, whence iffues a fmall ftream to the fouth, entering a large cedar fwamp, and running through that, empties into a large pond called Cedar Swamp Pond, which is environed on the eaft, north and weft, with faid fwamp; from this pond, on the fouth, there is an outlet which runs into Hopkinton, and aids in forming Sudbury, or Concord South River. It is worthy of notice, that the waters in this town, though they take different routs, finally unite in Concord, by the confluence of the north and fouth river in that town. In the northwefterly part of Weftborough is fituated Hobomocho Pond, not large, encircled with a meadow, bearing

bearing the fame name, and from this there is an outlet into the River Affabet, abovementioned.

Weſtborough is bounded on the eaſt, by Southborough and Hopkinton; on the ſouth, by Upton; on the weſt, by Grafton and Shrewſbury; and on the north, by Northborough.

UXBRIDGE.

THE town of Uxbridge was taken from the ancient town of Mendon, and was incorporated by an act of the Legiſlature, on the 27th of June 1727, and then received its preſent name. It was the weſterly part of that town. It was large at firſt, extending ten or twelve miles from north to ſouth; but has ſince been curtailed, having the north part ſet off in 1772, and made a diſtinct town, by the name of Northbridge.

Uxbridge ſtill remains a very conſiderable town in extent, and for the number of its inhabitants. When the cenſus was taken in 1791, there were 180 dwelling houſes, and 1310 inhabitants in the place.

The people took early care for the ſupport of the goſpel, and the inſtitutions of Chriſtianity among them; accordingly, ſoon after the incorporation of the town, viz. on the ſixth of January 1731, a church of Chriſt was here gathered under

the

the direction of the Rev. Joseph Dorr of Mendon; and on February third, 1731, the Rev. Nathan Webb, was invested with the pastoral office in the place. Mr. Webb continued the faithful minister of the town upwards of 41 years; being removed by death on the 14th of March 1772. The Rev. Hezekiah Chapman succeeded Mr. Webb in the work of the ministry in Uxbridge; whereunto he was solemnly separated January 27th, 1774; and from which he was dismissed April 5th, 1781. The Rev. Josiah Spalding, succeeded Mr. Chapman as minister of Uxbridge, being ordained on the 11th of September 1783: He continued with this people but about four years, being dismissed from his pastoral relation to them, October 23d, 1787. These two gentlemen were dismissed more on account of the peculiarity of their religious sentiments, than any thing beside. Mr. Spalding has since been installed at Worthington in the county of Hampshire. On the 17th of October 1792, the Rev. Samuel Judson was ordained Pastor, the fourth in succession, of the congregational society in Uxbridge.

In the town of Uxbridge there are a few families of the Anabaptist persuasion. And here also is a very considerable society, nearly one quarter of the inhabitants of the town, of the sect called Friends, who have a meetinghouse for the worship of God in their way, built with brick.

We will now give some Geographical Description of the town of Uxbridge.

This

This town is situated at the southern extremity of the county, and is bounded on the south, by the line between this Commonwealth, and the state of Rhodeisland ; on the west, by Douglass ; on the north, by Northbridge ; and on the east, by Mendon.

Uxbridge is 42 miles from Boston, somewhat to the southwest, and is 18 miles from the courthouse in Worcester, to the southeast.

The land in the town is pretty level, for the space of about one mile round the meetinghouse, being a plain, and rather sandy and light ; however, good for raising of grain of all sorts ; then it rises to hills on all sides, but not very high, nor very rocky ; these are moist and good for orcharding, and for grazing, and for English grass : There is a good proportion of interval and meadow lands upon the rivers, which are in general very good. There are three rivers in this town, all of them unite in the south part ; Blackstone, Mumford, and West River. Blackstone River has its source in Sutton ; and was particularly described in the account of that town. This river comes from Sutton through Grafton and Northbridge, and enters Uxbridge at the north end of the town, and running through the town, near the middle, passes into Rhodeisland State : This is a large and fine river. Mumford River has its rise in Rocky Woods, so called, in Douglass, being increased by streams from Badluck Pond, and from Manchaug Pond, in Douglass, and by springs and rivulets, and runs an easterly course into Uxbridge, then turns and
runs

runs southeasterly within a few rods of Uxbridge meetinghouse, where there are several sorts of mills and water works, in excellent order, and where much business is well performed. This river continues its course, and joins Blackstone River about one mile southeast of the meetinghouse.

West River is not large, its main source is a pond in the northerly part of Upton, and running through a part of Northbridge, it passes through the easterly side of Uxbridge, and falls into Blackstone River about two miles southeast from the meetinghouse. Besides these rivers, there are divers brooks and rivulets, by which this town is finely watered. There are also three small ponds in the town, covering ten or twelve acres of land each, and are called, Pout Pond, Mud Pond, and Shoelog Pond. Pout Pond is in the east part of the town, about one mile from the meetinghouse. Mud Pond is situated in the southeast part of the town, not far from Blackstone River, with which it holds a communication when the water is high. Shoelog Pond is situated in the southwest part of the town, from whence issues a small stream, which runs into Gloucester, in the State of Rhodeisland. Not far from this pond an iron mine has been discovered, and wherein persons have wrought to very considerable advantage. Upon the farm of Dr. Samuel Willard, in Uxbridge, there is a fine quarry of stone, of a greyish colour, easily split, and wrought into any shape for underpinning, door stones, &c. &c.

The

The growth of wood and timber in this town is pretty much like that of other towns in general: Oak of various forts, fome chefnut, walnut, poplar and pine.

The people of Uxbridge fubfift chiefly by the cultivation of the foil: They have, however, all the common forts of mechanicks, and a few dealers in European, Eaft and Weft India goods.

There is one road of confiderable travel, from Connecticut, directly through this town to Mendon, and fo on to Bofton.

This may be confidered as a large, wealthy, flourifhing place, and ftands forward in the lift of towns, according to the proportion which it pays to a State tax.

SOUTHBOROUGH.

THE town of Southborough, was taken from the ancient town of Marlborough, and derived its name from the circumftance of its lying about fouth from that town. It was incorporated, by act of Court, July 6th, 1727. A few years paft, a ftrip of land, belonging to Framingham, of about three hundred acres, and running up between Southborough and Hopkinton, was annexed to Southborough.

SOUTHBOROUGH.

The church of Chrift in this town, was embodied on the 24th of October 1730, and on the fame day the Rev. Nathan Stone was ordained their firft Paftor. He was a judicious, prudent, and faithful minifter of Chrift, and was continued ferving God in the gofpel of his Son, to the great fatisfaction of his people, until May 31ft, 1781, when he departed this life, in the 74th year of his age and 51ft of his miniftry. The people were deftitute of a fettled minifter for the long fpace of ten years, even until June 1ft, 1791, when the Rev. Samuel Sumner was folemnly feparated unto the paftoral office over the church and flock of God in Southborough.

We fhall proceed to give fome Geographical Defcription of this town. It is fituated on the eaft fide of the county, and is bounded by Marlborough on the north, Framingham on the eaft, Hopkinton on the fouth, and Weftborough and Northborough on the weft : It is 29 miles from Bofton, a little to the fouth of weft ; and 17 miles from Worcefter courthoufe, about eaft. It is not large in extent, but pretty well filled with people, who are generally good and wealthy farmers. They have about 120 dwelling houfes, 150 families, and 840 inhabitants. The town is not level, nor yet very uneven ; there are no extenfive plains, and no very high hills ; the foil is ftrong, good and rich, and productive, amply repaying for its cultivation. It is not very rocky, however, there is a fufficiency of ftone, perhaps on every farm, whereby it is, or may be walled in. In the South part of the town there is a hill, which, from the fteepnefs of its afcent,

cent, is called Breakneck Hill, over the steepest part runs a town road; it is rocky and rough, but covered with a large growth of young wood, and descends to the north. In the northeast part is situated what is called Pine Hill, which was covered with pines and timber until the year 1787, when, by a hurricane, the wood was chiefly destroyed. On the west side of the town there is a steep hill over which the county road lies, but not distinguished by any particular name.

The town is well watered by streams and rivulets. Stony Brook rises in the easterly part of Westborough, runs through Southborough in a course which in general is easterly; but not without several great angles; for what is worthy of remark, the road through the town to Boston crosses this stream three times within the space of four miles. This stream enters Framingham and there falls into Sudbury River. On this stream are two saw mills, in fine order, of profit to their owners, and benefit to the town. Upon the same brook are four corn mills. One in the westerly part of the town, nearest its source, and on the great road, can grind but about half the year, as raising a pond in the summer season would damage a large body of meadow land. But below this, at the distance of two or three miles, as the stream runs, stands another mill in good repair, and where much business is done, not only for the benefit of this, but the neighbouring towns. About two miles further down this stream, are two well constructed corn mills, the property of Col. Thomas Nixon, which

grind

grind all the year, except in a very dry feafon, as the waters of Angle Brook, and Broad Meadow Brook fall into this ftream above thefe mills. On this Stony Brook, clothiers' works have lately been erected in the eafterly part of the town where much bufinefs is well performed.

A fecond ftream is called Angle Brook, from its winding courfe. One branch of this ftream rifes near the meetinghoufe in Marlborough, and another branch a little further fouth, and foon uniting enters Southborough, and there joining with Broad Meadow Brook, in about the diftance of a mile, falls into Stony Brook, as abovementioned. There are many other ftreams lefs noticeable. But we muft obferve what is called Sudbury River, iffues from Cedar Swamp Pond, in the foutheafterly part of Weftborough, and when it leaves that town, is the boundary between Southborough and Hopkinton, on the fouth. The meadows on this river, in Southborough, are narrow, but produce large quantities of good ftock hay, being a mixture of meadow, and Englifh grafs. Thofe upon Stony and Angle Brooks are good, and yield moft excellent bank hay. There is but one pond in this town, in the weftern part, fmall, covering perhaps fix acres of ground. To this there is a fmall inlet, and an outlet to the fouth; and all the waters in this town run foutherly and eafterly, and empty into Sudbury, or Concord River. Here are no pot or pearlafh works.

The growth of wood is fufficient for the town, if prudently ufed, and confifts of white, red and black

black oak, fome walnut, and more chefnut: The low lands are all under cultivation. Upon the whole, this, though not large, its contents being but about 8350 acres, is a good town; and the people are induftrious and wealthy, in general; and hofpitable and peaceable.

SHREWSBURY.

IN the year 1717, November 2d, a grant was made to certain perfons, chiefly of Marlborough, who petitioned therefor, of all the lands lying between the original grant of Lancafter on the north; Marlborough, on the eaft; Sutton on the fouth; and Worcefter on the weft. Moft of the firft fettlers were from Marlborough. The tract of land was very long (about fifteen miles north and fouth) but not very wide (from three and an half to four and five miles.) The whole was called, by the proprietors, Shrewfbury from the beginning.

In about ten years from the date of the grant, it was fo flocked with inhabitants, as that the General Court incorporated it as a town, by an act which bears date December 19th, 1727, and gave it the name whereby it had all along been diftinguifhed.

The

The town so flourished and increased, as that in a little more than twenty years a second parish, in the northerly part, was formed, viz. on the 17th December 1742, which has since been made a distinct town.

The south part of this original grant which is now Shrewsbury, is about seven miles in length from north to south, and about three and an half or four miles in width ; and it is bounded by Worcester on the west ; by Boylston on the north ; by Westborough and Northborough on the east ; and by Grafton on the south. It is situated about six miles from Worcester courthouse, a little to the northeast, and from Boston 41 miles a little to the southwest. The post road from Boston to Worcester, and so on to Newyork, &c. passes directly through the town ; and the great road from Vermont, and from the upper part of Newhampshire, and northwestern part of the county, unites with the post road about a mile and an half west of the meetinghouse. Besides which there is a road of considerable travel from the northward, directly through Shrewsbury, to Providence.

The ecclesiastical history of this place is but brief, and is as here follows :

On the fourth day of December 1723, the church of our Lord Jesus Christ was gathered here, and on the same day the Rev. Job Cushing was ordained their first Pastor: He continued in peace and love with his people, and faithfully serving the Lord in the work of the ministry almost 37 years ; and was

was suddenly cut off, by a fit of the apoplexy, August 6th, 1760, in the 67th year of his age. And on the 25th of June 1762, the Rev. Joseph Sumner was solemnly invested with the pastoral office in this place; and who still continues to minister to them in holy things. There are a few Baptists in the south part of the town, but no church of that denomination.

Before we proceed to a Geographical Description of this town, I have thought that so remarkable and sorrowful an occurrence as took place in Shrewsbury, in its infancy, ought to be recorded in this history. I shall give it in the words of the account published in the only Newspaper (I have been told) then printed in Newengland, if not on this side Philadelphia. It was a small half sheet printed by B. Green.

"*Boston, August* 15th, 1723.

"An exact account of the awful burning of Capt. John Keyes's house, with five persons in it, at Shrewsbury, in the night between the 7th and 8th of this inst. taken from a letter of the Rev. Mr. Breck of Marlborough, and from the mouth of Mr. Ebenezer Bragg of the same, formerly of Ipswich, the only person of those who lodged in the house, who, by a distinguishing providence, escaped the flames.

"Capt. Keyes was building an house about nine or ten feet off his old one. It was almost finished. And Mr. Bragg aforesaid, the carpenter, with his brother Abiel, of 17 years of age, and William Oaks of 18, his apprentices, were working

ing about it. Capt. Keyes, with his wife and four daughters, lodged in the old one; and the three carpenters, with three sons of the Captain's, viz. Solomon of twenty, John of thirteen, and Steven of six years of age, lay in the new. On the Wednesday night, going to bed, they took a more than ordinary care of the fire, being excited thereto by the saying of one, *He would not have the house burnt for an hundred pounds*; and the reply of another, *He would not for two hundred*. Upon which, they carefully raked away the chips lying near it, and stayed till the rest were almost burnt out; and then they went all six together into three beds in one of the chambers; and were very cheerly and merry at their going to bed, which was about ten of the clock.

"But about midnight Mr. Bragg was awaked with a notion of the house being on fire, and a multitude calling to quench it; with which he got up, saw nothing, heard no voice, but could hardly fetch any breath, through the stifling smoke; concluded the house was on fire, perceived some body stirring, against whom he hit two or three times in the dark: And not being able to speak, or to breathe any longer, and striking his forehead against the chimney, he thought of the window and happily found it: When he gained it, he tarried a minute, holding it fast with one hand, and reaching out the other, in hopes of meeting with some or other to save them, till the smoke and fire came so thick and scorching upon him, he could endure no longer; and hearing no noise in the chamber, only, as he thought, a faint groan or two, he was forced to jump out, and, the window being fmall, head foremoſt; though he fuppoſes, by God's good providence, he turned before he came to the ground. As Mr. Bragg was juſt got up again, Capt. Keyes being awaked in the old houſe, was coming to this ſide of the new, and met him. But the flame immediately burſt out of the windows, and the houſe was quickly all on a light fire. No noiſe was heard of the other five who periſhed; and it is very queſtionable, whether more than one of them moved out of their beds. The old houſe was alſo burnt, and almoſt every thing in it: But the people were ſaved, through the great goodneſs of God. But a moſt dreadful fight it was in the morning, to ſee the five bodies frying in the fire, among the timbers fallen down in the cellar, till towards the evening, when the few almoſt conſumed fragments, without heads or limbs, were gathered, put into one coffin, and buried. Pſalm lxvi, 3, *Say unto God, How terrible art thou in thy works!* James iv, 15th, *Ye know not what ſhall be on the morrow.* Luke xii, 40th, *Be ye therefore ready.*" Thus far the newſpaper.

The Capt. Keyes abovenamed, was afterwards the well known and much eſteemed Major John Keyes, who died in Shrewſbury, not many years ſince, in a very advanced age. The new houſe which was burnt, ſtood on the great road about three quarters of a mile eaſtward from the preſent meetinghouſe. And upon the ſame ſpot a large dwelling houſe now ſtands.

Let

Let us now proceed to defcribe the town of Shrewfbury. Much the greater part of this town is upon quite high land. Indeed it is one large and extenfive hill, and the meetinghoufe ftands nearly upon the higheft part of it: The land falls but very little to the north: To the fouth, the defcent is long, but gradual: To the eaft, as the great road runs, there is a defcent towards Northborough, for the fpace of two miles or more, nay, even fome way into Northborough: To the weft, there is half a mile of rocky plain, and then a pretty fteep defcent to a fmall plain, before you come to the head of Long Pond, and beyond that the land rifes immediately, and there is quite a fteep hill before you leave Shrewfbury, on the way to Worcefter. The town is not very uneven confidered altogether, but is pretty rocky. There is a very large and extenfive profpect from the middle of the town, and all round the meetinghoufe, eaft and weft, north and fouth, and from fome parts of the town feven meetinghoufes can be difcerned. The land, in general, is rather rough and hard, but the foil is ftrong, rich, and very productive when fubdued. The higher lands are very good for orcharding, and fruit trees of all kinds, and for pafturage, and even for mowing; for the land is not dry, and it bears a dry feafon exceeding well. It is not fo well proportioned with tillage land; however, what they till is very productive, and richly repays the labour beftowed upon it. There is very little poor broken, wafte land in the town. And it is richly ftored with a fine young

young thrifty growth of the beſt of wood for fuel, ſuch as oak of all kinds, walnut and cheſnut, and the lower lands bear aſh, birch, maple, &c. &c.

The town is pretty well ſupplied with waters, by various ſprings and rivulets, although there is not one large ſtream which runs through the town. The largeſt ſtream in the town is that which iſſues from Sewall's Pond, which is within the limits of Boylſton, and running ſoutherly a mile and a quarter, falls into Long Pond, on the road to Worceſter, over which is the bridge at the head of ſaid pond. This pond, called by the natives, Quinſigamond, but commonly *Long Pond*, is a beautiful piece of water, in the form of a creſcent, nearly four miles in length, as it runs (though on a ſtraight line but three miles and twenty four rods) and it is from 100 rods to nearly a mile in width, although in one place, it be not more than forty rods. This pond lies almoſt wholly within the bounds of Shrewſbury, not more than one acre falling within the limits of Worceſter. It is, perhaps, the largeſt and fineſt pond in the county. Indeed, it may very fitly be denominated a lake. Upon the top of the hill, on the weſt ſide of Shrewſbury, it appears to travellers as a large river, ornamented with woods on each ſide. It affords great plenty of fiſh, as pickerel, large perch, eels, ſhiners, breams, &c. and the brooks which run into it, contain ſome trout. The water of this pond is in general deep ; in ſome places it has been found ninety ſix feet deep. In this pond there are a number of Iſlands of various ſizes.

The

The first, or uppermost, at the north end, is called Little Pine Island, has upon it a thicket of vines, and contains about a quarter of an acre. The second is Grafs Island, covered with grafs and willows, and which has been mowed in a dry feafon. The third is called Sherman's Island, and contains about one acre and an half, and has a growth of small timber and wood upon it, of different kinds. The fourth is called Bowman's Island, of about three acres, and is clothed with pine and other timber. The fifth is denominated Barberry Island, from the confiderable quantity of thofe berries which grow thereon; this contains about three acres. The fixth is another Grafs Island, having upon it willows and waterbufhes. The feventh is known by the name of Grape Island, of about the fourth of an acre, bears large quantities of grapes. The eighth, commonly called Sharp Pine Island, of three quarters of an acre, is covered with divers forts of wood. The ninth is known by the name of Ram Island, of two acres, covered with oak and chefnut. The tenth and laft is a very large ifland, and generally called Stratten's Ifland; this contains about 150 acres; a confiderable part of which is under cultivation; and there are three families living thereon, having good farms: Thefe are inhabitants of Shrewfbury. This ifland has oak, chefnut, walnut, and fome pine thereon. There are two or three other places in the pond where land appears in a dry feafon, but at other times are covered with water. This is bounded north and weft, by the Long or Great Pond;

Pond; southeast, by what is called Half Moon Pond; south, by Flint's Pond; east, by Round Pond, all which communicate with each other. From them runs a river, at the southeast, which passes into Grafton, whereon are a number of mills, and other water works. There is a small outlet from Long Pond, southerly, into Flint's Pond; and from Flint's Pond eastwardly, there is an outlet into the river just mentioned. And what is truly noticeable is this, while the water, more generally, runs out of Long Pond into Flint's Pond, yet in the drier seasons of the year, the water runs out of Flint's Pond into Long Pond; for Flint's Pond is fed by springs and rivulets, which keep it always full. There is a pond called Jordan Pond, lying about half a mile eastward of the great or Long Pond, and about midway of the length of it, and from this there is an outlet, by which waters some parts of the year empty into Long Pond. On the stream which runs from Sewall's Pond into Quinsigamond or Long Pond, there is a grist mill. Besides this, there is a stream which rises in the northwest part of the town, on which there are two saw mills: This runs southerly, and empties into Long Pond on the eastern side. There is also another stream, which rises from springs a little south of the meetinghouse, on which are mills, and running northeasterly, comes to the side of the great road, affording a fine watering place to travellers and teamsters, and there it is joined by two other rivulets, and taking a

southeast

southeast direction, and running through the southwest angle of Northborough, there empties into the River Assabet.

In this town there are both Pot and Pearl Ash works, and where large quantities are made in a year.

The people in Shrewsbury are generally farmers, though they have a due proportion of traders in European and Westindia goods, and mechanicks of various sorts. On the great road the buildings are large and handsome; and the town makes a pretty appearance; and the number of inhabitants, when the census was taken, was 963.

LUNENBURG.

ON the 4th of November, 1719, the General Court, at the request of a number of gentlemen, made a grant to them of this territory for a valuable consideration, reserving, however, college, school, and ministerial rights of land; as also a right to the first ordained minister.

There is a hill, in the middle of the town, called *Turkey Hill*, on account of the great number of wild Turkies which frequented the place in that day. It still retains the name; and gave denomination to the whole tract, previous to its incorporation; which took place on August 1st, 1728, when the name of *Lunenburg* was given to it, in compliment to George II, who, the preceding year, came to the British throne; and was styled Duke of Lunenburg, as having in his German dominions a town of that name.

The first settler in this place, was a Mr. Samuel Page, who was dubbed governor Page, and is mentioned by that title to this day: He lived to a great age, and died in September, 1747. Many of the first settlers were emigrants from Ireland and Scotland; whose descendants, by intermarriages, are now blended and incorporated with the other inhabitants.

The Ecclesiastical History of the place is as follows. Like people in general, at that day, who came to America for the sake of enjoying the sacred rights of conscience, they were fond of supporting the publick institutions of religion, and took early care to settle a minister: Accordingly, here a church was gathered, and the Rev. Andrew Gardner, (who had been the first minister at Worcester) was installed their first minister on the 15th of May, 1728, a little before the incorporation of the town. Mr. Gardner continued not four years in the ministry here; being dismissed the 22d of February, 1732. After his dismission, he moved up nigh to Connecticut River, in Newhampshire State, where he died, but a few years since, in a very advanced age.

The second minister of Lunenburg, was the Rev. David Stearns, who was ordained April 18th, 1733; and died of a peripneumony, March 9th, 1761, in the 52d year of his age, and 28th of his ministry.

ministry. As he lived greatly beloved, he died no less lamented.

He was succeeded, for a few days, by the Rev. Samuel Payson, who was separated unto the sacred work of the gospel ministry September 8th, 1762; and died February 14th, 1763, of an atrophy.

He was succeeded by the Rev. Zabdiel Adams, who was solemnly consecrated unto the service of God, in the gospel of his Son, on the 5th of September, 1764, and who is still living.

During the administration of these ministers there have been baptized, of infants and adults, down to the present time, no less than 2400 persons: And the church here is comparatively large, containing very little short of two hundred communicants.

The growth and increase of Lunenburg was rapid and great; for in the year 1764, the whole town of Fitchburg was taken from it. It is now bounded by Townsend, in the county of Middlesex, on the north; by Shirley, in the same county, on the east; by Leominster, on the south; and by Fitchburg, on the west. It is about 44 miles distant from Boston, over Charles River bridge, to the northwest; and 25 miles north by east, from the courthouse in Worcester.

The soil of this town is sweet, and as productive as is usually found in so northern a situation. For though the land be in general high, yet by reason of its cohesive texture, and having a clayey stratum within a few feet of its surface, it retains moisture sufficient for vegetation through the whole summer,

summer, unless in seasons of severe drought. The soil is friendly to the growing of wheat, rye, Indian corn, oats, &c. The wheat raised on the hills is of the first quality. Many parts of it bear hemp and flax luxuriantly. The mowing and pasture lands are equal to what are generally found in the county. It is a place famed for cyder; as their high lands are excellent for orcharding: But the canker worms beginning to infest the trees, threaten them with a scarcity of this kind of fruit.

The natural growth of wood and timber in the town is oak, white, red, black and gray. Of walnut there is considerable plenty; and of chesnut a large proportion. In the low lands there is ash, also rock and white maple, black, white and yellow birch, some beach and other hard wood. Nevertheless, as there is very little waste land, and the people are numerous, fuel will in a few years be scarce and dear. White and yellow pines were plenty in the infancy of the plantation; but from the great and long consumption of both, a scarcity is sensibly felt. Although the surface of the town is uneven, and may be denominated hilly; yet it is not rocky; there being, take the town in general, not more than stones sufficient to wall in the several inclosures.

From the elevated situation of the land, and its proximity to those lofty mountains, the Grand Monadinock in Newhampshire, and the Watchusett in this county, being about twelve miles from the latter, and twenty five from the former, the air is keen and piercing in winter, pleasant in summer,

and

and through the whole year very falubrious. Here are little or no ftagnant waters; but few meadows; and but few brooks and ftreams. In confequence of which they are in a great degree exempted from fogs, from deleterious vapours and exhalations; and having the air ventilated by high winds, the inhabitants are remarkably healthy, and free from thofe diforders of the putrefcent kind which fweep off many in other places; and they double their numbers in lefs than 25 years. This occafions large emigrations, and as the farms are fmall in general, being on an average not more than 75 or 80 acres; this, together with the fecundity of the people, produces a large number of paupers, with which the town is burdened more fo, perhaps, than any other town in the county; creating an expenfe beyond that of fupporting the gofpel. However, the greater part of the people live comfortably, and a few may be faid to be opulent. The people are induftrious and economical, generous, hofpitable to ftrangers, and much given to convivial entertainments.

The town labours under other difadvantages befides thofe already mentioned. For though the directeft route from the northerly part of Connecticut River, and from the State of Vermont, to Bofton, be through Lunenburg, yet from difficulty in the road for a fhort fpace of way, and the influence of certain men, the travel paffes to the north or fouth of it; whereby the people are left deftitute of all the benefit arifing from travellers depofiting their money among them.

Befides

Besides this, they labour under the want of sufficient water to carry their corn and saw mills. Though there are several small streams on which there are mills, yet they are generally inoperative a considerable part of the year. Mulpus, so called, is but a small brook, which, originating in the west part of the town, runs east about twelve miles, and then empties itself into the River Nashaway, in the north part of Shirley. This deficiency of water obliges some of the inhabitants to carry their grain to other towns to be ground, a certain part of the year. But while we speak of this singular deficiency of water, we are constrained to mention a Mr. Wetherbee, who, having built both corn and saw mills, in the southwest part of the town, on what is called part of the north branch of Nashaway River, and finding, by several years experience, that the water was not sufficient to carry his mills, except in the spring of the year, or in rainy seasons, was at great expense to dig a canal, in length about a mile, to convey water from a larger branch of the same river, (which comes from Westminster) into his mill pond; which enables him in a wet season, to grind for all; and, in a dry one, for most of his numerous customers. An instance of so spirited and laudable enterprize is worthy to be transmitted to posterity. This man, it is thought, makes the best wheat flour within the compass of Newengland; and has grain brought to his mill from remote places.

In the southwest, south, and southeast parts of the town, are three ponds, which, retaining their
Indian

Indian names, are called Onkeſhewalom, Maſſapog, and Catatoonamug; The firſt of which is nearly two miles and an half; the ſecond, two miles, and the laſt not more than one mile in circumference. From theſe ponds, the neighbouring anglers draw from time to time, pickerel, perch, roach, bream, and other freſh water fiſh, not only ſo as to give themſelves a delicious repaſt, but ſometimes a quantity to ſell to their townſmen.

Mines, minerals or foſſils, there are none in the town; nor furnaces, or forges. The blackſmiths bring their iron from a diſtance. The nailing buſineſs has been carried on here to advantage.

In giving an account of Lunenburg, we ought not to omit the mention of Edward Hartwell, Eſq; who early came into the place, and poſſeſſing advantages above people in general, was promoted in the town and county; he was a deacon of the church; and, paſſing different grades of office, was Major of a regiment of militia; a juſtice of the peace; a Judge of the Court of Common Pleas; and a repreſentative of the town, with few interruptions, for a great number of years; in which ſtation he continued until a very advanced period of his life; and, finally, he died in the 97th year of his age, as full of piety as of days. This gentleman was much engaged in the Indian wars, and was very helpful to the neighbouring towns in ſcouring the woods, and driving off the ſavages. In Lunenburg, indeed, he had little work of this kind to perform. For, though the Indians aforetime inhabited this territory, as is evident by veſ-

tiges

tiges thereof remaining to this day, yet they never much annoyed the English; they did, indeed, so put them in fear, that between the years 1740 and 1750, the inhabitants frequently went armed to the house of God on the sabbath. There were also a few troops stationed in this town at garrisoned houses, to which the people retired at night for safety. In the summer of the year 1749, the Indians came into the northwest limits of the town, and killed two soldiers, Jennings and Blodget, who were stationed there, and carried Mr. John Fitch and his family into captivity, who all returned in safety, after enduring incredible hardships and fatigues, except Mrs. Fitch who sickened and died in Canada.

Lunenburg is almost wholly settled: The town contains but 14000 acres of land; and on this space, when the late census was taken, there were 192 houses, and nearly 1300 souls.

I shall close the account of Lunenburg in the words of the Rev. Mr. Adams, in a letter to the author. " The town is much more remarkable for the health than the wealth of its inhabitants. Almost destitute of travel through it, the people live an independent, but solitary life. In their ecclesiastical affairs they have been remarkably peaceable. They dismissed Mr. Gardner; but because he was unworthy. Two of their ministers died in rapid succession. None of them were so long in the ministry, nor so old, as myself. Almost thirty years have I lived among them in profound peace."

DUDLEY.

DUDLEY.

THE grant of this township was originally made to the Hon. Messrs. Paul and William Dudley, of Roxbury, while yet in the possession of the aborigines, the tribe known at this day, by the name of the Pegan Tribe. It was to comprise all the lands between Woodstock, or the colony line, south; Oxford, north; the grant to Medfield, now Sturbridge, west; and Newsherburne, now Douglass, east. This tract of land was incorporated by act of the Legislature, on the 2d of February, 1731, and the name of *Dudley* was given to it, as a token of respect to that family, who were principal proprietors of the soil, and great benefactors to the first settlers in their infancy. Since the incorporation of Dudley, an addition was made to it by a strip of land taken from Oxford, and annexed thereto. The present extent of this town is nearly east and west about nine miles; north and south about four miles. It is now bounded, north, by Oxford, and Charlton; east, by Douglass; south, by the state line, or Woodstock; and west, by Sturbridge.

Dudley has but one religious society, viz. congregational, although there may be about thirty families of various other persuasions, in the place. The church of Christ here was founded in the year 1732, and the Rev. Perley Howe was solemnly invested

vested with the sacerdotal office in the year 1735. He was dismissed from his particular relation to the church and flock of God in Dudley in 1743. The Rev. Mr. Howe was afterwards installed at Killingsley in Connecticut. He was succeeded in the pastoral office at Dudley by the Rev. Charles Gleason, who was ordained October 31st, 1744. He continued the worthy, faithful and beloved minister of the town until his death, which took place May 7th, 1790. The Rev. Joshua Johnson, who had been for a short time minister of the north parish in Woodstock, was installed Pastor of the church and congregation in Dudley, as successor to Mr. Gleason, December 1st, 1790.

The congregational meetinghouse, which is the only one in this town, was erected in the year 1734. It stands on an hill, which commands a south prospect of extensive farms even to the distance of twelve miles. Four acres of land on the summit of this hill were given to the town for publick uses, by the Pegan tribe of Indians, on condition that all of their tribe, who should ever inhabit the town, should have the right to convenient seats in the meetinghouse on days of public worship. This tribe still exists, to the number of ten or twelve, and hold about 200 acres of excellent land near the middle of the town; but their whole interest is constantly taken care of by a committee of the General Court.

The general face of this town is hilly, but not mountainous. It is richly and beautifully interspersed with hills, valleys, and streams of water. The

DUDLEY.

The hills are of eafy afcent, paffable with teams, and moft of them fuitable and good for cultivation. The foil in general is good and fertile, producing all forts of grain and fruit, and grafs in plenty; and the land affords a fufficiency of ftones for fencing in the farms. There is one hill in the town, not very high, famous for yielding great quantities of moft beautiful building ftones. They are taken out in fquare edged flabs, of any manageable length or width, with one natural face, fmoother than can be wrought; they are capable of being fplit, cut, or hammered into any fhape or thicknefs. The colour of thefe ftones is a very fine light gray; and they are much ufed for jambs, hearths, mantle pieces, under pinnings, for fteps and door ftones, and cellar walls.

The forefts, are principally of oak, chefnut, and walnut, yellow pine, and fome white pine.

This town abounds with ponds, ftreams, rivers and fprings. There are four large ponds, well ftored with all the ufual forts of fifh : But there is one efpecially in the eaft part of the town, called by the Indians Chaubunagungamaug: This is five miles in length, and one in breadth. Through the weft part of the town, from northweft to the foutheaft, runs the rapid river Quinebaug, of about twenty yards in width, coming from Sturbridge, and paffing down on the eaft of Woodftock, Pomfret, &c. to Norwich. Through the eaft part of the town, from north to fouth, runs *French* or Stony River. This is about fifteen yards in width. On this are fine interval and meadow lands, which being

ing in spring and autumn overflowed, become very excellent mowing and arable ground. This river comes from Oxford, and falls into Quinebaug ten miles below this town.

This is a large and flourishing town, the people subsist chiefly by farming, except the usual mechanicks, and a few traders ; and when the enumeration of the Commonwealth was made, there were 160 houses and 1114 inhabitants in the place. Dudley is situated upon the State line, sixty miles from Boston, lying about southwest, and from Worcester it is eighteen miles, nearly south.

HARVARD.

THE town of Harvard is situated on the eastern side of the county, thirty five miles from Boston, a little to the north of west, and is twenty three miles from the courthouse in Worcester, to the northeast. It is bounded by Groton on the north ; by Lyttleton on the northeast ; by Boxborough on the east ; by Stow on the southeast ; by Bolton on the south ; and on the west by the river Nashaway, which separates it from Lancaster, and Shirley. Harvard was not an original grant, but taken from Lancaster, Stow and Groton, principally from the two former. From the circumstance

cumstance of its being made up of the corners of other towns, it was rather irregular in its shape; but before the incorporation of Boxborough, which took off the easterly angle of this town, it was nearly equal to seven miles square: It is now more than six. The bill for the incorporation of this tract of land passed the Legislature, June 29th, 1732, when it was called Harvard, to bear up the name of that excellent and worthy minister of Charlestown the Rev. John Harvard, who died in 1638, who laid the foundation of Harvard University in Cambridge, bequeathing thereto 779*l*. 17*s*. 2*d*. when by a special order of court, it took the name of Harvard College. At the time of the incorporation of the town of Harvard, it consisted of about 50 families.

The town of Harvard is very hilly and uneven; the land is rough and hard to subdue, but the soil is warm and strong, rich and fertile. It produces good crops of grain of all kinds. Such broken land, however, is better adapted to the raising of wheat and rye, than Indian corn. As the township is rocky, the farmers are induced to appropriate a large proportion of their land to grass and pasturage. The principal articles carried hence to market, are beef, pork, butter, and cheese. The high lands are particularly fertile in chesnut trees, whose fruit yields the owners no inconsiderable profit. And as the lands are excellent for orcharding, many farmers pay particular attention to raising all kinds of fruit, which they have in plenty, and of the best quality.

There are about 1000 acres of what is called interval land in this town ; though perhaps half of it may more properly be ftyled meadow.

Although there are feveral hills in this place, yet there are but three which have names, or merit particular notice. The firft we fhall mention is called *Pin Hill*, from its remarkable form which is pyramidical. The perpendicular height of this hill, from the brook which runs at the foot of it, is judged to be two hundred feet. In the bowels of this hill are contained vaft quantities of blue or flate ftone. It leafes to the ftone cutters in this and a neighbouring town for 6*l*. 10*s*. per annum. The ftones taken hence, are not fo eafily wrought, as fome of a fimilar kind : But on this account, however, they are more valuable for jambs and hearths, as they in the fame proportion, do the more refift the heat of fire. Thefe ftones are chiefly ufed, for grave and tomb ftones ; and are carried to a great diftance.

Thofe called Bear Hill, and Oak Hill, are not, ftrictly fpeaking, diftinct hills, but links only in a chain of hills, which begins in the weft part of Lyttleton, and extends fouthwefterly through Harvard, as far as the centre of Bolton. Oak Hill, however, which rifes in the eafterly part of the town, is the fummit of this range, and affords a profpect fingularly diverfified and extenfive. The land upon thefe hills is moftly exceeding good.

The general growth of wood in Harvard, is the fame as in other towns of fimilar foils. Chefnut, oak of all kinds, and walnut, conftitute the principal

pal part on the high lands. They have some white pine, and in the northerly part, confiderable pitch pine. In the low lands they have much elm, some butternut and button wood, birch, ash, &c.

Harvard is like other hilly, rocky places, not dry, but moift land, and well watered indeed by numerous fprings and rivulets, running about among the hills, and which caufe them to rejoice on every fide.

Nafhaway, or Lancafter River, flows along the confines of Harvard upwards of fix miles. The depth of the water, when the bed of the river is full, is about twelve feet; and about fix feet at low water. This river, an humble imitator of the Nile, overflows its banks at certain feafons, and greatly fertilizes the bordering lands.

Still River originates in fome marfhes and quagmires in the wefterly part of Bolton, and is joined by a brook running from the interval lands in Lancafter, near the river. Thefe two ftreams unite in Harvard, and compofe what is called *Still River*, or long pond, or lake, which paffes in a filent and almoft imperceptible manner, for three miles, (one mile or more of which is in Harvard,) and then by a fmall outlet, empties itfelf into the river Nafhaway.

There are two or three ponds of fome notoriety in this town. The largeft of thefe begins but a little fouthwefterly of the meetinghoufe, and very nigh the feat of Col. Bromfield, and extends away foutherly. It is called *Bear Hill Pond*, as it lies upon the wefterly fide of that hill. Its figure is oblong:

oblong: Its circumference more than three miles. In this pond are two small islands of about three acres each. The greatest depth of this pond is not more than twenty feet.

At the north west angle of the town, is situated what is commonly called *Hell Pond*, from its amazing depth, being ninety five feet in one place, by measure; and between eighty and ninety feet in general, all over the pond, and immediately as you launch from shore. This pond is nearly circular. Its diameter is about three hundred yards. Fish were never caught here until within a few years, when pike and perch were put therein, which have since multiplied exceedingly. Near this is a small pond, with which the former is supposed to maintain a subterraneous communication. There is also another, in the north part of the town, called *Robbins's Pond*; but this is not remarkable for size or depth. About an hundred rods from Hell Pond, is a spring, known by the name of *Cold Spring*. The waters hereof are always pure and cold, and never freeze. The head of this spring is two or three yards broad. Bear Hill Pond emits a stream from its north side, which almost winds around Pin Hill; and which, within the limits of Harvard, supplies with water, four grist mills, one saw mill, one clothiers' works, one forge, and one trip hammer. These are all in the north part of the town. In the south part, there are two grist mills, and one saw mill, furnished with water from two streams which issue from the east side of the chain of hills above described.

It

It is worthy of particular mention, that the eastern side of the above hills is uniformly steep, while the opposite side has a gentle and gradual declivity.

At the foot of Oak Hill, on the eastern side, there is a mine which may be justly deemed a curiosity. Early in the year 1783, when a rage for the treasures, thought to be hid in the bowels of the earth, was prevalent in the country, it was thought by some persons, from the colour of the earth in this place, and from the working of the mineral rods, that silver ore might be obtained not far beneath the surface of the ground. Accordingly some gentlemen in this town and its vicinity, (twenty five in number) formed themselves into a mine company for the purpose of descrying those hidden treasures, and enriching themselves therewith. Under the conduct of certain men, Messrs. Ives and Peck, they began their operations in July following. These were continued, though with frequent interruptions, until sometime in the year 1789. During this time, they had, with some difficulty, digged through a considerable quantity of condensed gravel, until they came to a solid rock: Into this they penetrated more than forty feet. But, either from the unskilfulness of the mineralists, or for want of perseverance in their employers, the shining ore has not yet been discovered. The company, after expending one thousand one hundred dollars in the process, is amically dissolved. The sides of this cavity are almost rectilinear. It is about six feet high, and half as wide. The excavation

cavation was made, partly by heating the rock to a great degree, and then cooling it fuddenly with water; but the greater portion of it was effected with powder. Pieces of the earth, which they dug before they entered the rock, had the appearance of yellow lead, and were confiderably fulphureous. This cavern now refts a deferted monument of fuccefslefs toils. Its mouth opens to the eaft; and the rifing fun, to a perfon in the other extremity, renders the profpect highly delightful.

The town of Harvard is large and numerous, here are 200 dwelling houfes, which, like thofe of moft country towns in this State, are fcattered over the place without much order; and confift of fome good and more ordinary buildings. The inhabitants are 1400; thefe are chiefly farmers, who are frugal and induftrious, and fome are become wealthy. They have two or three traders in foreign goods, and all the ufual forts of mechanicks.

This town difcovers great folicitude for the good education of its children. The inhabitants divide themfelves into eight diftricts: In each there is a neat and commodious fchoolhoufe; and fix of them, in the winter feafon, are furnifhed with latin grammar inftructors; the other two with Englifh grammar mafters. In the fummer, the very young children are taught by approved females; while they who are more advanced, are handling the plough and the diftaff. Here a library company has lately been formed. They have at prefent, about one hundred volumes in their library. No doubt it will foon be confiderably augmented.

There

There is alfo here a focial club eftablifhed, confifting of twelve of the principal inhabitants, who have monthly meetings. In them they endeavour to acquire information on the common, as well as on the moft important affairs agitated in the world.

The principles and modes of religion in Harvard, are uncommonly numerous. Within the limits of the town dwell congregationalifts, anabaptifts, prefbyterians, epifcopalians, univerfalifts and fhakers. Until after the commencement of the late war, they were all of the denomination firft-mentioned ; and this ftill comprifes five fevenths of the fouls in the town.

The congregational church in Harvard was imbodied by an ecclefiaftical council, October 10th, 1733, and the Rev. John Seccombe was, the fame day, ordained their firft Paftor. He continued until September 7th, 1757 (almoft twenty four years in the facred office here) when he was difmiffed from his paftoral relation to this people. Mr. Seccombe was afterwards employed many years in the work of the miniftry in the province of Novafcotia, where he died in 1792, aged eighty four years. Mr. Seccombe was fucceeded in the work of the miniftry at Harvard, by the Rev. Jofeph Wheeler, who was confecrated thereunto December 12th, 1759. In a few years Mr. Wheeler was afflicted with bodily infirmities, which peculiarly affected his voice, in confequence whereof he folicited a difmiffion from that facred employment, which accordingly took place by advice and under the direction of a mutual council, July 28th, 1768.

1768. Mr. Wheeler was foon after, and for feveral years employed by the town as their reprefentative in the General Court. He was alfo a worthy Magiftrate, and Regifter of Probate in the county of Worcefter, from 1776, until February 10th, 1793, when he died in the fifty eighth year of his age. On November 1ft, 1769, the Rev. Daniel Johnfon was ordained to the paftoral office in Harvard. He was fuffered to continue but a little time, being removed by death on the 23d of September 1777. After Mr. Johnfon's deceafe, the Rev. Ebenezer Grofvenor was inftalled their Paftor on the 19th of June 1782. He had been before Paftor of the firft church in Scituate almoft feventeen years. Mr. Grofvenor was not fuffered to continue long at Harvard, being tranflated by death to a better world May 28th, 1788, in the forty ninth year of his age.

The town was deftitute of a fettled minifter near four years, when the Rev. William Emerfon was feparated unto that facred office, May 23d, 1792, the fifth Paftor in fucceffion. In this church of Harvard 1805 perfons have been baptized, and 540 have been admitted to church communion.

In the year 1776 an anabaptift fociety began to collect in Harvard. It was eftablifhed in 1778, when Mr. Ifaiah Parker, who is alfo a phyfician, was ordained their teacher, and ftill continues. The number of this fociety has fince been fomewhat increafed by perfons from the fkirts of the adjacent towns. This fociety have a pretty meetinghoufe

inghoufe in the fouthweft part of the town, near to Still River, in a pleafant confpicuous place. The epifcopalians, prefbyterians, and univerfalifts are but few, and have no diftinct and feparate focieties.

Sometime in the year 1780, the leaders of that fect of religionifts, called fhakers, came into this town; and as there are few of them indeed in any other part of the county, it is highly fitting and proper to give a full account of them in this place.

They fixed themfelves down in a corner of Harvard, where fuperftition and enthufiafm had confiderably flourifhed under the aufpices of one Mr. Ireland. A part of this man's followers kindled at this new torch of fanaticifm, while the majority of thefe old fafhioned enthufiafts at the fight of the fhakers' diftraction became more rational and fober. Since their beginning in Harvard, they have been continually making reforms in their fentiments, modes of worfhip and manners. In a religious and political view they have greatly meliorated. From grofs indecencies in their rites and behaviour, they are become moderate and civil. Formerly they were indolent and troublefome in fociety; now they are the moft induftrious and peaceful members of the community. The number of fhakers in Harvard is about one hundred and fifty. Thefe are divided into three orders; or as they call them, *gifts*. The firft of thefe orders confifts principally of the youngeft and faireft of them who are gathered. Thefe are under the moft rigid rules poffible. They are

never

never to fee any of the world's people, nor converfe with them of the lower orders. All their actions, words and fteps, are narrowly infpected by their fpiritual teacher, who almoft perfuades them to believe that he is converfant with their thoughts. They of the firft order are privileged with his oral addreffes; to the others he ufually communicates his monitions by a meffenger.

The fecond order is compofed of them who are gathered, but who are more advanced in years, and otherwife lefs vigorous and alert in labour and in devotion.

The loweft order are they who live about in families.

Extreme fimplicity in drefs and manners characterizes this fingular religious fect. They are neat in their apparel and furniture. The houfes which they have erected in this town, are large and commodious, and approach to fomething like elegance. Their floors and ftairs are all covered to prevent making a noife. They imitate the Moravians apparently more than any other denomination; particularly in their modes of government and fubordination. They affect to be wholly under the dominion of the Spirit; and to crucify even the innocent defires of the flefh, infomuch that they neither marry nor are given in marriage. So ftrict are they in their laws of abftinence from women, that the two fexes are not permitted to live in the fame houfe, nor even to enter the fame door. Inftances of inchaftity, efpecially among the governed, feldom or ever occur. The orders are

are under the moſt complete ſubjection to their leaders. The utmoſt preciſion and regularity are obſerved in their eating, ſleeping and working. Hence they are making quite rapid proficiency in the lower kinds of the mechanick arts ; and ſuch is their agricultural ſkill and perſeverance, that they have reduced the moſt rugged and indomable part of Harvard to a ſtate reſembling that of a garden.

We conclude this account with only remarking, that it is not a little ſtrange, that the leaders of this deluded ſect, who certainly can claim no preeminence above ordinary men in point of capacity and improvement, ſhould thus keep bound in ſervitude ſo great a number of their brethren in the very heart of Newengland. But it will be ſtranger ſtill, if in ſuch an era as this, the majority of the ſhakers, who now pant for liberty, ſhould long continue in ſhackles of bondage to their elders.

Having ſaid what may be thought quite ſufficient upon the ecclefiaſtical and religious ſtate of Harvard, we ſhall cloſe our account of this place, with ſaying it is a large, proſperous and wealthy town ; and notwithſtanding the diverſity of ſects, the people are peaceable and happy.

GRAFTON.

GRAFTON.

THIS is that tract of land of four miles square, which was reserved for the Indians when the town of Sutton was granted to the English. It was called by the Indians Haſſanamiſco, and known by that name only until April 18th, 1735, when it was incorporated by an act of the Legiſlature, and called Grafton. Since its incorporation one half a mile of land was taken from Shrewſbury and added to Grafton, on the north, and about half a mile of Sutton, on the ſouth, was annexed to it; ſo that Grafton is now five miles in length, from north to ſouth, and four in width from eaſt to weſt. This town is bounded, on the north, by Shrewſbury; on the eaſt, by Weſtborough and Upton; on the ſouth, by Upton and Sutton; and on the weſt, by Sutton.

At firſt there were divers Indian families here: As they diminiſhed, the white people became proprietors of the ſoil, by purchaſe; and a grant from the General Court, upon theſe conditions, however, that they ſhould always provide preaching and ſchooling, and ſeats in the meetinghouſe, for the remaining Indians. And as the people hold the lands of the original four miles ſquare, on ſuch conditions, they muſt all of whatever perſuaſion, be equally bound to contribute to the ſupport of a goſpel miniſter in the place. The General

GRAFTON.

ral Court has from the beginning, appointed a committee of three, called the truftees of the Indians' intereft ; their bufinefs is to take care of their property, both real and perfonal, and difpofe of the fame to the beft advantage, for the fupport and maintenance of the Indians. This committee, at prefent, have little to do in the execution of their truft, as the lands have by length of time, and various concurring circumftances, chiefly paffed into the hands of the white people. There are indeed feveral farms in the poffeffion of the heirs of the Indians, married to negroes ; but it is faid there is not one male in the town at this day, who is all of Indian extract or blood.

The Indians very foon decreafed in this place, and the whites became poffeffors and occupiers of the foil ; and fo early as the 28th of December 1731, a Chriftian congregational church was imbodied here, and on the next day, the Rev. Solomon Prentice was ordained their firft Paftor. He became what was called in that day, a zealous newlight, or more properly, a raving enthufiaft. He was difmiffed from his paftoral relation to Grafton, July 8th, 1747, and became an itinerant preacher. He was fucceeded in the work of the gofpel miniftry at Grafton by the Rev. Aaron Hutchinfon, who was folemnly confecrated hereunto on the 6th of June 1750. Mr. Hutchinfon continued upwards of twenty two years as Paftor of Grafton, and was difmiffed from his relation to that church and people, November 18th, 1772. He has fince generally been employed in preaching

ing the gospel, and is still living. The Rev. Daniel Grosvenor succeeded Mr. Hutchinson as Pastor of the church and flock of God in Grafton, to which office he was separated by the laying on of the hands of the presbytery, on the 19th of October 1774. By reason of great bodily infirmities of long continuance, he requested a dismission from his particular relation to the church and people of Grafton, to which they acceded with great reluctance, and which took place January 1st, 1788. No minister is since settled in the place. Mr. Grosvenor's health, being in a good measure restored, he is most constantly employed in preaching in neighbouring vacant parishes.

Some years ago there was an anabaptist society and church established in Grafton, and they had a regular minister of publick education settled with them*; but now there is neither minister nor church of that denomination in the town, and very few anabaptist families.

Let us now proceed to some Geographical Description of Grafton. It is a most excellent township of land. The face of the town is hilly and uneven, and in general rocky; but the soil is moist and strong, rich and very productive: It is good for Indian corn, wheat, rye, oats, barley, and flax: The lands are naturally warm and not subject to frosts; and as they are high and rocky, they are well adapted to orcharding and all kinds of fruit trees. There are three noticeable hills in the town. The first to be mentioned, is called Chesnut Hill, as abounding in that sort of wood.

This

GRAFTON.

This is situated but a little east of the meeting-house, and is the highest land in the town, hiding Grafton from Westborough: This is not large; the land is moist and good. On the easterly side of the town lies George Hill, two miles and an half in length. It took its name from one George Misco, an Indian who dwelt upon it. This is a hill of most excellent land; and there are a number of very fine farms upon it. A third is denominated Brigham Hill, from a number of that name who have lived upon it: This lies in the westerly part of the town, is high, about two miles in length; has upon it several excellent and large farms, though some parts of it are rough, broken lands.

The general growth of wood is walnut, oak of all kinds, chesnut, some pitch pine, butternut, button wood, black and white ash, and birch. There is some pine plain land in the town near the rivers.

Blackstone River, from the north parish in Sutton, enters Grafton in the southwesterly part of the town; this is then become a large and beautiful river, and runs about three miles in the southerly part of Grafton, and then passes into Upton. Little River, or more properly Quinsigamond, being the outlet from the pond of that name, runs along on the west side of the town, within about half a mile of the meetinghouse, and between that and Brigham Hill; and about one mile and an half south from the meetinghouse joins Blackstone River. On these rivers, before and after the junction, there are considerable bodies of good meadow;

and

and rich interval lands. The River Affabet, which runs northeaft, and empties into Merrimack, has its fource in Grafton, about one mile and an half northeaft from the meetinghoufe: This paffes through the northweft angle of Weftborough, into Northborough, &c. Befides thefe, on the weft fide of George Hill, runs George Brook, which rifes in the northerly part of Grafton; this paffes to the fouth. On this ftream there are large and good meadows. There is no pond in the town. Upon the feveral rivers and ftreams abovementioned, there are four grift mills, feveral faw mills, three trip hammers, and one fulling mill. The town abounds with rivulets and fprings of water.

The people fubfift mainly by the cultivation of the foil, and they are amply recompenfed for all their labour. They have one or two traders in foreign goods, and the ufual tradefmen and mechanicks; and here pot afh making is carried on. Grafton, though not a large tract of land, yet being a rich and good foil, is pretty well filled with people, and they are become wealthy. There were nearly 900 inhabitants when the cenfus was taken about two years ago. This town reaps confiderable advantage from the travel through it. A road much ufed, leading from Connecticut to Bofton, paffes through this town; as alfo the poft road from Worcefter to Providence. Grafton is forty miles from Bofton, to the fouthweft: It is thirty four miles from Providence, to the northweft, and eight from the courthoufe in Worcefter, a little to the fouth of eaft.

UPTON.

UPTON.

THIS town was not an original grant, but taken from several other towns, part from Mendon on the south, part from Sutton on the west, and part from Hopkinton on the east. It is bounded by Westborough on the north. The post road from Worcester to Providence passes through this place, about a mile southwest of the meetinghouse. It was incorporated by an act of the Legislature on the 14th of June, 1735, and contains upwards of 13000 acres of land; and when the census was taken there were 126 dwelling houses, about 150 families, and about 900 inhabitants in the place.

As no church records are to be found of what took place in the earlier days of this town, so the precise time when the congregational church was formed here cannot be ascertained; but it was soon after the incorporation of the town, when the Rev. Thomas Weld was ordained their first pastor. This gentleman continued in the ministry among this people but a few years, being dismissed from his pastoral relation to them; and was afterwards installed at a parish in Middleborough, in the county of Plymouth. From hence also he was removed, and soon after entered the army, in the last French war, in the capacity of chaplain, where he died. He was succeeded at Upton, in the work of the gospel ministry, by the Rev. Elisha Fish, who was solemnly separated unto this sacred employment on the 5th of June, 1751, and who, having obtained help of God, still continues, faithfully serving the Lord in the gospel of his Son. There is a considerable society of anabaptists in this town, and has been for many years. For early in the year 1751 they ordained one Mr. Abraham Bloss for their teaching elder, who continued there but a few years before he left them; after which the society and church dissolved. However, a few individuals remained, who called themselves anabaptists, who rarely had any meetings for religious worship among themselves for several years, but occasionally attended upon teachers of that denomination in other towns. But early in the year 1787 there arose a considerable number, very suddenly, who called themselves anabaptists, and still remain as a distinct society, to whom one elder Ingalls first ministered; and since they have the occasional instruction of Mr. Simeon Snow who has been ordained at large. However, there is not, so far as I can learn, any church so gathered among them as to celebrate the Lord's supper by themselves.

In the town of Upton there are also a number of the people called friends or quakers, but no distinct society of that denomination is formed there.

We shall proceed to some Topographical Description of Upton. Some parts of the town are very rough and uneven, others more level. The soil is generally strong, rich and good, favourable
for

for orcharding, and fruit of moſt kinds, and for paſturage and graſs; and there are a number of rivulets paſſing about in the valleys, between the hills, whereby it is pretty well furniſhed with water. There is one river, which has its ſource in Grafton, and paſſing through the weſt part of Upton, in a ſoutherly courſe, known by the name of *Weſt River*: This is emptied into Blackſtone River in the lower part of Uxbridge. On this river there are ſome good meadows; alſo mills. A little north of the meetinghouſe, there is a ſmall pond fed by rivulets and ſprings, from the ſouth end of which there iſſues a fine ſtream, on which there is a corn mill within a few rods of the meetinghouſe, whereby the inhabitants are greatly accommodated and benefited; this falls into Weſt River. The growth of wood is ſimilar to that of other towns of like kinds of ſoil. The high lands have plenty of oak of the ſeveral ſorts; conſiderable quantity of walnut; ſome cheſnut: The low lands have birch, maple, elm, alder, &c. There is much pitch pine in the place, and alſo conſiderable white pine remaining even at this day. This town is ſituated about thirty eight miles from Boſton, to the ſouthweſt; and fifteen miles from Worceſter courthouſe, about ſoutheaſt; and is bounded on the north by Weſtborough; on the eaſt, by Hopkinton and Milford; on the ſouth, by Mendon; and on the weſt, by Northbridge and Grafton.

HARDWICK.

HARDWICK.

FOR the sum of 20*l.* Newengland currency, *John Magus* and *Lawrence Naffowanno*, two noted Indians, so early as in the year 1686, December 27th, gave and signed a deed of a large tract of land to Messrs. Joshua Lamb, Nathaniel Page, Andrew Gardner, Benjamin Gamblin, Benjamin Tucker, John Curtiss, Richard Draper, and Samuel Ruggles, of Roxbury. This tract of land included what is now Hardwick. In consequence of the abovementioned deed, the heirs of those gentlemen petitioned the General Court, and obtained a grant of this township on the 17th of June, 1732. It was called Lambstown, from the first named proprietor, until it was incorporated and made a town by an act of the Legislature, which bears date January 10th, 1738, when the name of *Hardwick* was given to it.

This town contains, according to its original grant, about six miles square, notwithstanding a part on the easterly side of the place was set off more than forty years ago, to help in making up the town of Newbraintree. Hardwick is now bounded on the north, by Petersham and Barre; on the east, by Barre, Newbraintree and *Ware River*; on the south, by Ware River, and the town of Ware, in the county of Hampshire; and on the west, by Greenwich in that county.

After

After the location of this grant a number of settlers immediately entered upon the lands, and others followed fo rapidly, as that they foon had the gofpel preached among them, and as early as November 17th, 1736, a little more than four years from the date of the grant, the church of Chrift was gathered, and the fame day the Rev. David White was ordained their firft Paftor. He died January 6th, 1784, in the 74th year of his age, and the 48th of his miniftry. He was fucceeded in the facred office by the Rev. Thomas Holt, who was feparated unto that high and holy calling on the 25th of June, 1789, after a vacancy of five years and almoft fix months.

The people of Hardwick, confidering their number, are remarkably united in their fentiments refpecting religion. There are a few antipedobaptifts in the place; as alfo a few profeffed univerfalifts.

We proceed to fome Topographical Defcription of Hardwick. The town is of a good form and fhape, being nearly fquare. The face of the town is rather rough, hilly and uneven: Although there are no very great and remarkable hills. The foil is, in general, deep, loamy, and very fertile. The lands produce all kinds of grain in fufficient plenty for the inhabitants; but they are beft adapted to grafs and pafturage: Here vaft quantities of butter and cheefe are made, and moft excellent beef fatted for the market. All kinds of fruit trees flourifh here.

The principal growth of wood is oak of all sorts, chesnut and walnut; but in the north western part of the town, there is some white and pitch pine. The land is generally rocky and moist; and it is finely watered in every part by springs, streams and rivulets, which run about in the valleys among the hills; but there are no streams of note or distinction in the town, although they furnish water for all sorts of water works; and there are within the town, five corn mills, four saw mills, and two clothiers' works, where much business is performed to the great advantage of the people.

Ware River, which is large, runs on the east and south of the town, and is the boundary between this town and Newbraintree, and also between Hardwick and the town of Ware. The interval on this river, in the eastern part of the town, may contain perhaps as much as two hundred acres of very excellent mowing land. On this river a furnace was erected several years ago, and where much hard ware has been manufactured; but at present there is no business done thereat.

There are two considerable ponds in the town; one called *Pottapoug*, in the northerly part, is about two miles in length, and nearly one third of a mile in breadth; this is stored with fish. It has an inlet which comes from Petersham; its outlet passes through the northwestern part of Hardwick, and falls into Chicabee River. The other, called *Muddy Pond*, is about one mile in length, and about half a mile in width in the southerly part.

It

It has plenty of good fish. It has a small inlet; its outlet is into Ware River.

The roads of travel are from Boston, either through Worcester or Rutland, to Hardwick, and so on to Northampton. Another road from the southwest, with one from the southeast, form a junction near the centre of the town, and then passing northward, through Petersham into the States of Newhampshire and Vermont. Hardwick is situated a little southwest from Boston, distant from the State house seventy two miles, and from the courthouse in Worcester twenty five miles, a little to the northwest. It is a very large, flourishing, wealthy town, and contained, when the census was taken, 245 houses and 1725 inhabitants; and was the fifth town in the county in the proportion it paid to a State tax in 1790.

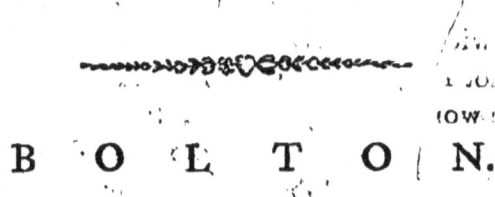

BOLTON.

THIS town was taken from the ancient town of Lancaster; and was incorporated on the 24th of June, 1738, by act of the Legislature, when it received its present name. The tract of land was large at first: In the year 1784, the district of Berlin, to the south, was set off from it: Still it is large enough to make a very respectable figure among the towns in the county. It contained,

ed, when the continental cenfus was taken, 125 houfes, and 861 inhabitants. It is bounded by Lancafter on the weft; by Harvard, on the north; by Stow, in the county of Middlefex, on the eaft; by Marlborough on the foutheaft; and by Berlin, on the fouth. It is diftant from Bofton about thirty four miles, nearly weft; and from the courthoufe in Worcefter, it is about eighteen miles, lying to the northeaft.

The Ecclefiaftical Hiftory of Bolton is as follows. The church of Chrift here was gathered on the 4th of November, 1741; on which day the Rev. Thomas Gofs was ordained their firft paftor, who continued until January 17th, 1780, when he died in the fixty third year of his age, and thirty ninth of his miniftry. He was fucceeded, a fhort fpace of time, by the Rev. John Walley, who had been before for feveral years minifter of a parifh in Ipfwich. Mr. Walley was difmiffed from Bolton, not long before his death. He was fucceeded in the work of the gofpel miniftry in this place, by the Rev. Phineas Wright, who was folemnly feparated hereunto October 26th, 1785, and who ftill lives. The people are peaceable and happy, profperous and flourifhing.

In Bolton, and the diftrict of Berlin, there is a fociety of friends, or quakers, confifting of a large number of moftly wealthy families; their houfe of worfhip ftands within the limits of Bolton, near to Berlin line.

We fhall proceed to give fome Geographical Defcription of Bolton. The town in general is

good

good land, not level, nor yet has it any very high hills. The higheft lands in the town are rich and moift; excellent for orcharding and pafture land. It is not very rocky, however, there are ftones fufficient to wall in all their farms. The people raife rye, wheat, Indian corn, barley, oats, flax, &c. &c. upon their lands, in fuch plenty as richly to repay their labour in the cultivation thereof. About half a mile from the centre of the town, to the weft, begins the great hill, known by the name of Wattoquottock Hill, which extends fouthwefterly into Berlin. This long, large hill, is not very high; it is in general very good land, and there are divers fine farms upon it. The great road from Lancafter to Bofton paffes over the north end of this hill, upon its declivity, where it is very moift, confifting of clay and loam, fenfibly felt by travellers in the wet feafons of the year. On the wefterly fide of this hill, about halfway from its foot to the fummit, is a cavity opening to the fouthweft, parallel with the main courfe of the hill, near the upper end of which is a pool, or fmall pond of water, known by the name of Welch Pond. This pond is of a circular form about twenty feet in depth, and occupies the fpace of about one acre on its furface. It is fuppofed to have diminifhed about one half, both in depth and circumference within forty years paft. People now mow confiderable grafs, where they went with boats and canoes half a century ago. On the foutheafterly fide of this hill, and nearly oppofite to Welch Pond, iffue a number of rivulets, which
foon

soon unite in the low lands, and form a considerable brook, taking a southeasterly course, till it falls into Assabet River, in the northerly part of Marlborough. This brook has water sufficient to carry two mills, in the wet seasons of the year, at the distance of less than one mile from the hill. There is a glade of most excellent meadow on each side of this stream, its whole length, with but few small interruptions, by hard land. The higher parts of these meadows, next the hill, are known by the name of Wattoquottock Meadows. At a small distance from the northeasterly foot of Wattoquottock, begins another large hill, with a gradual ascent, which extends northeasterly through Harvard into the boundaries of Lyttleton, in the county of Middlesex. By some, this is called Bear Hill, by others Oak Hill. This hill has been thought to contain mines and minerals, and has, consequently, for a number of years engaged the attention of a respectable society of mineseekers; but their expectations have far exceeded their gains: For though its bowels have been explored with much painful labour, and sanguine hope, yet the mountain has not even to this day brought forth a mouse. At the intersection, between this last mentioned hill and Wattoquottock, is a narrow bar of hard land, about fifteen rods in width; and on each side of this bar, is a small piece of low, sunken, boggy ground, in which arise several springs, soon forming a rivulet each way. That on the northwestly side, runs a northerly course, about a mile and an half, with a continual increase of waters,

waters, and empties into *Still River*, fo called, within the boundaries of Lancafter. The rivulet on the foutheafterly fide runs an eafterly courfe; the waters of which being augmented by fmall additions, become fufficient to carry mills, where much bufinefs is done, at the diftance of two miles from their fource, except in the fummer months, and they are emptied into the river Affabet, about two miles foutheaft from Stow meetinghoufe; previous to which, however, the road to Bofton croffes this ftream three times. On this brook are feveral bodies of meadow, but not equal in goodnefs to thofe beforementioned. In the northeafterly part of Bolton, about two miles and an half from the centre of the town, is fituated the large and extenfive hill, called Rattle Snake Hill, belonging to the heirs of the late Gen. John Whetcomb. In the fouth fide of this hill is a body of limeftone; and here are annually made about one hundred and fifty hogfheads of the very beft of lime. In the eafterly part of the town is a large hill, known by the name of Long Hill. It lies clofe on the fouth fide of, and runs parallel with the great road, about one mile and an half, to Stow line, with a gradual afcent to the fouth of about half a mile to its fummit. There are two fmall ponds, of a circular form, at the diftance of about eighty rods from each other, in the eafterly part of the town, fuppofed to cover, one about forty, and the other about thirty acres of ground. The largeft of thefe lies near the weft end of Long Hill, in fight of the great road, and known by the name of

Weft's

West's Pond, from a person of that name formerly living on its shore. In the northwest angle of Bolton, mainly, is situated a large body of almost stagnant water, and therefore called Still River, but might be more properly denominated a lake, or very long pond. It is various in its width and depth. It begins within the boundaries of Lancaster, in the great intervals (about twenty rods east of the great bridge over the Nashaway, after the junction of its two branches) and proceeds in a circular course, upwards of three miles, across the northwest corner of Bolton, into Harvard, from the north end of which there is a very small outlet into the river Nashaway. On the south side of this lake, and between this and the river Nashaway, is a very large body of most excellent interval land, part of which is within the limits of Bolton, used for tillage, mowing and pasturing: And which is often laid several feet under water by spring and fall floods, presenting the appearance of a small sea.

Various are the conjectures of people respecting Still River, Lake, or Long Pond, above mentioned. Some suppose the bed of the south branch of Nashaway once was here, and that by some great freshet it was cut off above, formed a new channel, and joined the north branch the sooner, where the junction now is. Be this as it may, it is certain these branches have shifted their beds, in various places, and of considerable lengths, in the revolution of ages. There are several rivulets fall into this lake on its easterly side; but there is no inlet at its upper end, except what appears to rise

directly

directly out of the ground; and the great probability is, that a ſtream, which begins in Bolton, feeds this Lake by a ſubterraneous paſſage; for while this ſtream is conſtant, briſk and lively, for half a mile, coming to a ſpot of pine, ſandy land, it diſappears, and no water is diſcernible for near two miles. There is a ſmall inlet into this lake on the eaſtern part of Lancaſter intervals, in wet ſeaſons, but in the ſummer no water runs in this, and yet the lake appears no way to be affected thereby.

Let us leave this lake, and finiſh our Deſcription of Bolton.

There are two pot aſh works in this place, and one of pearl aſh. Here are two famous brickyards where above two hundred thouſands of bricks are annually made. The town is very well wooded. On the high lands there is plenty of walnut, cheſnut, and oak of all ſorts: And here vaſt numbers of barrels and hogſheads are manufactured yearly; and great quantities of hoops are carried to market. In the low lands there is much maple, but little aſh; ſome birch. There are ſome plains covered with pitch pine, very little white pine.

Upon the whole, this is a town of rich, ſtrong and good land, and the people are increaſing in number wealth and reputation. They are now building a large elegant meetinghouſe, upon the modern conſtruction, with a ſteeple to it, to which Meſſrs. Joſhua and James Richardſon, formerly of Boſton, have generouſly contributed 100*l.* and bought their pews, as others, at vendue, but upon

this

this condition, that they should not be taxed to the building said house. The pews will pay for the house. The underpinning of this meetinghouse is very beautiful, and equal to any in the county, if not in the whole State. It is a white and free stone, easily split into any size, and was discovered just when wanted.

STURBRIDGE.

THIS is styled in the act for erecting the county of Worcester, "The land lately granted to several petitioners of Medfield," and many of the first settlers here were from the town of Medfield, and hence the place was called Newmedfield, until its incorporation, which was, by an act of Court, on the 24th of June, 1738, when it received the name Sturbridge.

This town is large in its dimensions, containing by actual survey, about 28929 acres. It is situated in the southwest corner of the county, and is divided from Woodstock and Union, on the south, in the state of Connecticut, by the state line; and bounded west, on Holland and Brimfield, in the county of Hampshire; on the north, by Brookfield; and on the east, by Charlton and Dudley. The grant of this tract was made in the year 1729, in the month of August, but it was thought scarcely ly habitable by reason of its broken rough state; and the soil, for the most part, requiring hard and great labour to render it productive; but the first settlers being a robust, resolute, sober and industrious set of men, were determined to get an honest living, by "the sweat of their faces," and, through the blessing of God, they soon converted this wilderness into a fruitful field. The original proprietors built a house for the worship of God, which was raised on the 20th and 21st days of June, 1733, and on the 3d of September following it was consecrated by the Rev. Joseph Baxter of Medfield, who preached from Isaiah lxiii, and 5th. From that time the place increased fast in the number of good and industrious people, who very quickly obtained to live comfortably; and like others of that age, early sought for a teacher of piety and morality. On the 29th of September, 1736, the Rev. Caleb Rice was ordained to the pastoral office over the church and flock of God in the place. He was a pastor after God's heart; sound in faith; a good preacher, endued with excellent ministerial gifts, and very exemplary in life, as well as social and benevolent in his deportment. He lived in great harmony with his people, in the fore part of his ministry: But about the year 1747, a number of the brethren and inhabitants, conceiving they had received *new light*, different from what was common among their neighbours, separated from him, which rendered his work more arduous, and his life uncomfortable. From separatists they became anabaptists:

N   But

But it pleafed the Great Head of the church to remove Mr. Rice from his labours, by death, on the fecond of September, 1759, whofe praife was then through all the churches, and his memory is ftill dear to many. He was fucceeded in the work of the gofpel miniftry, in the congregational church and fociety in Sturbridge, by the Rev. Joſhua Paine, who was feparated hereunto on the 17th of June, 1761, and ftill continues the faithful and beloved paftor thereof. The people here have furprifingly flourifhed and increafed; for there are now about 1800 fouls in the place. The congregational church is large, confifting of about 150 members of both fexes. On the 29th and 30th days of June, 1785, they raifed a large new meetinghoufe, which is elegant and well finifhed; in which the firft fermon was preached by the Rev. Mr. Paine on January 7th, 1786, from firft of Kings, viii. 27.

There is in the town a very refpectable fociety of anabaptifts, comprifing about one fifth part of the inhabitants. Thefe alfo have built them lately a handfome meetinghoufe. As great peace and harmony fubfift between the two focieties, as can well be expected under fuch circumftances: Difference of fentiments, as to modes and rites of religion, fcarcely injures good neighbourhood; nor does it prevent their mixing in families, or friendly focial circles.

The inhabitants at prefent are induftrious and frugal, charitable, and given to hofpitality. The great precepts of the Chriftian religion, moral virtue,

tue, and the inftruction of their youth, they make their ftudy and care. They live in peace and love.

However hilly, rough and uneven the town was at firft, yet, by induftry and frugality, the people are become wealthy, fubfifting chiefly by the cultivation of the earth. By hard labour the foil is become fruitful. It is good for orcharding and grazing. Much butter and cheefe are made here; efpecially the former, which has obtained high credit in the markets. The land is pretty good for grain. The growth of wood is fimilar to that of the towns in the vicinity, oak of all forts, walnut, chefnut, pine in confiderable plenty, efpecially in its earlier days; afh, beech, birch, maple, elm, &c.

The town is in general well watered by fprings, brooks, rivers and ponds. The River Quinebaug, which has its fource in Brimfield, runs through this town near the centre, from weft to eaft. On this there are large bodies of good interval, and valuable meadow lands. There are valuable ponds in the town, well ftored with the ufual forts of frefh water fifh.

Near one of thefe ponds, called Lead Mine Pond, a number of adventurers from Europe, fome years paft, dug deep for ore. A confiderable quantity of which they carried with them to England; but they have never returned to their purfuit.

Sturbridge is fituated at the fouthweft angle of the county, on the ftate line, about twenty miles from the courthoufe in Worcefter; and it is fixty five miles from Bofton, and confiderably to the fouth of weft.

HOLDEN.

HOLDEN.

THE town of Holden was taken wholly from the town of Worcester, being included in their original grants; and was the northwesterly part thereof.

It was incorporated on the 9th of January, 1740, when the name of Holden was given to it to perpetuate the name and deeds of the Hon. Samuel Holden, Esq; one of the directors of the Bank of England; and of his lady and their amiable daughters; who had been great and generous benefactors to the literary and religious interests of this country.

This worthy, benevolent man, transmitted to Newengland for charitable purposes, in books and bills of exchange, to the amount of 4847*l*. Newengland currency. After his decease, Mrs. Holden and daughters sent over in value, 5585*l*. for the same noble and pious uses. With part of this latter sum *Holden Chapel*, in the University of Cambridge, in Massachusetts, was erected in the year 1745. There are nineteen volumes, chiefly octavos, in the hands of the Rev. Mr. Avery, given by Mrs. Holden and her daughters, to the minister of Holden, and his successors. This town was said to be laid out six miles square, but it considerably exceeds that: From east to west it is about seven miles across: From the south point at Leicester

cester it is ten miles. It is bounded northerly, on Princeton and Sterling; easterly, on Worcester and Boylston; southerly, on Worcester, Leicester and Paxton, and westerly on Rutland and Paxton. We shall next present the reader with the Ecclesiastical History of Holden.

The church of Christ in this place was formed on the 22d of December, 1742, and on the same day the Rev. Joseph Davis was ordained their first pastor. He was dismissed from his pastoral relation to that people October 18th, 1772. Since that time he has been employed in preaching the gospel in various places; and on Wednesday the 2d day of January, 1793, he preached a special lecture to the people of Holden, as on that day half a century, from the imbodying the church and his ordination, expired.* Mr. Davis was succeeded in the sacred office at Holden, by the Rev. Joseph Avery, who was publickly separated thereunto December 21st, 1774, and still continues in the ministry there.

We go on to a Geographical Description of the town of Holden. The soil of this town is somewhat various, yet in general of a loamy kind: The land in the outskirts of the town is the most springy and natural to grass. The general produce is rye, Indian corn, spring wheat and oats. Some farms produce good barley. Flax is raised with various success; when there is a failure of a crop, it is generally owing to other causes than the nature of the soil. Though the town is rather hilly and uneven, yet not very much so. Such land

* The discourse was printed.

land is generally good for fruit; and, accordingly, here are very large and valuable orchards indeed, but they are chiefly at a considerable distance from the centre of the town; the middle not being so fruitful, and more exposed to destructive frosts. There is a brickyard two miles and an half northeast of the meetinghouse, where are made annually about sixty thousands of bricks. The clay is very strong and good. There are two pot-ash works about three miles east of the meetinghouse; one of them lately erected. The growth of wood in Holden is mainly chesnut and oak of all kinds. In former years there was a great quantity of excellent white pine timber, but the most of it has been cut off. There still remains, chiefly in the northerly part of the town, considerable yellow pine. There are other kinds of wood in various parts of the town. Some walnut, hemlock, hornbeam, white maple, ash, and some valuable rock-maple.

At the northwest part of the town there is a Pond called Quincpoxet, the greater part of which is in Princeton: A narrow fordable strait of water issues from this into a lesser pond, perhaps fifty rods in length; from this there is an outlet into a second pond; from this second an outlet into a third; and from the third, into a fourth pond. These lesser ponds are in Holden; and from them proceeds a river called Quincpoxet, which holds an easterly course, and passes out of Holden into Boylston, where, quite on the west side of that town, it joins Still River which comes from the foot of of Watchusett-Hill, and from thence takes the name of the south branch of the River Nashaway. Just below the abovementioned ponds in Holden, and on this River Quinepoxet, stands a fine saw mill. There is another pond about two miles and three quarters northeast of the centre of the town, called Lily Pond, which has neither inlet nor outlet. There is a fine stream coming from the west and southwest parts of the town, part of which is derived from Asnebumskit Pond in Paxton, and crossing the main road leading to Rutland, one mile and an half west of the meetinghouse, joins Quinepoxet River, about that distance north of it. On this stream are three saw mills and two grist mills. Another stream, which has its rise mainly, a mile and upwards south of the centre of the town, takes a circuitous course, crosses the great road about two miles east of the meetinghouse, and falls into Quinepoxet about two miles northeast of said house. It was formerly called Cedar Brook. On this are two saw, and two grist mills. On a branch which enters it, and about two miles southeast of the middle of the town, stands another saw mill. In the south part of the town rises a stream which holds a southeasterly course, and passes into Worcester, called Turkey Brook. On this there is a saw mill, and also a grist mill. There are no extensive intervals in Holden; but yet, in several parts of the town, there are farms whose value is much enhanced by the meadows and pieces of interval which lie on the river and streams mentioned above.

About three miles northeast from the centre of the town is situated *Malden Hill*, where there is a large quarry of most excellent stone for underpinning, &c. and which may be wrought into any form, although they do not hew very easy. In the west part of the town is a hill called Pine Hill. In the southwest part of the town the foot of the famous *Asnebumskit* Hill, which is mostly in Paxton, falls within Holden limits; and east of this, and stretching southeast and northwest, lies *Stone House Hill*, so called, whose sides in some places are very steep, and exhibit horrid cliffs of rocks, noticeable for affording dens for rattlesnakes; they are however, mostly destroyed, and rarely seen at this day. Winter hill lies in the southeast part of the town, and is partly in Worcester.

This town is large, increasing in number and wealth, and when the census was taken contained 1080 souls. It is fifty one miles from Boston, nearly west, and seven miles from Worcester courthouse, to the northwest. It has one large road running through it, from Boston to Connecticut river, Vermont, &c.

LEOMINSTER.

THIS town was taken from Lancaster, and was part of what was called Lancaster new grant. It was incorporated on the 23d of June, 1740.

The

The Ecclesiastical History of Leominster is as follows. The church here was imbodied on the 14th of September, 1743: And on the same day the Rev. John Rogers was ordained their pastor. He was a sensible, worthy man, and used his natural right to examine, think and believe, for himself. And what he thought to be the truth as it is in Jesus, that he preached to his people; always appearing to act uprightly and conscientiously. However, a number of the church and people, apprehending Mr. Rogers delivered doctrines contrary to the gospel, called in a large council for advice in July 1757, consisting of fifteen churches. The council judged the brethren had reasons for dissatisfaction, but advised them to attend on Mr. Rogers's ministry for three months, and if he did not retract his errors, as they called them, in that time, then they advised the church to dismiss him; which they accordingly did, and shut him out of the meetinghouse. Upon this Mr. Rogers preached to such as were disposed to attend on his ministry, in his own house. At length Mr. Rogers sued the town for his salary: And after a long contest in the law, the dispute was compromised in this manner, viz. Mr. Rogers relinquished all claims upon the town as their minister; the town to pay to Mr. Rogers whatever sums of money his adherents had been obliged to pay towards supplying the pulpit after he had been shut out of it; and, finally, that all who wished to have Mr. Rogers for their minister, should be made a poll parish; about a fifth part of the town were accordingly

made

made a distinct, but poll parish, by an act of the Legislature; after this settlement of their unhappy controversy, the church and town proceeded to the choice of a minister, and on the 22d of December, 1762, the Rev. Francis Gardner was ordained their second pastor; in whose ministerial labours the people have been very happy for more than thirty years already; and during this period they have been peaceable and prosperous. And when the town, a few years since, erected a large and elegant new meetinghouse, Mr. Rogers's adherents contributed their full proportion to the building of it. The Rev. Mr. Rogers, having obtained help of God, continued to preach and administer special ordinances to the people of his parish until the year 1788; when, finding his age and bodily infirmities so great, he wished to be excused from the sacred labours, to which his people consented, and generously paid him three years salary in advance: Whereupon, by an act of the Legislature, this poll parish was dissolved, and the whole town now form but one church and congregation under the ministry of the Rev. Mr. Gardner.

The Rev. Mr. Rogers lived but a little while after he ceased from his publick labours. He departed this life October, 1789, in the 47th year of his ministry.

Let it now be observed, there was no way to avoid giving this particular detail, and yet mention the two religious societies which for a time subsisted in Leominster. Our plan, truth, and impartial justice, required the mention of them. And

nothing

nothing derogatory of any one has been said. Nay, the defign has been to pay tribute due to worthy characters, to Mr. Rogers and Mr. Gardner, and to the people, who once were two parties and focieties. The majority of the church and town difmiffed Mr. Rogers, that the truth and purity of the gofpel, as they thought, might continue with them. The friends of Mr. Rogers fuppofed him to be a good and faithful minifter of Jefus Chrift; and therefore adhered to him to the laft; and treated him with all poffible refpect, kindnefs and generofity, until the Great Head of the church was pleafed to remove him from this world. And now he is gone to be here no more, we find the two focieties cordially receiving and embracing each other, and cheerfully attending upon and fupporting one and the fame minifter, the Rev. Mr. Gardner. The moral character of Mr. Rogers was never impeached. Had he lived in the prefent day, perhaps fuch a controverfy would never have been heard of. We have feen in Mr. Rogers a uniform character, and an honeft upright man, whofe integrity, and firm attachment to what he thought were important truths, were fuperior to the trials he met with, and by which perfons of more eafy virtue might have been overcome.

 Some Geographical Defcription of the town of Leominfter fhall here be prefented to the reader. Leominfter contains about as much as five miles fquare, and is fituated in the northeaftly quarter of the county, and is diftant about nineteen miles from the courthoufe in Worcefter; and from Bofton,

ton, it is a little to the northweſt, at the diſtance of fifty miles. It is bounded on the north and northeaſt, by Fitchburg and Lunenburg; on the eaſt, ſoutheaſt and ſouth, by Lancaſter; and on the ſouthweſt and weſt, by Sterling, and a gore of land. This town is pretty plain and level in the middle of it, and for a mile and a half or two miles round the meetinghouſe, and indeed all the way ſouth of the meetinghouſe towards Lancaſter; to the north, towards Fitchburg, it is not quite ſo level; yet the land is pretty good, and the ſoil is clayey: Upon the eaſt, and eſpecially on the weſt, the land becomes hilly and more uneven, and the land is proportionably better. The farms in the middle of the town, are by no means poor; but thoſe in the ſkirts of the town are very excellent indeed; and the land is equal to that in any town. The land is well adapted to all kinds of grain, and the hilly parts to graſs and paſturage; and the town abounds with famous orchards, and all kinds of fruit, and much cyder is made in the place. The land is not very ſtony and rocky in general, except it be ſome particular part of ſome of the hills: Of theſe none are famous or worthy of particular notice, except one in the weſterly part of the town, called Wauhnooſnook Hill; this is about two miles in length, and a mile or more from the meetinghouſe in the neareſt place: It is pretty high and ſteep: And although there is ſome broken and unimproveable land upon it, yet there are many very fine farms thereon: This hill is famous for affording vaſt quantities of moſt excellent

ſtone,

stone, of a grayish colour, pretty free, and easily split and wrought, and some have natural faces, sixteen, eighteen and twenty feet in length. This store is perhaps inexhaustible. In the south part of the town there is a very large body of plain land covered with pitch pine; and there is considerable white pine within the town: But the main growth of wood consists of oak of all kinds, chesnut in plenty, much walnut, elm, butternut, shagbark, &c. &c.

The town is very well watered in every part, by numerous springs and rivulets. There are two streams which claim a particular mention: One is Wauhnoosnook Brook, so called from the hill of that name, as it originates at the foot of this hill, at the north end, and runs all along on the east side of the hill, and on the westerly side of the town, and finally falls into the river Nashaway. The other is the north branch of the river Nashaway, which coming in from Fitchburg, at the northwest angle of the town, runs about a mile east of the meetinghouse, and at the southeast angle of this town passes into Lancaster. There is some good interval land on this river, but in many places the banks of it are high and very steep. There is but very little meadow land in the town. On this river and the streams there are two grist mills, five saw mills, one oil mill, and clothiers' works very excellent. There are only a part of two ponds fall within the limits of this town, and these were mentioned in giving an account of Lunenburg.

It

It has been mentioned before that the soil of this town is clayey. There are indeed vast bodies of the best of clay in the town: And upwards of two hundred thousands of bricks are made here in a year. These bricks are said to endure the fire longer than any made in the county. The people of Leominster live mostly by the cultivation of the earth; and their farms and buildings proclaim their industry, and indicate a good degree of wealth. They have all the mechanicks and tradesmen in common with other places. And besides, the manufacturing of combs is here established, in two or three places, and the work is carried on to great perfection and profit. About twenty persons work, more or less at this trade; about ten are constantly employed therein, and they manufacture about six thousand dozen in a year. Mr. Jotham Johnson, a trader here, employs five men in this work, who make twenty five hundred dozen per annum. Among these, is one who makes ivory combs, equally good perhaps, as any imported from any country. Here are several stores and shops filled with European, East, and West-india goods. There is much travel through this town, from the north part of the county of Hampshire and of Worcester, by the way of Westminster, and from Vermont State, and the western part of Newhampshire, by the way of Fitchburg; these roads unite in the northwesterly part of Leominster, and come to the meetinghouse, where they part again; one turns nearly east, leading on through Harvard to Boston; the other runs south,

bearing

bearing a little to the east into Lancaster, and so on to Boston. The county road from Leominster to Worcester runs southwesterly through Sterling. Leominster is a growing, flourishing town; it stands about the middle of the towns of the county in the proportion it pays to a state tax; and when the late census was taken there were 166 dwelling houses, and 1190 inhabitants in the place.

WESTERN.

THIS town was taken from Brookfield, Brimfield and Palmer, and was incorporated on the 16th of January, 1741. In this place a congregational church was formed in the year 1748, and on the last of January, 1744, the Rev. Isaac Jones was ordained their first pastor. He died July, 1784, in the 67th year of his age, and 41st of his ministry. Mr. Jones was succeeded in the sacred office by the Rev. Stephen Baxter, who was separated hereunto March 9th, 1791.

Western is situated at the southwest angle of the county, and is bounded on the north and east by Brookfield, on the south by Brimfield, and on the west by Palmer: It is about seventy three miles from the statehouse in Boston to the southwest, and from the courthouse in Worcester it is about twenty ty eight miles, and on the post road from Boston to Springfield, although this road does not pass through the centre of the town, or by the meeting-house. From Brookfield this road enters Western on the northeast, about one hundred and twenty rods from the River Quaboag on the south side thereof, and runs nearly parallel therewith for about the space of two miles; then the road to Northampton parts from this, taking a northwesterly direction across the abovenamed river. The left hand, or post road, bears a southwestern course to Springfield. The town does not lie in a square and regular form. The lands in general, are very uneven: There are some small meadows on the several brooks, and some good interval lands on Quaboag River which runs through the town; also some small swamps and morasses, but the principal part of Western is high land. The middle of the town is broken and rough. A hill, by the name of *Mark's Mountain*, of about two miles in circumference, on its base, and terminating unequally in ragged cliffs, greatly injures the prospect of the middle of the town. A body of land in the northwest angle of the town, known by the name of *Coy's Hill*, is most excellent for grazing. Part of this hill falls within the limits of Brookfield, and over this hill passes the road to Northampton. On the west and southwest, this town is separated from the towns of Ware and Palmer, by a chain of rocky hills and mountains. The inhabitants in general, are farmers; and the lands, though rather rough, produce large crops of Indian

dian corn, rye, and oats; and some considerable wheat is raised in the town: But much the greater part of the land is best adapted to English grass and pasturage. The soil is propitious to the cultivation of fruit trees of all kinds; and the height and uneven surface of the lands, are a great security to the grain and fruit from frosts. Western has its proportion of unimproveable lands; some of which are dry and rocky; some almost entirely inaccessible, by reason of vast ledges of rocks; yet almost all the unimproved and unimproveable lands are covered with wood and timber. On the high lands grow chesnut, oak and walnut; and in the lower lands grow ash, birch, maple, elm, pine, hemlock, &c. &c. Western is sufficiently watered by springs, brooks and rivulets, which run about in the valleys among the hills.

The river Quaboag, from Brookfield, enters this town on the northeast, and passing through it about a mile west of the centre, goes out at the southwest angle, and falls into Chicabee. A great number of brooks and rivulets are emptied into Quaboag River in its course through Western. Salmon were formerly taken from this river within the town; but now their course is obstructed by several dams which extend across it, for the accommodation of mills and other water works: However, the river and other streams afford all the various kinds of fish which are common to fresh water. About a mile from the centre of the town, are fixed on this river, two grist mills, one saw mill, one scythe mill, one fulling mill, and one forge; and the town affords some ore for the supply of the forge. Besides the manufactory of iron, there is no other which claims a particular mention, except it be that of silk. Several gentlemen are turning their attention to the cultivation of mulberry trees. Col. Joseph Jones, from about thirty trees, has for three seasons past, fed upon an average about 30,000 worms; their produce has been between three and four pounds of raw silk annually. And when manufactured, after making all deductions for labour and trouble, has yielded a clear profit yearly, of sixty dollars, which is an annuity of two dollars per tree. A sample of the sewing silk, manufactured by Col. Jones, and presented to the writer, is equal to any imported.

There have been some vestiges of the aboriginals discovered on an extensive hill in the easterly part of this town, which was taken from Brookfield. On ploughing the ground a few years since, large beds of clamshells were discovered under the soil, which appeared to be placed at equal distances from each other; these, together with Indian utensils found there, prove this was a place of their resort and dwelling.

This town is very flourishing, and is growing in number, and increasing in wealth. When the census was taken two years ago, there were 124 dwelling houses, and 900 inhabitants in the place.

DOUGLASS.

DOUGLASS.

THIS was an original grant, and was prior to that of Sutton. It is about feventy years fince fome families fettled in the place. The firft fettlers came from Sherburne, in the county of Middlefex, whence it was called *Newſherburne*, until its incorporation, which was in the year 1746, when it received the name of *Douglaſs* to perpetuate the name and deeds of William Douglaſs, M. D. of Bofton, originally from Scotland, educated there, a famous phyfician in his day, and who alfo wrote a Hiftory of Newengland in two vol. 8vo. a proprietor, and confiderable benefactor.

The firft perfon born here is yet living, almoft feventy years old.

The lands in this place were not fo pleafing and inviting as fome others, and were therefore but flowly fettled. The lands were burnt over yearly in the fpring, for the purpofe of turning cattle from the neighbouring towns, to feed thereon. Hereby the growth of timber was greatly injured, and the land became hard to fubdue. Hurtleberry and whitebuſh fprung up, together with laurel, fweetfern and checkerberry, which nothing but the plough will deftroy. For thirty five years paft the inhabitants have greatly increafed, have prevented the fires running, have cultivated the lands, erected decent buildings; and are induſtrious

dustrious and prosperous. When the general enumeration of the Commonwealth was made in the year 1791, there were in the town 165 dwelling houses, and 1080 inhabitants. This town is bounded on the north, one mile by Oxford, and five miles by Sutton; on the east, by Uxbridge, six miles; on the south, by Gloucester, in the State of Rhodeisland, seven miles; on the west, two miles, by Thompson, in the State of Connecticut; two miles by a gore of land, and two miles and an half by Oxford. It lies 47 miles from Boston, about southwest; and about sixteen miles from the court-house in Worcester, nearly south. The lands of Douglass, in general, are better for the growing of Indian corn, rye, oats and flax, than natural to grass. They are exceedingly adapted to the growth of apple trees, and all the other kinds of fruit trees common in this part of the country. The natural growth of wood in the town is, in the swamps and low lands, cedar, spruce, &c. in some; in others, hemlock, white pine, ash, birch, beech, hornbeam, and maple: On the uplands, walnut, gray, white and yellow oak, chesnut, and chesnut oak, (its leaves like the chesnut, and bark like the oak) maple, pine, elm, locusts, balm of Gilead, so called, &c. &c. and almost every kind of tree, shrub, and bush, which is to be found in any of these northern States. The town has greatly abounded with good timber, and in the west part thereof there are almost four thousand acres of rocky woods; and in the place, potash, hoops and barrels are made in plenty; some shingles are manufactured

factured here, and pine boards fawed. The general face of the town is uneven; hills and vales interfperfed; there are many fteep, pine, fandy hills; good building fpots abound; and fmall hills defcending every way; dry cellars, and yet on fuch fpots, eighteen feet is deep enough to find conftant water for wells, and that within two rods of the top of the higher lands. The town is exceedingly well watered: Rivulets and fprings every where abound; and the people reap great advantages indeed, by turning and fpreading the water over their lands at their pleafure. The brooks and ftreams run eafterly, until they fall into rivers which go to the fouth.

In the fouthweft part of the town is Wallump Pond, fo called; it has a fmall inlet at the north end, and an outlet at the fouth end, in the State of Rhodeifland. This pond lies two miles in Douglafs, and one mile in Gloucefter, and is about three quarters of a mile in width. Badluck Pond, fo called, in the border of rocky woods, in the wefterly part of the town, covers about one hundred and fifty acres of ground. In this pond great rocks appear above the water, even in the midft of it. This is fuppofed to contain much ore, and may be eafily drained. It has an inlet at the fouth, and an outlet on the north, which paffes into Mumford River. Manchaug Pond, in the northwefterly part of the town, is about one mile long, and one quarter of a mile wide in Douglafs, the remainder of it lies in Sutton. This has feveral inlets on the weft and north; the outlet is on the eaft, east, runs in Sutton, becomes a river, turns south and comes into Douglass, and finally unites with Mumford River. Mumford River rises in rocky woods, increasing by streams from the ponds and from springs, and runs east into Uxbridge. There is a spring in rocky woods, a little southwest from Badluck Pond, which issues out of an apparently dry hill, and forms a stream, which runs southeast, never dry, and never known to freeze. This passes one rod and an half south of the great road, and is greatly admired for its pleasantness and refreshing nature. The soldiers in the late war, called it the White Oak Tavern. There is considerable interval land on Mumford River; there are four hundred acres in one body, near the head of it; further down there are divers other pieces, some of them large: Also, on this same river, there are works for making refined iron, near to Uxbridge line, and a corn and saw mill, very profitable. There are four hills in the town, large and noticeable. The first we shall mention is a little north of the meetinghouse, large and considerable; originally well clothed with timber, but now affords good tillage, mowing, and pasture land. On the west side of this hill, at the bottom near a swamp, the Indians, in old time, had their Wigwams and a fort, the remains of which are yet visible, and their tools are still found in the fields. About forty rods north of this hill, lies another hill, larger, but not cleared. Wallump Pond hill, near the pond of that name, in the southwest part of the town, is large but not very high;

high; this the people are beginning to settle and improve. In the southeast part of the town is situated Bald Hill, taking its name from the barrenness of its summit. This hill is now become fruitful in corn, rye, &c.

We shall now give some account of the Ecclesiastical state of Douglass. The congregational church here was gathered November 11th, 1747, and on the 16th of December, the same year, the Rev. William Phipps was ordained their first pastor. On the 10th of July, 1765, he was dismissed; he was succeeded in the gospel ministry by the Rev. Isaac Stone, who was separated hereunto October 30th, 1771, and still continues with them in peace and harmony. Here are a number of families of the anabaptist persuasion.

NEWBRAINTREE.

THE General Court of Massachusetts having granted six thousand acres of land to certain persons of the ancient town of Braintree, in the county of Suffolk, for services by them done to the publick, it was called and known by the style of Braintree Farms. This tract of land, together with a part of Brookfield, and a part of Hardwick, was incorporated January 31st, 1751, and the name

Newbraintree was given to it. The people who first settled this territory took early care for the support of the gospel, and the enjoyment of all the instituted means of religion; they accordingly erected a house for the publick worship of God, and on the 18th of April, 1754, the church of Christ in this place was imbodied, and the Rev. Benjamin Ruggles, their first minister, was installed the same day. Mr. Ruggles had been, for a number of years before, minister of the second parish in the town of Middleborough, in the county of Plymouth. The Rev. Daniel Foster, the present pastor of the church and congregation in Newbraintree, was ordained a colleague with Mr. Ruggles, on the 29th of October, 1778. The Rev. Mr. Ruggles died suddenly, of an epilepsy, or apoplexy, Lord's day morning, May 12th, 1782, in the 82d year of his age, and the 62d of his publick ministry. There is but one religious society in the town, nor any sectaries excepting only two families of anabaptists. The first meetinghouse ever built here is now standing, and on a beautiful eminence in the centre of the town, from whence there is a very extensive prospect. This house was a few years since repaired, and is now very decent and commodious. The people in this place are particularly attentive to the education of their children and youth: They have eight reputable school houses and in the winter season, as many instructors; two Latin grammar masters; and in the summer, they have generally two or three masters, and as many mistresses: And they
expend

expend more annually in supporting schools, than in supporting their publick teacher of piety, religion and morality, though he is honourably maintained.

We shall now present a Geographical Description of Newbraintree.

This town contains about 13000 acres of land, and is bounded south, on Brookfield; west, by Ware River, which separates it from Hardwick; north, on the town of Barre; and east, on the towns of Oakham and Spencer: It lays much in a triangular form.

The town is neither remarkably hilly nor level; but agreeably interspersed with moderate hills and valleys. There are two hills of name and note; one on the westerly side of the town, and is steep, with large ledges of rocks on the east side of it, called *Rattle Snakes' Rocks*, from the great number of those venomous serpents, which, in the infancy of the town, inhabited them; but their race is now almost extinct. The other is situated in the southeasterly part of the town, and is called *Mohawk Hill*. On the westerly side of the town, is what is commonly called a plain, though not very level; its natural growth of wood is pitch pine; and it is excellent for grain, and good roads. The soil of the town is in general rocky, moist, loamy and warm, and genial to wheat, rye, barley, oats, Indian corn, peas, flax, hemp, &c. &c. It is most excellent for orcharding; and, for its bigness, rather exceeds, perhaps, any other town in the county in fine grazing lands, as is evinced by the annual

annual produce of the dairy and of beef. Before the settlement of this place, the fires made in the woods, had destroyed almost the whole growth of timber ; and it was feared there would be a scarcity ; but by the care and prudence of the inhabitants there have, within a few years, sprung up fine groves of wood, and now there is a plenty. The common timber upon the upland, or hilly parts, is oak, walnut and chesnut ; in the low lands, swamps and marshes, there is maple, ash, birch, hornbeam and some spruce and hacmatack.

Newbraintree is very finely watered by rivers, brooks, rivulets and springs. Ware River runs along on the west side of the town, and is the boundary between Hardwick and this place. On the westerly side of the town there is also a large brook, called Meminimisset Brook, which is formed entirely by springs from the adjacent hills, and running north empties itself into Ware River. On this brook there is an extensive and luxuriant meadow of several hundreds of acres, called Meminimisset, the name given to it by the Indians when a hideous swamp : This was the head quarters, and the chief place of rendezvous of the savages, at the time when Brookfield was destroyed ; and near which place eight brave men were killed, and three mortally wounded by the Indians, August 2d, 1675, as has been more particularly related in the account of Brookfield : And hither Mrs. Rowlandson was carried captive, who was taken by the enemy at Lancaster, February

ary 10th, 1676, and here she buried her wounded child, on the 18th of that month.*

This meadow beforementioned produces exceeding great crops of most excellent hay. At the easterly part of the town lie two very considerable tracts of meadow land, through which run two brooks which arise from springs; these brooks, one of which carries a corn mill, after passing said meadows, and running near the south line of the town, unite, and then carry a saw mill: This stream then runs into the north part of Brookfield, and after several windings and meanderings, and carrying two more mills, it again visits the south part of this town, and runs through another large tract of excellent meadow, called Ditch Meadow, and carrying another corn mill in Newbraintree, it leaves the town, and falls into a large pond in the west parish in Brookfield, called Wickoboaug Pond. The air of this town is accounted good, and salubrious, and the people prosper, flourish and increase. Excepting a few of the usual mechanicks, and one or two traders in foreign goods, the people are farmers, and have the reputation of being good husbandmen, frugal and industrious, and they live much independent. According to the late enumeration the number of souls amounted to 940; and their houses are in general neat and commodious. This town is sixty six miles from Boston, a little to the south of west; and it is nineteen miles from the courthouse in Worcester, a very little to the north of west. There is considerable

* See this account as related under the head of Lancaster.

able travel through the place. A road from Connecticut river, through Hardwick, passes through Newbraintree and on to Rutland, and so on to Boston. A road also from the northward leads through this town to Brookfield, and so on to the southward.

SPENCER.

THE whole of this town was included in the original grant of Leicester. It was made a parish or precinct early in the year 1744, and was called the westerly parish of Leicester, until its incorporation on the 3d of April, 1753, when the name of Spencer was given to it. In this place a church was gathered May 17th, 1744; and over the flock of God in this place the Rev. Joshua Eaton was ordained November 7th, 1744, who continued in the work of the gospel ministry until April 2d, 1772, when he died in the 28th year of his pastorate. Mr. Eaton first turned his attention to the law, and was, for several years, an able and skilful attorney in the county of Worcester; but chose at length to forsake that gainful employment, for the more high and honourable one of serving God in the gospel of his Son. He made a conspicuous figure in the sacred office. The Rev.

Rev. Joseph Pope succeeded Mr. Eaton, as an ambaſſador of Jeſus Chriſt, being conſecrated unto this holy calling October 20th, 1773, and ſtill continues therein.

Spencer is ſaid to be eight miles in length, and four miles in breadth, on a ſtraight line. The town is conſiderably uneven, abounding in hills and valleys, although there are no hills very high or large, or called by any particular names. It is an exceeding fertile townſhip, and the inhabitants are induſtrious, proſperous and wealthy. It is become more numerous and opulent than the town from whence it was taken, as it is larger in lands, becauſe ſeveral years after the incorporation of Spencer, the northweſterly part of Leiceſter was with the ſoutherly part of Rutland, ſet off to form the town of Paxton.

This town is watered by many excellent perennial ſtreams which run through the ſeveral parts of it, ſome of which are ſufficient to carry mills, but none of them are large. There are three in the northerly part; one proceeds from a large and fine pond, which lays partly in Spencer and partly in Rutland, called Browning's Pond: Its courſe, for ſeveral miles, is ſoutherly. Another to the eaſtward of it, has its ſource in Rutland, and runs for ſome miles in the ſame direction with the former. A third iſſues from a pond in the north part of Leiceſter; and running a weſterly courſe for a conſiderable ſpace, then unites with the ſecond; after this junction, turning ſouthweſt, they fall in with the firſt mentioned ſtream. The general courſe of theſe waters

ters still being southwesterly, they are emptied into Podunk Pond, so called, in Brookfield; whence issues a river which runs into Chicabee River, which falls into Connecticut river, in the north part of Springfield. There are also in the south part of this town, two streams, one of which uniting with the streams mentioned above, falls into Connecticut river; the other running southerly, falls in with French River, which is emptied into the sea at Newlondon, in the southeast angle of the State of Connecticut. All these streams have one or more mills standing on them. There are likewise in Spencer, two clothiers' works, where much business is performed to great publick advantage; also, there are two potash and pearlash works.

The growth of wood in the town is of the usual various sorts. On the high lands, oak, walnut and chesnut are the chief. The swamps are covered generally with maple, birch and elm. In the infancy of the town, there was a large quantity of excellent pine timber, but this is mainly worked up.

The number of the people in Spencer, according to the late census, was computed at 1322, and the number of houses was 192.

Spencer lies about eleven miles southwesterly from Worcester, on the post road to Springfield, and fifty eight miles from Boston to the southwest.

Spencer is bounded on the north, by Paxton; on the east, by Leicester; on the south, by Charlton; and on the west, by Brookfield.

PETERSHAM.

PETERSHAM.

This was an original grant made by the General Court, in the clofe of the year 1732, or beginning of 1733, to John Bennett, Jeremiah Perley, and others, as a compenfation for fervices performed by them in the Indian wars, under a Capt. John White of Lancafter. The firft meeting of the grantees was held on the 10th of May, 1733. Some time after the grant was made, to quiet the Indians who claimed the foil, the proprietors made them a fatisfactory confideration therefor. It is rather more than fix miles fquare. It had been a feat for Indians, and was called many years by its Indian name, which was *Nichewaug*; and in the fouth part of the town lies *Nichewaug Hill*, fo called by the natives, whereon, as in fome other parts of the town, they had formerly planted fields of Indian corn, of which there remained evident traces when the firft Englifh fettlers began there.

The original proprietors being fome of them wealthy and enterprizing, they encouraged and drove on the fettlement of this then infant plantation, although there were no fettled towns nearer than Lancafter on the eaft, and Rutland to the foutheaft, and Brookfield to the fouth, except a few new fettlers in Lambftown, now Hardwick. But the land being excellent, divers perfons foon began to work upon lots; the proprietors built a meetinghoufe, meetinghouse, and so early as the year 1738, they contracted with and settled a minister for the inhabitants, and who was supported by them until its incorporation. Although the prospects from the soil were very promising, and settlers moved in fast, yet they laboured under many and exceeding great disadvantages, being then so remote from any white people, from whom they could procure the necessaries of life, or derive any aid and support. While in its infancy, and struggling for life, so early as 1744, a French war broke out; and the Indians, being always in the interest of the French, they became hostile, and began to commit depredations in various parts of the land, which occasioned the few inhabitants great fear, terror and danger, obliging them to build forts in different parts of the town, round certain houses, into each of which a number of families moved for safety and defence, and soldiers were stationed there as a guard to the inhabitants, and to reconnoitre the country. The people used to labour on their lands, in small parties, changing works with one another, having their guns by them, and these also they were, for a long time, obliged to carry with them whenever they went to the house of God for religious worship, and also to place centinels at the doors. But although they were often alarmed, yet no white person was ever known to be killed in the place. When peace was settled between England and France, and danger and fear from the Indians ceased, the settlement of the plantation went on very rapidly, and the people

ple were become so numerous and able, as that the place was incorporated with all town privileges April 20th, 1754, and received the name of Petersham. The church of Christ in this place was gathered, and their first minister, the Rev. Aaron Whitney, was ordained December, 1738, who continued until September 8th, 1779, when he died in the 66th year of his age, and the 41st of his ministry. The year following, October 25th, 1780, the Rev. Solomon Reed was solemnly separated unto that office and work, and who still continues therein. Here also is a society of baptists, who have for their teacher Mr. John Sellen.

The town of Petersham has been one of the most prosperous and flourishing in the county, if not in the Commonwealth. Although the grant of the township was subsequent to the formation of the county, yet it has so flourished and increased that it is become one of the foremost towns in the county for wealth and number. There are but seven towns who pay more to a State tax; it contains about 1520 souls, according to the late census. The natural situation of the town is exceedingly beautiful; it is very high, but not hilly and uneven: The body of the town lies upon the highest land in it, which is a large long flat hill, upon the highest part of which the great road runs from the south to the north, eight rods wide, and set with trees on both sides, and for three or four miles in length affords a most commanding prospect, not only of the whole town, but of all the adjacent towns; the houses are large and well finished, ed, standing on either side of the street, from whence the land falls each way east and west, about a mile and an half to a stream, and then rises again, especially to the east, where it is fully settled; is in clear view on the main street, and appears like another town. Here they have lately erected a large and elegant meetinghouse, standing on a most conspicuous situation, so as to be seen from divers of the contiguous towns; soon after it was built, Mr. Eleazar Bradshaw, now of Brookfield, made them a present of a large bell, the weight whereof is 913℔, and the cost thereof was 96*l*. 6*s*. 8*d*. So noble and publick spirited a deed, ought to be perpetuated for the honour of the donor, and to stimulate others to like generous acts.

This town is thought by some to be the pleasantest, for an inland town, of any in the State, affording to the eye, a general, extensive, and agreeably variegated prospect.

The land in this place is exceedingly favourable to the growth of all kinds of fruit trees, being high and warm; and here are large and excellent orchards, and much cyder is made here, beyond what the inhabitants consume; but they find a ready market for the surplus in the newer settlements. Having mentioned their fine orchards, I would duly notice one very remarkable natural curiosity relative to this subject. There is now growing in an orchard, lately belonging to my honoured father, the Rev. Aaron Whitney, deceased, an appletree, very singular with respect to its fruit. The apples are fair, and when fully ripe of of a yellow colour, but evidently of different taftes, four and fweet. The part which is four is not very tart, nor the other very fweet. Two apples, growing fide by fide, on the fame limb, will be of thefe different taftes, the one all four, and the other all fweet: And which is more remarkable, the fame apple will be four on one fide, end, or part, and the other fweet; and that not in any order or uniformity; nor is there any difference in the appearance of the one part from the other. And as to the quantity, fome have more of the acid, and lefs of the fweet, and fo *vice verfa*. Neither are the apples fo different in their taftes, peculiar to any particular branches, but are found promifcuoufly on any and every branch of the tree. The tree ftands almoft in the midft of a large orchard in a rich and ftrong foil, and was tranfplanted there about fifty years ago. There is no appearance of the trunk, or any of the branches having been ingrafted or inoculated. It was a number of years after it had borne fruit, before thefe different taftes were noticed; but fince they were firft difcovered, which is upwards of thirty years, there has been conftantly the fame variety obferved in the tafte of the fruit of this tree. For the truth of the above account, an appeal may be made to many perfons of diftinction, and of nice taftes, who have travelled a great diftance to view the tree and tafte the fruit; but to inveftigate the caufe of an effect fo much out of the common courfe of nature, muft, I think, be attended with difficulty. The only folution I can conceive is, that the corcula, or hearts of two feeds, the one from a four, and the other from a fweet apple, might fo incorporate in the ground, as to produce but one plant, or that farina from bloffoms of thofe oppofite qualities, might pafs into, and impregnate the fame feed. But leaving this to the difcuffion of naturalifts, I proceed with our defcription of Peterfham.

The foil is rich and fertile, and the lands bear all kinds of grain, but moft natural to grafs and pafturage, and from the appearance and face of the town, we muft judge the inhabitants to be induftrious and wealthy, who fubfift mainly by the cultivation of the earth. Though the town lies very high, yet the land is not dry, but ftony and moift, abounding with fprings and brooks of water; there are, however, but two noticeable ftreams: Swift River, which rifes from fprings in Gerry, runs to the fouthweft, through the eafterly and foutherly part of Peterfham, into the northweft part of Hardwick.

Weft Brook, a confiderable ftream, rifes in the northwefterly part of the town, and runs through all the weft fide of it, and then enters Greenwich, in the county of Hampfhire. On each of thefe there are both corn and faw mills, and clothiers' works; and by the fides of both there are confiderable bodies of good meadow land. Here are works for making pot and pearl afh, where much bufinefs is profitably carried on, and many perfons employed. On the high lands the growth of wood is oak, more chefnut, and a great deal of walnut of later years. In the fwamps and low lands,

lands, there is birch, beech, maple, afh, elm, and hemlock.

This town is fituated fixty fix miles from Bofton, nearly weft, and about twenty eight miles from the courthoufe in Worcefter to the northweft, and is bounded on the north, by Athol; on the eaft, by Gerry and Barre; on the fouth, by Barre and Hardwick; and on the weft, by Greenwich and Newfalem, in the county of Hampfhire.

CHARLTON.

THIS town was taken wholly from Oxford, and was the wefterly part thereof: It was incorporated November 2d, 1754, and then received its prefent name.

As much of the land in Charlton lies in the hands of the original proprietors, its fettlement was greatly retarded for many years. However, in April, 1761, the congregational church here was imbodied, and the Rev. Caleb Curtis was folemnly ordained to the work of the gofpel miniftry in this place, on the 15th of October, 1761. He continued their paftor fifteen years, and was difmiffed from his office by a mutual council, October 29th, 1776. The people remained deftitute of a fettled minifter upwards of fix years, until January 8th, 1783, when the Rev. Archibald Campbell was installed

installed their pastor. This Mr. Campbell was, ordained pastor of the church and congregation in Easton, in the county of Bristol, on the 17th of August, 1763, where he continued nineteen years, being dismissed from his pastoral relation to that people, August 11th, 1782. Mr. Campbell continued in the pastoral office in Charlton, until April 9th, 1793, when he was dismissed by council, at his special request.

There is a large anabaptist church and society in this town, but at present they are destitute of a settled minister, as well as the congregational church and society.

We proceed to a Topographical Description of Charlton.

This town was not in high repute at first, and was thought by some to be hardly worth settling upon: As it was very rough in its natural state, and hard to subdue. But such land is almost always found to be strong and to wear well. This being the case with Charlton, from small beginnings and an inconsiderable figure, it has risen up, in the space of thirty or forty years, to renown among the towns of the county. It is computed to be nearly seven miles square, being much larger in extent than Oxford from whence it was taken, and in general a better tract of land. The people are become very numerous, there being 1965 souls in the place when the census was taken in the year 1791, which is more by several hundreds than any town in the county, except Brookfield, Sutton and Worcester, and it is become exceedingly wealthy,

wealthy, as in the laſt State tax there were but ſix towns which paid more. There are 300 dwelling houſes in the town. The people ſubſiſt chiefly by the cultivation of the earth ; and they have great encouragement to labour, for the ſoil is ſtrong and rich, and the lands are fertile and very productive: Here they raiſe grain of all kinds in plenty ; beef and pork are fatted ; butter and cheeſe are made in quantities equal to, if not ſurpaſſing any other town in the county. The lands are well and naturally adapted to orcharding and fruit of all kinds. The hills are moiſt and ſpringy ; the hills and valleys are well proportioned and agreeably interſperſed. The town is well watered by ſprings, brooks and rivulets, none of which claim particular mention : But there is one large river in the weſtern part of the town, near to Sturbridge, which runs from the north to the ſouth, and is called Quinebaug. This river is almoſt an inconceivable advantage, not to Charlton only, but to many adjacent towns, by ſupplying great plenty of water for all the mills and water works in the drieſt ſeaſons. On this river, within the limits of Charlton, there are ſome rich interval, and good meadow lands.

There are ſeveral hills in this town worthy of particular mention ; one by the name of Ponnakin. Another called *Maſhymuggett* ; this is high, for on its ſummit buildings in about twelve adjacent towns may be diſcerned. This hill is ſituated about three quarters of a mile from the congregational meetinghouſe. There is a third, known by the name of *Blood's Hill*. The fourth and laſt we ſhall mention, is called Craige's Hill.

There are no ponds in the town worthy of notice, nor mines or minerals as yet diſcovered.

The wood and timber which grow in Charlton is white, black, and red oak, and walnut and cheſnut in great plenty; ſome white pine, and ſome pitch pine: In the low lands there is aſh, birch, maple, &c. &c.

In Charlton there are a few dealers in European and India goods, as is uſual in country towns; and they have alſo all the common tradeſmen and mechanicks. But there are two tanners in the town to be noticed, who carry on their buſineſs to a very conſiderable degree, and in the moſt advantageous manner, viz. Capt. Iſrael Waters, and Mr. Aſa Corben; and eſpecially the former, in the northerly part, who carries on his work to great perfection. He has an excellent bark mill, carried by water, and upon a new conſtruction, whereby he grinds all his bark. On the ſame ſtream, a little below, there is a gin ſtill, a brewery, malt houſe and corn mill, under the ſame roof, the property of Mr. Eli Wheelock, who erected ſaid works in the year 1792, and where he carries on each branch of buſineſs very largely to his own and the publick intereſt. On the ſame ſtream there are ſeveral griſt and ſaw mills, and other water works, and moſt of the mechanicks live in this north part of the town. There are alſo a number of pot and pearl aſh works in different parts of the town, where large quantities of pot and

pearl

pearl ash is annually made and exported. Charlton is in many respects, one of the foremost towns in the county. It is situated southwest from Boston at the distance of sixty miles; and from Worcester courthouse it is fifteen miles, a little to the southwest. It is bounded north, by Spencer; east, by Oxford; south, by Dudley; and west, by Sturbridge.

WESTMINSTER.

THIS must be " the south town laid out to the Narraganset soldiers,"* as expressed in the act for erecting the county of Worcester. It was granted in the year 1728, as a reward to a number of people who did service in what was called the Narraganset, or King Philip's war, or to their heirs, and was styled Narraganset, No. 2, until its incorporation, which was on the 20th of October, 1759, when the name of Westminster was given to it.

---

* Having mentioned this grant, it is fitting to give a history of the whole matter in brief. In the year 1728, application was made to the General Court for a reward for services done in the Narraganset war, and the Court immediately granted two townships of six miles square. But notice was given to all who did service in said war, or the legal heirs of such as were deceased, to bring in a list of their names at the next sessions of the Court; when eight hundred and forty appeared, and were approved as legal claimants. Being so numerous, two townships were judged inadequate; and upon further

WESTMINSTER.

The first meeting of the proprietors of this grant (who consisted chiefly of the inhabitants of Cambridge, Charlestown, Watertown, Weston, Sudbury, Newton, Medford, Malden and Reading) was held December 3d, 1733, when all officers were chosen necessary to manage the affairs of the proprietors. The first committee of the proprietors of Narraganset No. 2, were John Cutting, James Lowden, and Joseph Bowman. From this time, to the year 1737, little was done to forward the settlement of the place. In March this year, Capt. Fairbanks Moor moved his family into it. He was the first planter. In June, Deacon Joseph Holden moved his family into the place. These two families contained fifteen souls. It being an exposed plantation, settlers moved in but slowly. In the year 1739, the proprietors erected a decent meetinghouse, which was dedicated at a proprietors' meeting, June 6, 1739. The few settlers were desirous of, and forward for settling a minister; accordingly, on the 4th of August, 1742, they made choice of Mr. Elisha Marsh, in which the

further application, the Court granted five townships more in 1732, assigning one hundred and twenty proprietors to each, on condition, that sixty families be settled in each place, with a minister, in the space of seven years from the date of the grant, reserving in each, one right for the first minister, one for the ministry, and one for the school; the government to be at the expense of laying out the townships.

The whole society of petitioners, or claimants, met at Boston on the common, June, 1732, and, dividing themselves into seven classes, agreed to draw lots for the townships. A committee of the General Court laid out the townships, and numbered them. No. 1, was located back of Saco and Scarborough. No. 2, north of Watchusett hill. No. 3, at Souhegan, west; No. 4, at Amariscogan. No. 5, at Souhegan, east. No. 6, west of No. 2, and No. 7, was not then located.

WESTMINSTER. 227

the proprietors concurred. The church of Chrift in this place was formed, and the Rev. Elifha Marfh was ordained their firft minifter October 20th, 1742. Mr. Marfh continued with them but a few years. An unhappy controverfy arifing between him and the people, he was difmiffed from his paftoral office, 1757. Mr. Marfh was afterwards Judge of the Court of Common Pleas, in the county of Chefhire, in the State of Newhampfhire ; and died but a few years fince, at Lancafter, being on a journey.

The town remained in a broken ftate until October 16th, 1765, when the Rev. Afaph Rice was confecrated paftor, the fecond in fucceffion, of the church and congregation here, and ftill continues in that office ; and in peace and love with his people.

Previoufly to his fettlement in Weftminfter, Mr. Rice had been a miffionary among the Indians.

At the time of Mr. Marfh's ordination, the place was in its infancy, few in number, ftruggling for life, and expofed to Indian depredations, and its population went on flowly. About the year 1743, the General Court granted 400*l*. to fortify the place, with which ten forts were erected, and foldiers ftationed there for the defence of the inhabitants. In 1746, fome of the people of the place were put under pay, as a town fcout. From 1744, to the clofe of the year 1748, the fettlers met with great difcouragements, and endured fevere trials, although no perfon in the place was ever cut off by the enemy.

After

After that period, the people increased, and the place flourished exceedingly, so that in the space of half a century, notwithstanding their dangers, distresses and difficulties, and the smallness of their first number, only fifteen souls, they have spread and extended their branches, and covered the town, and are become a great people, as at this day; having, when the census was taken in 1791, 177 dwelling houses, and 1176 inhabitants. The original grant was six miles square; however, the measure was rather large, for by actual survey, including ponds, rivers, &c. it contained 27000 acres; but of late, 7000 acres of land, with the inhabitants thereof, were set off to aid in forming the town of Gardner, to the northwest. This town is still large, and is bounded on the west and the northwest by Gardner, on the north by Ashburnham; on the northeast by Fitchburg; on the east, by some farms not belonging to any town; on the south by Princeton; and on the southwest, by Hubbardston.

Westminster is situated on the height of land between the rivers Merrimack and Connecticut, having streams arising in the town, and running into both. The town is interspersed with hills and valleys; and with springs, brooks and rivulets, very convenient for watering the land, and for carrying of mills. The northwesterly part of Watchusett hill falls within the limits of this town. And what is called the middle of the place, or centre of the town, is a large and high hill, the top of which is nearly level; this is a square of

six

six acres, left by the proprietors, as a convenient place for a training field, and for the meetinghouse. A little north of the centre of this square stands their new, large and elegant meetinghouse, directly in front of which passes the great road from Connecticut River to Boston. At the southeast angle of this square stands an elegant house belonging to the Hon. Judge Gill; on the westerly side of the square stands the minister's house. On the sides of this square are shops well stored with English and Westindia goods. In the town they have all the usual tradesmen and mechanicks. Here also are three grist mills, three saw mills, one oil mill, one fulling mill, one clothiers' works, and one trip hammer; also works for cutting nails, and works for the manufacture of iron are now erecting. The soil of this town is strong, rich and fertile; the high lands are well stored with stones, suitable and sufficient for walling in the farms, and are good for orcharding, and almost all kinds of fruit. Here are lands for the various purposes of mowing, ploughing and pasturing. And the town has been, and still is well furnished with wood. The high lands have all sorts of oak, some chesnut, some walnut, which is increasing; they have had great plenty of white pine, which is chiefly cut off; some yellow and pitch pine: The low lands are stored with ash, beech, birch, maple, and hemlock.

There are four ponds within the town, one called Watchusett Pond, lies at the foot of that hill, on the northerly side. The line of the town crosses this

this pond, leaving part thereof in Princeton ; this is of confiderable bignefs, and well replenifhed with frefh water fifh. A ftream iffues from the northwefterly end of this pond, and runs northerly through the eafterly part of Weftminfter, receiving feveral ftreams in its courfe ; and leaving the town it runs in a northeafterly direction into Fitchburgh, forming a confiderable branch of the Nafhaway, or Lancafter River. Another very fmall ftream runs at the northeaft corner of the pond, and running foutheafterly falls into a ftream, rifing out of a large body of meadow, and continuing its courfe, empties into Stillwater River in Sterling. There is a ftream arifing in another body of meadow land, which falls into this pond, on its fouthwefterly fide. This pond is fed and fupplied chiefly, perhaps wholly, by fprings and rivulets iffuing from the great hill *Watchufett*. There is another large pond, near the centre of the town, in front of the hill, on which the meetinghoufe ftands ; this is called Long Pond, being one mile and twelve rods in length, and about half as much in width. This being a very rocky pond, is not well furnifhed with fifh. No conftant ftream empties into this pond : A fmall ftream iffues from the foutheafterly corner of it, and running eafterly, unites with the ftream which runs out of Watchufett Pond. There is a fmall pond, in the eafterly part of the town, called Graffy Pond, into which there is no vifible inlet : There is a fmall outlet, which, running foutherly, falls alfo into that which comes from Watchufett Pond.

Pond. The fourth pond is in the northern border of the town: No stream of any consequence runs into it; a small one issues from it, and running south, falls into a large stream, which rises in Westminster, and running easterly, is known by the name of North River; and continuing an eastern direction, unites with the stream which comes from Watchusett Pond. There is another stream, called the Most Northerly River, which rises in Ashburnham, and running through the northerly part of Westminster, receives various brooks and rivulets in Westminster, and helps to form the northerly branch of the river Nashaway. The last stream which deserves our notice, is called Otter River, which issuing from a swamp or low land in Hubbardston, runs northerly, through the westerly part of Westminster, into Gardner, receiving several streams in its way, then turning, runs westerly through the north part of Templeton, Athol, Warwick, and the southerly part of Northfield, and falls into Connecticut River. This stream unites with Miller's River in Winchendon, as may be seen more particularly in the description of Templeton.

Westminster is large, and become populous, and is continually increasing in number and wealth. It is situated about fifty five miles from Boston, a little to the north of west, and about twenty two miles from the courthouse in Worcester, nearly north.

PRINCETON.

PRINCETON.

ON the 20th of October, 1759, the General Court of Massachusetts passed an act for incorporating the east wing, so called, of Rutland, together with sundry farms, and some publick lands, contiguous thereto ; and gave the place the name of Princeton, to perpetuate the name and memory of the late Rev. Thomas Prince, colleague pastor of the old south church in Boston, and a large proprietor of this tract of land, whose daughter and only surviving child the Hon. Judge Gill married for his first wife.

The town contained about 19000 acres : And at the time of its incorporation there were about twenty families in the place. It was in the month of May, in the year 1751, when Mr. Robert Keyes, now living, removed with his family from Shrewsbury, and fixed down near the foot of Watchusett hill, on the east side, being the fourth family which settled in the place. Upon the 14th of April, 1755, a child of his, named Lucy, aged four years and eight months, attempting, as was supposed, to follow her sisters, who had gone to Watchusett Pond, about a mile distant, and having nothing but marked trees to guide her, wandered out of her way in the woods, and was never heard of afterwards. The people for nearly thirty miles round collected immediately, and in companies traversed ed the woods, day after day, and week after week, searching for her, but never made the least discovery. Many journeys were taken by the father, in consequence of reports, but all in vain. Various were, and have been the conjectures of people respecting the fate of this child. Divers concurring circumstances render the following most probable, that she was taken by the Indians, and carried into their country, and soon forgat her relations, lost her native language, and became as one of the aborigines.

Let us return to Princeton. The people who had settled in this town laboured at first under very great difficulties, by reason of the mountainous, rocky, and naturally moist state of their lands, from want of passable roads, and by reason of the prodigious quantities of heavy timber with which the ground was covered, (sure indications of a rich and fertile soil,) however, they attended to their roads, and increased in number, and on the 30th of June, 1762, raised the frame of their present meetinghouse, hired preaching, and were attentive to their religious interests.

On the 12th of August, 1764, the church of Christ was imbodied in this town, and after various fruitless attempts to settle a minister, the Rev. Timothy Fuller was ordained their first pastor on the 9th of September, 1767. In about eight years a general disaffection to Mr. Fuller took place, which ended in a dissolution of the pastoral relation between him and the people of Princeton on the 19th of April, 1776. Various attempts for a resettlement of the gospel ministry were unsuccessful,

ful, until the 28th of June, 1786, when the Rev. Thomas Crafts was ordained paftor of the church and flock of God in this place. In the fpace of about three years, Mr. Crafts's health failed, and for nearly two years he was unable to preach, when all hope of his being recovered, fo as to carry on the work of the facred miniftry being cut off, the paftoral relation between him and his people was amicably diffolved at his fpecial requeft, on the 14th of March, 1791. The people remain without a fettled minifter.

In Princeton they have a very handfome focial library eftablifhed, of the value of upwards of 70*l*. ten pounds whereof were given by the Hon. Judge Gill.

In a little more than thirty years from its incorporation, Princeton is become very confiderable among the towns of the county. It has furprifingly increafed in number and wealth. When the cenfus was taken in 1791, there were 144 dwelling houfes, and 1016 inhabitants in the place. The foil being excellent, people had every encouragement from that confideration, to fettle and cultivate the lands; and their farms are moftly large and good. The land is naturally moift and fpringy, hilly and rocky, exceedingly well adapted to pafturage, and the growth of Englifh grafs: Hence the fineft of beef is fatted here, and vaft quantities of butter and cheefe are produced in the town : Some parts of the place afford grain in plenty; and from the appearance of their buildings and farms, we muft judge the people are very induftrious.

induſtrious. Many of their houſes are large and elegant.

This leads to a particular mention, that in this town is the country ſeat of the Hon. Moſes Gill, Eſq; who has been from the year 1775 one of the Judges of the Court of Common Pleas for the county of Worceſter, and for ſeveral years a Counſellor of this Commonwealth. His noble and elegant ſeat is about one mile and a quarter from the meetinghouſe, to the ſouth. The farm contains upwards of 3000 acres. The county road from Princeton to Worceſter paſſes through it, in front of the houſe, which faces to the weſt. The buildings ſtand upon the higheſt land of the whole farm ; but it is level round about them for many rods, and then there is a very gradual deſcent. The lands on which theſe buildings ſtand, are elevated between 1200 and 1300 feet above the level of the ſea, as the Hon. James Winthrop, Eſq; informs me. The manſion houſe is large, being fifty by fifty feet, with four ſtacks of chimnies : The farm houſe is forty feet by thirty ſix : In a line with this ſtand the coach and chaiſe houſe, fifty feet by thirty ſix : This is joined to the barn by a ſhed ſeventy feet in length—the barn is two hundred feet by thirty two. Very elegant fences are erected around the manſion houſe, the outhouſes, and the garden.

The proſpect from this ſeat is extenſive and grand, taking in an horizon to the eaſt, of ſeventy miles at leaſt. The blue hills in Milton, are diſcernable with the naked eye, from the windows of this

this superb edifice, distant not less than six miles; as also the waters in the harbour of Boston, at certain seasons of the year. When we view this seat, these buildings, and this farm of so many hundred acres, now under a high degree of profitable cultivation, and are told that in the year 1766 it was a perfect wilderness, we are struck with wonder, admiration and astonishment. The honourable proprietor hereof must have great satisfaction in contemplating these improvements, so extensive, made under his direction, and I may add, by his own active industry. Judge Gill is a gentleman of singular vivacity and activity, and indefatigable in his endeavours to bring forward the cultivation of his lands; of great and essential service, by his example, in the employment he finds for so many persons, and in all his attempts to serve the interests of the place where he dwells, and in his acts of private munificence, and publick generosity, and deserves great respect and esteem, not only from individuals, but from the town and country he has so greatly benefited, and especially by the ways in which he makes use of that vast estate wherewith a kind Providence has blessed him. Upon the whole, this seat of Judge Gill, all the agreeable circumstances respecting it being attentively considered, is not paralleled by any in the Newengland States; perhaps not by any on this side the Delaware.

Return we to our more general description of Princeton. Having said the soil is rich, strong, and very productive; it is to be added, the growth

growth of wood is oak of the various kinds, chefnut, white afh, beech, black birch, and maple; and near the Watchufett hills, fome butternut is to be feen, as alfo fome walnut, which will undoubtedly increafe and fpread.

The hills of Princeton merit a particular defcription; they are three. Firft, *Pine Hill*, fituated about two miles from the centre of the town, contains perhaps about thirty acres, and is moftly unimproveable; but its bowels afford a very great quantity of moft excellent ftones for buildings, &c.

The fecond, is Little Watchufett Hill, this is fituated near the centre of the town, perhaps half a mile diftant, to the northward. This contains 237 acres, chiefly pafturing; though fome parts of it, being ledgy and mountainous, are unimproveable.

The third, is the Great Watchufett Hill, or Mountain. This is fituated about two miles from Princeton meetinghoufe, to the north; the northwefterly part hereof falls within the limits of Weftminfter. This is an exceedingly high mountain, and is fome of the firft land difcovered by people on board veffels at fea, when making for any of the fea ports in Maffachufetts; and it is to be feen from the higher lands, in a greater part of the towns in the Commonwealth, efpecially in thofe between the fea and Connecticut river. It contains feven or eight hundred acres; about four hundred acres of which being the fummit, and being province land, were given to the Rev. Mr. Fuller,

Fuller, by the General Court, in confideration that he was the firſt miniſter, and ſettled upon a ſmall ſalary, in the infancy of the town. This was no trifling gift; for although one hundred acres of it be worth little or nothing, yet moſt of the remaining three hundred acres will make conſiderable paſture land, and ſome parts very good. The higheſt part of the mountain is a flat rock, or a ledge of rocks, for ſome rods round, and there is a ſmall pond of water generally upon the top of it, of two or three rods ſquare; and where there is any earth, it is covered with blueberry buſhes for acres round; and as you deſcend the hill, there are very low and ſmall trees, with flat tops, like thoſe on the ſea ſhore, occaſioned no doubt, in part, by the ſtate of the air; for it is ſeveral degrees colder, at any time, on the top than at the bottom of the mountain; the further you deſcend, the taller are the trees, until they become of the common ſize. Upon the ſoutherly ſide of this hill it may be aſcended to the very top with horſes, but upon the eaſt, north and northweſt, it is very ſteep, broken and ledgy; and many acres utterly unimproveable any way at preſent. Perhaps its bowels may contain very valuable hid treaſure, which in ſome future period may be deſcried. There are very conſiderable improvements upon ſome ſides of this hill near the bottom of it, and ſome very valuable lands yet uncultivated. The circumference of this monſtrous maſs is about three miles, and its height is 3012 feet above the level of the ſea, as was found by the Hon. John

Winthrop,

Winthrop, Esq; L. L. D. in the year 1777: And this must be 1800 or 1900 feet above the level of the adjacent country.

This town is exceedingly well watered by springs and rivulets, as is generally the case with hilly, rocky land; but there are no streams of any great bigness, although several large and fine rivers have their sources here. One branch of the Nashaway begins at the foot of Watchusett Hill, and runs through Sterling and Boylston to Lancaster. Piss River, so called, springs up at the foot of this mountain, on the westerly side, and runs through Hubbardston, and joins Ware River. There are several places in the town where springs issue and the waters divide, running some into Merrimack, some into Connecticut river. There is but little meadow land in Princeton, when compared with towns in general, but there are considerable tracts of interval which afford good hay; however, the greatest part of their hay is produced from upland mowing. There are two ponds only in this town, or rather a part of two: Watchusett Pond, about three miles north from the meetinghouse, at the north end of that mountain; it covers about one hundred acres, only about twenty of which are in Princeton, the greater part in Westminster. It is fed by springs from the hill; its outlet is in Westminster. Quinepoxet Pond is situated in the southwest part of the town, some of which falls within the limits of Holden. It contains perhaps seventy or eighty acres. Its inlets are several small streams; its outlet is the

River Quinepoxet, as described in the account of Holden. In Princeton there are four grist mills, five saw mills, and one fulling mill, and clothiers' works. This town is situated fifty two miles from Boston, about due west; and fifteen miles from the courthouse in Worcester, nearly north, and bounded on the north, by Westminster; on the east, by Sterling; on the south, by Holden; on the southwest, by Rutland; and on the west, by Hubbardston.

TEMPLETON.

THIS was an original grant to certain persons who did service in what was called the Narraganset, or King Philip's war, or to their heirs, and was accordingly known by the name of *Narraganset* No. 6, until its incorporation, March 6th, 1762, when the name *Templeton* was given to it. The first meeting of the proprietors of this tract of land was held at Concord October 29th, 1733. The grant was designed to include as much as six miles square, but the measure was made rather large. Its settlement was greatly retarded through danger from the Indians, in that then infant state of this part of the country; and especially in the French war, in the years from 1740, to 1746. After that period inhabitants came in very

very faft; fo that a church of our Lord Jefus Chrift was gathered here December 10th, 1755, and the fame day the Rev. Daniel Pond was ordained to the work of the gofpel miniftry in this place: He continued in the facred office not four years, being difmiffed by advice of an ecclefiaftical council, Auguft 2d, 1759. He was fucceeded by the Rev. Ebenezer Sparhawk, who was feparated unto that high and holy calling on the 18th of November, 1761, who ftill continues faithfully ferving God in the gofpel of his Son.

This town flourifhed and increafed fo faft, and not lying in the beft fhape to continue one religious fociety, it was divided into two parifhes, February 16th, 1774. The new or fecond parifh lay on the weft fide, and being foon after made a diftinct town, we fhall leave it for the prefent, and proceed in our defcription of Templeton. Although this town is not a level, champaign tract of land, yet it is not fo uneven as many; it has no remarkable hills or eminences diftinguifhed by particular names, except one on the fouth fide towards Hubbardfton, called *Mine Hill*, from its abounding in good iron ore; and fuppofed alfo to be rich in other more valuable mines and minerals; this was granted to a Capt. Andrew Robinfon, of Gloucefter, fome time before the original grant of the townfhip; it was foon fold, and now a great number of perfons have a right therein: it is a long, rocky hill, and very fteep on one fide.

There is but one pond in the town, and that is fmall, in the fouth part, from whence there is an outlet,

TEMPLETON.

outlet, on which are mills, this forms what is called Otter River, on which are clothiers' works, and where the bufinefs is well and profitably carried on. This river runs foutherly into a corner of Hubbardfton, then turning northeaft, runs back into Templeton again, and through an angle of Gardner, where feveral ftreams join it. It is fome way a boundary between Gardner and Templeton; then it takes a northwefterly courfe in Templeton, and is joined by Trout Brook; and from thence running through an angle of Winchendon, there falls into Miller's River. The main branch of the river Burnfhirt, fo called, rifes from a pond on the eafterly fide of Gerry, at its northeaft end, and runs through meadows to the foutheaft, where there are good mills, and within the bounds of Templeton, joins the eafterly branch of Burnfhirt, and foon after becomes a boundary between Templeton and Gerry, for almoft two miles; and then runs through a corner of Hubbardfton into Barre, where it unites with Ware River. Conneyftow, another ftream, rifing from fprings in the fouth part of this town, runs foutherly into Hubbardfton, where are mills, and then falls into Burnfhirt. On thefe ftreams and rivers there are excellent meadow and interval lands.

   The general growth of wood in the town is of the following kinds, oak, chefnut, white and pitch pine, afh, beech and birch; walnut, within a few years, has fprung up, and is fpreading. The lands are rich and good in general, producing all forts of grain, and yield pafturage and grafs in great plenty.

plenty. In this town the bufinefs of making potafh is carried on. Here are the ufual neceffary tradefmen; but the inhabitants chiefly fubfift by the cultivation of their lands, and are a profperous and flourifhing people. This town is fituated about fixty miles from Bofton, a little to the north of weft; and is twenty eight miles from the courthoufe in Worcefter, a little to the weft of north.

The number of its inhabitants was 950, when the general cenfus was taken in 1791.

Templeton is bounded on the weft, by Gerry; on the north, by Winchendon; on the eaft, by Gardner; and on the fouth, by Hubbardfton; and contains ftill about 17000 acres of land, notwithftanding the greater part of Gerry, and a part of Gardner was taken from it.

ATHOL.

WHEN the grant of this townfhip was made by the General Court, cannot now be afcertained, as the firft proprietors' book was fome years ago loft. The prefent book has recorded that the original proprietors, being fixty in number, met at Concord June 26, 1734, and, in the prefence of a committee of the General Court, whereof the Hon. William Dudley was chairman,
drew

drew their house lots in the township of Pequoig, or Payquage, as the natives called the place at that time; and by this appellation it was known in all publick acts and records until its incorporation by an act of the Legislature, on the 6th of March, 1762, when it received the name of Athol. This tract was a seat for the Indians, and at the time of its being granted, was a frontier township, and greatly exposed; and the settlement of the place was obstructed by the French and Indian war, which commenced in 1744, and continued several years. Previously to the breaking out of that war, several families had seated themselves here, but they were greatly distressed with fear, by reason of the Indians; they were obliged, as other infant plantations, to live in garrisons for several years, and to labour at their various occupations with their military armour by them. Although this place was thus exposed, yet I cannot find that any persons were killed here, except a Mr. Ezekiel Wallingford, who being on some occasion at a distance from his garrison, was discovered by the enemy; and seeing them, he turned to run to the fort, but was stopped short by a fatal ball, August, 1746. In the month of April, the year following, a Mr. Jason Badcock was taken captive by the Indians, and carried to Canada: From whence he returned in a few months.

The church of Christ in Athol was imbodied in the presence, and under the countenance of three neighbouring pastors and churches, August 29th, 1750; and the Rev. James Humphrey was consecrated

ATHOL.

consecrated their first pastor on the 7th of November following. The Rev. Mr. Humphrey, after serving the church and people of this place faithfully upwards of thirty one years, was, at his request, dismissed from his pastoral relation to them on the 13th of February, 1782, on these conditions, viz. The inhabitants voted to free his person and estate from all kinds of taxes during his natural life ; and gave to him and his heirs a good pew in the present meetinghouse, so long as it should stand.

The town remained destitute of a settled pastor until November 21st, 1787, when the Rev. Joseph Estabrook, was solemnly separated unto the work of the gospel ministry, as successor to the Rev. Mr. Humphrey.

There are about ten families of anabaptists in this town, but there is no church, nor any stated teacher of this denomination in the place : There are also three families of universalists, and one of episcopalians here.

We shall now go on to some Geographical Description of Athol. This township was originally granted to sixty proprietors, with a reserve of a right of land for the first settled minister, a right for the use of the ministry, and one for a school : It was to contain as much as six miles square. A part of the town was set off, at the southeast angle, to aid in forming the town of Gerry, and a part at the northwest corner, to help form the district of Orange ; but still the town of Athol is more than five miles square, and contains 16000 acres of land.

It

It is very uneven, rocky, and hilly, though there are no famous or remarkable hills in the place; nor any with names, except one in the east part of the town, called *Walnut Hill*, from the confiderable quantity of walnut wood and timber growing thereon. The foil of this town is not fo good as fome: It is rather cold, confequently not extraordinary for grain of any kind, for orcharding, or for mowing: It is faid to be very good for grazing; and much beef is annually fatted in the place. There is fome pitch pine plain in the north part of the town; there is alfo confiderable white pine remaining in the wefterly part of the place; but oak, chefnut, afh, beech, birch, hemlock, and maple, conftitute the principal growth of wood. The town has its full fhare of water. Miller's River, fo called by the Englifh, in confequence of a man by the name of Miller, who was drowned herein, well towards a hundred years ago, in attempting to pafs this river in his way to Northfield: But the natives called it Payquage or Bayquage—this river is large, and its current in many places rapid; it comes into Athol in the northeafterly quarter of the town, and paffing within half a mile of the meetinghoufe, it runs wefterly into Connecticut River; in the fouthwefterly part of Athol, there is fome good meadow on this river. The next ftream for bignefs is Tully Brook; (or rather *River* if its appellation had not been eftablifhed) this has its origin in Fitzwilliam in the State of Newhampfhire, comes through Royalfton into the northerly part of Athol, and joins Miller's River

River about one mile northweſt from the meeting-houſe. On this ſtream, and after the junction, there are ſome very good meadows. Mill Brook, ſo called from its having upon it many convenient ſeats for mills, riſes from various ſprings in the ſouth-eaſterly part of the town, and runs northweſterly, and falls into Miller's River in the weſt part of Athol. In the ſoutheaſterly part of the town riſes a brook ſufficient to carry mills, which runs to a pond of thirty acres or more, which the line between Newſalem and Athol croſſes in the ſouth-weſt part, and from this pond there is an outlet which runs north, and empties into Miller's River. There is alſo another pond in the north part of the town, from whence there is an outlet into Tully Brook : This is ſmall, covering perhaps twenty or thirty acres.

Upon the rivers and ſtreams abovementioned, there are in the town, four griſt mills, ſix ſaw mills, one fulling mill, and one trip hammer. We muſt not omit to mention, there is a very fine ſpring in this town, which iſſues out of a high bank upon the ſide of Miller's River, (perhaps twenty feet above the ſurface of the river) the water whereof is medicinal. Many perſons who have drank freely thereof, have found it operate as a gentle cathartick; and ſome who have been poiſoned, have been ſpeedily cured by waſhing the parts affected therewith. Several who have been afflicted with rheumatick complaints, bathed in the waters of this ſpring, in a ciſtern, ſome few years ago provided to receive them, and found great relief.

And

And what is worthy of notice is this, these w[...] have the same efficacy and virtue without soap, in washing of persons, which other waters have with. We close the account of Athol with saying, it is situated in the northwestern extremity of the county, about thirty five miles from the courthouse in Worcester, to the northwest, and from Boston it is seventy two miles, a little to the north of west. It is bounded on the north, by Royalston; on the east, by Gerry; on the south, by Petersham; on the southwest, by Newsalem; and on the northwest, by Orange. The number of inhabitants in this town, when the census was taken, was 850.

OAKHAM.

THE whole of this town was included in that tract of land of twelve miles square, which was purchased of the Indians, confirmed to the petitioners, and called Rutland, in the year 1713. After the town of Rutland was incorporated, this part was called *Rutland West Wing*, until the year 1759, when the inhabitants had certain privileges granted them, and the place was called the Precinct of Rutland West Wing, until its incorporation by an act of the Legislature, June 7th, 1762, when the name of Oakham was given to it.

The

The church of Christ in this place was imbodied, in presbyterian form, August 28th, 1767, and the Rev. John Strickland was ordained their pastor, April 1st, 1768. He was dismissed by the presbytery, and a vote of the town, June 2d, 1773. After Mr. Strickland's removal, the presbyterian church was dissolved, and a church on the congregational plan was imbodied, June 23d, 1773, and the Rev. Daniel Tomlinson was separated to the work of the gospel ministry among them, June 22d, 1786. Mr. Strickland removed from Oakham to Nottinghamwest, in the State of Newhampshire, where he was installed, and continued a number of years; from thence he was dismissed, and removed to Turner, in the county of Cumberland, and the district of Maine, where he is again settled in the presbyterian mode.

In Oakham they have a social library established, containing towards sixty volumes.

The reader shall now be presented with some Geographical Description of Oakham.

Although the shape of the town is not an exact square, yet it contains about four miles and an half square; and it is bounded by Rutland, on the east; by Barre, on the north and northwest; by Newbraintree, on the west and southwest; and by Spencer, on the south and southeast. The general face of the town is hilly and stony. The natural soil is not inferior perhaps to that of the neighbouring towns in general; but not being settled so early as Rutland, it was greatly injured by fires. The first settlers of Rutland used to set

R   fires

fires in Oakham annually, or frequently, and then turn their cattle thither to feed through the summer season. There are no remarkable hills, nor any extensive plains in the town. The produce is, Indian corn, wheat, rye, flax, &c. &c. and whatever is common to this country. The land is well adapted to orcharding, and all kinds of fruit trees; for it is high, sweet, and in general not exposed to frosts. The growth of wood and timber is oak of all sorts, abounding especially in white oak, walnut, chesnut, and whatever is common to the high and low lands in other towns.

Some parts of the town are high and rather dry; nevertheless, the lands bear a drought well; and in general there are sufficient springs, rivulets, and streams of water. There is one river which has its source in the easterly part of the town, called *Five Mile River*; it runs from the north to the south; it is not large, yet there is one corn, and one saw mill standing thereon in the southerly part of the town; and on this stream there is some meadow land. The northerly part of Oakham borders on and near a river, which is large, called Ware River; on this there is some little interval and meadow land. There is but one other meadow in the town of any considerable bigness; this is situated about a mile southeast from the meetinghouse, and is known by the name of Clammour Meadow. In the northeasterly part of this town, near to Rutland, is situated Muddy Pond, so called, not large; from this pond issues a stream, which running from the southeast to the northwest,

OAKHAM.

northweft, falls into Ware River; on this ftream there are two faw mills.

There is a large pond, called Browning's Pond, fituated in the foutheafterly quarter of this town, and lies, partly in Rutland and partly in Spencer, but the greater part in Oakham. To this there is an inlet, and at the fouth end an outlet which runs into Spencer, and fo to Quaboag River. Thefe ponds and ftreams are well ftored with fifh.

There are feveral roads through different parts of the town; one through the north angle of the town, leading from Peterfham to Rutland and Worcefter; another about a mile north of the meetinghoufe, leading from Rutland to Hardwick; another which leads from Rutland to Brookfield, paffing about half a mile eaft of the meetinghoufe; another leading from Newbraintree to Worcefter, called the New County Road; this runs near the fouth fide of the town.

This town is fituated fifteen miles from Worcefter courthoufe, a little to the northweft; and from Bofton it is diftant fixty two miles, nearly weft. When the cenfus was taken there were 772 inhabitants in the town.

FITCHBURG.

FITCHBURG.

THIS place was originally a part of the town of Lunenburg, and wholly included in the grant made to the proprietors of Turkey Hill. It was made a distinct and separate town on the 3d of February, 1764. A part of Fitchburg, to the north, was set off in the year 1767, to aid in forming the town of Ashby, in the county of Middlesex. It is now bounded by Ashburnham and Ashby, on the north and northwest ; by Lunenburg, on the east ; by Leominster, on the south and southeast ; and by Westminster, on the west and southwest.

This is a very hilly and uneven, but fertile town. On the eastern part it is not so very uneven, resembling Lunenburg, from whence it was taken ; but in the other parts of the town, the hills are large, high, and steep ; however, on them there is not much broken, poor and waste land. In general the soil is excellent ; and the town in many respects is superior to Lunenburg. By the late census the dwelling houses were found to be 166, and the inhabitants 1151, spread over a territory not much exceeding 13000 acres. Most of the people live in comfortable and easy circumstances, possessing all the necessaries, and many of the conveniences of life. They are industrious, and having a good soil to labour upon, live independent, and, for an inland town, several families

among

among them may juftly be deemed rich. The people near the meetinghoufe are fettled pretty thick, and there much bufinefs of various kinds is performed: For here runs, a few rods fouth of the meetinghoufe, the north branch of Nafhaway River. One part of this river comes from Afhburnham, the other part from Watchufett Pond; thefe unite a little weft of Fitchburg meetinghoufe. After this junction, and juft below the meetinghoufe, there is one corn mill, one faw mill, one fulling mill, one clothier's works, one trip hammer, and works for grinding fcythes: Thefe occafion a great refort of people there to tranfact their various concerns. A little fouthweft from the meetinghoufe, is a high, rocky hill, covered principally with pine, called *Rollftone Hill*. Here alfo is a hill, ufually denominated *Pearl Hill*, and is compofed of a rock of a peculiar quality, not common in this part of the country. It produces ifinglafs, or talc, in great plenty. The appearance encourages a hope that there are valuable mines, either of gold or filver, or both, imbofomed there. Attempts have heretofore been made to explore and poffefs them; but for want of wealth or perfeverance in the undertakers, they have not obtained the defiderata. All valuable mines in this part of the world, as in moft other parts, lie deep in the bowels of the earth, and much labour is neceffary to reach them. In the prefent ftate of our population, riches, in thefe northern parts, are with much greater facility procured from the furface of the earth, by the various inftruments of cultivation,

cultivation, than from deep and latent mines of the richest ore. When the country becomes overstocked with inhabitants, and support from the soil shall not be so easily obtained, it is not improbable, that from this mountain will be dug large quantities of those shining metals, as every thing, at present, favours the conjecture. Besides the river abovementioned, which runs from the northwest to the southeast, through the town, there are several other streams which pass through it, which occasion the inhabitants great expense in building and repairing bridges. From the northwest part of Connecticut river the people travel much through this place, in their way to Boston; and at present they have a stage which runs between them and Boston, and goes and comes twice in the week.

The church of Christ in this town was imbodied, and their first and only, and present minister, the Rev. John Payson, was ordained January 27th, 1768.

This is a growing, flourishing place, and the people have hitherto been peaceable and happy; they are indeed very much so; and if they continue in peace and unity, they will still greatly increase in number and wealth. They subsist chiefly by husbandry; there are, however, the usual mechanicks, and a few dealers in European, East and West India goods.

The growth of wood in this town is very excellent: Oak, walnut and chesnut, constitute the

principal

principal part thereof, although there is some white and yellow pine.

Fitchburg is situated northwest from Boston, at the distance of fifty miles over Charles's River bridge; and it is almost north from the courthouse in Worcester, distant about twenty three miles.

WINCHENDON.

ON the 10th of June, 1735, a grant of land, to be equal to six miles square, was made by the Legislature of Massachusetts, to Lieut. Abraham Tilton, and others: Preference, however, was to be given to the descendants of the officers and soldiers who served in the expedition to Canada, in the year 1690. This tract was to be laid out into sixty three equal shares; one for the first minister, one for the use of the ministry, and one for the use of a school; the others, for sixty proprietors. As these all, excepting eight, belonged to *Ipswich*, in the county of Essex, in Massachusetts, it was called Ipswich Canada, until its incorporation by an act of the General Court, which passed June 14th, 1764, when it was made a town, and called Winchendon. The proprietors received this grant on conditions of erecting sixty small houses, together

gether with a suitable, convenient meetinghouse, and settling a learned and orthodox minister in five years from the laying out of the township. These conditions were not punctually fulfilled; however, in the year 1752, ten families had fixed down here. But the settlement of the place was immediately retarded by what is commonly called the last French war. Most of the settlers left the place; they who remained were obliged to keep in garrisons. The proprietors set up the first meetinghouse, thirty five by forty five feet, in the spring of the year 1762. The church of Christ in this place was imbodied, and the Rev. Daniel Stimpson was ordained their first pastor, on December 15th, 1762. Mr. Stimpson continued not six years in the ministry; the Great Head of the church saw fit to remove him hence by death, July 20th, 1768. He was succeeded in the pastoral office by the Rev. Joseph Brown, who was separated hereunto May 24th, 1769. Mr. Brown continues in his work, and enjoys the affection and esteem of his people. The first house for publick worship being too small for the inhabitants, they on the 24th and 25th of May, 1792, erected a large new one, fifty by sixty feet, and having completed it, met in it for the first time January 1st, 1793, when it was solemnly dedicated to the service of God.

In this town a foundation is already laid for a social library, which bids fair to be large and very considerable in time.

WINCHENDON.

When this township was first located it was supposed to extend northerly to Newhampshire, but upon running the line afterwards between the two States, it was found there was a mile in width for the whole length of this town left to Massachusetts. Upon the granting of Royalston, some years after, this strip of land was annexed to that town, and called Royalston Leg. When a number of families had got seated thereon, at their request, it was in 1780 set to Winchendon. It contained 3840 acres. In June, 1785, a piece of land of 3680 acres, was taken from the southeasterly part of this town, to help form the town of Gardner; Winchendon, however, still remains more than six miles square.

The present extent and boundaries of Winchendon are as follow. Beginning at the northeast angle of the town, on the State line, thence south twelve degrees west, five miles and an half on Ashburnham line, to the northeast corner of Gardner: Thence west twenty eight degrees south, three miles and eighty five rods on Gardner line, to a corner in Templeton line: Thence north thirty six degrees west, two miles one hundred and forty four rods on Templeton line, to a corner: Thence north seventy eight degrees west, six hundred rods on said Templeton line, to a corner in Royalston line: Thence north twelve degrees east, on Royalston line, five miles two hundred and sixty rods, to the northeast corner of said Royalston, on the State line, or the line between Winchendon and Rindge: Thence east twelve degrees south, six miles on the State line, to the first mentioned bound.

The

WINCHENDON.

The soil of Winchendon is deep and good, and produces rye, barley, oats, flax, and all kinds of vegetables : Wheat is not raised here in so great plenty as in some other towns ; yet more at present than formerly. Indian corn is not so easily raised, as the land is rocky, and some of the extreme parts of the town are much subject to frosts. The town is not very uneven, and there are no remarkable hills in the place.

The general growth of wood on the high lands, is red oak, beech, rock maple, and black birch, interspersed with white pine and hemlock. On the low lands, white pine, hemlock, hacmatack, ash of all kinds, and yellow birch, interspersed with red oak and beech. On some of the lowest lands, there is little or nothing but pine, hemlock, and hacmatack. In some parts of the town there is chesnut, and in other parts pitch pine, but neither of them in plenty.

Mines or minerals, none as yet have been discovered in the town : There are two or three springs, however, of the mineral kind ; one especially in the northerly part of the town, which is thought by physicians and others acquainted with such things, to be equal to many in great repute for their healing virtue. It is certainly of the medicinal kind, and rather seems of a chalybeate quality. There is but one pond which is wholly within the limits of this town, called *Denison's Pond*, it covers perhaps as much as one hundred and fifty acres. It has an inlet from the north, and an outlet towards the south into a river which runs within

WINCHENDON.

within an hundred rods of said pond. It abounds in fish of various kinds. There is one river, known by the name of Miller's River, the principal source whereof is a large pond, lying chiefly in the northeasterly part of Rindge, a small part only falling within the bounds of Winchendon, where the outlet is. This pond is known by the name of *Monomenock Pond*. The outlet from this pond, together with some small streams from ponds in the northwesterly part of Ashburnham, uniting in the northeasterly part of Winchendon, form Miller's River, which runs westerly, southwesterly and southerly, half round the town; in no place nearer than one mile of the meetinghouse, and in some places three miles and more from it. It leaves this town in the southwesterly part thereof, not far from the pond above described, the outlet of which, as we have said, falls into this river. Otter River, so called, which runs through the northerly part of Templeton, just touches on Winchendon, in the southwesterly part thereof, and runs nigh the bounds of the town about a mile and a half, and unites with Miller's River, but just before it leaves Winchendon. There are two large streams in the westerly part of this town, taking their rise in Fitzwilliam. One of them joins Miller's River in Winchendon, near to Royalston: This is not distinguished by any particular name. The other, still larger, runs into Royalston, and some considerable way in the easterly part thereof; then turns and enters Winchendon, and after running several miles, joins

Miller's

WINCHENDON.

Miller's River juft above Denifon's Pond. This ftream might have been denominated a river from its largenefs, had it not early received the appellation of Prieft's Brook. This name was given to it from the circumftance of its running through a tract of land, now lying in Royalfton, formerly granted by the General Court of Maffachufetts to a Jofeph Prieft, to induce him to fet up an houfe of entertainment for the benefit of travellers from this ftate to the Afhuelots (Keene and Swanfey) and to No. 4 (Charleftown) in the ftate of New-hampfhire. The houfe of this Prieft, was called *The Half Way Houfe.*

Thefe two ftreams, efpecially the latter, abound with falmon trouts. This fort of fifh is alfo found in many parts of Miller's River, as alfo pickerel and perch.

Befides the abovementioned, there are many other ftreams and rivulets running in every part of this town, whereby it is exceedingly well watered.

There is but little meadow land, perhaps not more than one hundred and fifty acres in the town of Winchendon.

Interval land on Miller's River there is confiderable, and what is improved is of a very good quality. But of this there is not fo much as might have been expected; for the high lands in moft places fhut down quite clofe upon the river. Upon the rivers and ftreams in the town there are two grift mills, fix faw mills, and one clothier's works. There are alfo in the town, two potafh works.

Roads

Roads in various directions centre at, or near the meetinghouse. The greatest road is from Boston, through Winchendon, and so on through Fitzwilliam to Charlestown; this road a stage passes weekly through the summer season. Another road leads from Winchendon, through Gardner, Westminster, and so on to Worcester. Another runs south through Templeton; another westerly through Royalston, and another northerly through Rindge. Winchendon is situated about sixty two miles from Boston, by the nearest route, to the northwest: And from Worcester courthouse it is thirty five miles, a little to the west of north. When the census was taken, there were in the place 150 houses, and 950 inhabitants; and it will no doubt still greatly increase and multiply.

ROYALSTON.

This is, as to the original grant and settlement, doubtless by many years, the youngest town in the county. It was in the year 1752, or very soon after, granted to the Hon. Messrs. Hubbard, Erving, Royal, Otis, and others, and was to include all the unappropriated lands between Newhampshire line, on the north; Warwick, on the west; Athol and Templeton, on the south; Winchendon, on the east and south; and Ashburnham, on the east. This grant was known by the name of Royalshire, until its incorporation, which was on February 16th, 1765, when it was called *Royalston*, in compliment to the late Col. *Isaac Royal*, one of the original proprietors. Before the last French war, some who intended to settle here, began to work upon their lands, but the breaking out of that war put an entire stop thereto. Towards the close of that war some people began to work here again; and in the year 1762 several families moved into the place; the first of which came in, in the month of June. Its increase was truly surprising; for in less than three years, it was incorporated with distinct town privileges; and in the close of the year 1767, there were about forty families in the town. The number of families at this time is 195, and the number of souls about 1130; besides that, there were a number of families with their estates set off to aid in forming the district of Orange, in the county of Hampshire. As early as the year 1766, on the 13th day of October, a congregational church was imbodied here, under the countenance, and in the presence of the churches in the vicinity; and on the 19th of October, 1768, the first and present pastor, the Rev. Joseph Lee, was ordained to the work of the gospel ministry among them.

There were nine or ten families of the baptist denomination among the first settlers. At what time

time they imbodied into a church state is not known to us. A Mr. Elisha Rich was their teacher, but he was never ordained among them. He was succeeded by Mr. Whitman Jacobs, who was installed December 13th, 1770. He lived in Athol, to which town part of his society belonged, and there he now resides: Mr. Moses Kinney is now the ordained teacher of the baptists in Royalston.

The lands in this town consist generally of hills and valleys; and the soil is very excellent, being suitable for tillage, pasturage, mowing and orcharding. The natural growth of wood is of various kinds, as oak, chesnut, beech, ash, white, black and yellow birch, maple, or sugar tree, bass, alder, and the ever greens, as pine, hemlock, hacmatack and spruce, &c.

This town is exceedingly well watered by rivers, rivulets and springs. Miller's River runs through this town from the east. And there are a number of considerable brooks or streams, which uniting, form what is called Tully River in Athol. In the southerly part of the town one of the streams which helps to form Tully River, has very observable falls. In the course of forty or fifty rods, the whole fall of water is more than a hundred feet. In one place it is twenty feet, or more. On these several streams before mentioned are large quantities of rich interval, or excellent meadow lands.

There are two ponds in the town; one small, a little west of the meetinghouse; the other about a mile further westward, called *Long Pond*. A small stream runs out of the lesser into the greater.

Although the distance between these ponds is but little more than half a mile in a direct line, yet the little pond is at least an hundred and fifty feet higher than the other. There are in both ponds, various sorts of fish, and in great plenty; those in the larger are most excellent. The distance of this town from Boston is, by the nearest route, about seventy miles, to the northwest; and from the courthouse in Worcester it is forty miles, and is bounded on the north, by the State line; on the east, by Winchendon; on the south, by Gerry and Athol; and on the west, by Athol and Warwick.

ASHBURNHAM.

ON the 10th of June, 1735, a grant was made by the General Court, to Thomas Tilestone and others, for and in consideration of services done by officers and soldiers of the ancient town of Dorchester, in the expedition to Canada in 1690, under Capt. John Withrington. This grant was to be equal to six miles square, and went by the name of *Dorchester Canada*, until its incorporation,

incorporation, which was on the 22d of February, 1765, when it received its prefent name. To the original grant were afterwards added Lexington farm of a thoufand acres, Cambridge farm of a thoufand more, Rolfe's farm of fix hundred, and another of about a thoufand acres.

The church of Chrift in Afhburnham was gathered April 23d, 1760, and the fame day the Rev. Jonathan Winchefter was ordained their firft paftor. This gentleman was fomewhat advanced in life when he was fettled in the work of the miniftry; and he continued but a fhort fpace therein, leaving the world November 27th, 1767. To him fucceeded in the facred office and work, the Rev. John Cufhing, who was folemnly confecrated hereunto November 2d, 1768. In the town there are about twenty families of baptifts, who manifeft far greater catholicifm than formerly. The whole number of families is about 150, and of inhabitants about 970, befides a number who were fet off to Afhby, in the county of Middlefex, with about 3000 acres of land, and a number to the town of Gardner, with about 2000 acres more.

In this town are fituated two large hills, or mountains, *Great* and *Little Wetatick*. Great Wetatick lies in the northeaft part of the town, and Little Wetatick to the fouthweft from it.

There are feven ponds within the limits of Afhburnham, which divide it nearly into two equal parts, north and fouth. Two of them are large, viz. Great and Little Naukheag. The others are not diftinguifhed by any particular names. Here are

are no rivers ; but thefe ponds are fources of feveral ftreams, which take different routes, and contribute to the formation of feveral large rivers. From Little Naukheag, which is near the centre of the town, a rivulet empties into Great Naukheag, whence a ftream iffues to the weft, which makes part of Miller's River. About three quarters of a mile eaft of Little Naukheag begins another ftream, which runs foutheaft, and joining in Fitchburg with another ftream from Weftminfter, and other fmall ftreams, helps to form the north branch of Nafhaway River. Northeaft from this laft mentioned ftream, arife two more, which, joining foon, run through Afhby into Newipfwich, in the State of Newhampfhire, and become a large branch of Souheagan River, which empties into the great river Merrimack. Hence it appears that this town is upon the height of land between Connecticut river on the weft, and Merrimack on the eaft. And what is worthy of particular notice is this, that fcarce any water runs into this town : It being conjectured that all which comes in, from all quarters, would pafs through a man's boot. On ftreams iffuing from three of the ponds in Afhburnham, there are mills, and a fine feat for more on the ftream which runs out of Great Naukheag, not yet improved. On the banks of Little Naukheag is a white fand, equal in finenefs and whitenefs to that on the banks of Capeanne, and which it is judged would make glafs.

There is much broken land in this town. Some parts abound in hemlock, fpruce, white and pitch pine ;

pine; this is the cafe more efpecially in the weftern part; however, there is much good land for grafs. Where the growth of wood is oak, hard and foft maple, beach, birch and chefnut, the land is moift and good for grazing. It has been a noted place for lumber: The beft pine timber is moftly worked up: There yet remain great quantities of white and pitch pine, fuitable for boards. There are five faw mills, and four corn mills in the town. Here are potafh works, and have been from its infancy; and the firft complete ton of this article carried into market was from Afhburnham. Here are no remarkable fprings, or other natural curiofities. They have an elegant new meetinghoufe. The former houfe of publick worfhip was, about twenty years ago, wrecked by an hurricane, and moved three or four feet to the north and eaft; a barn, about fixty rods to the fouth, was torn down, while the owner within it efcaped unhurt. This hurricane paffed from the weft to the eaft, extending about half a mile in width, and upon the hills fwept all before it. The town enjoys a fine air, and is remarkably healthy.

Its diftance from Worcefter, is thirty miles to the north; and from Bofton, by the neareft route, is fifty five miles, but through Lancafter and Stow, it is fixty miles, and lies to the northweft.

Afhburnham is bounded on the north, by the State line; on the northeaft, by Afhby; on the eaft, by Fitchburg; on the fouth, by Weftminfter and Gardner; and on the weft, by Winchendon.

PAXTON.

PAXTON.

THIS was taken from the towns of Leicester and Rutland, in nearly equal parts; and was incorporated on the 12th of February, 1765, when it received its name.

The ecclesiastical state of this town has been somewhat singular, from the gathering of the church of Christ in the place, to the present time, as will appear by the following account.

The church in Paxton, was imbodied September 3d, 1767. The Rev. Silas Biglow was ordained their first minister the same year, viz. October 21st, 1767. He was much beloved and respected by the people of his charge; but the Great Head of the church suffered him to continue but a little more than two years in office, being removed by death, November 16th, 1769.

He was succeeded in the work of the gospel ministry by the Rev. Alexander Thayer, who was solemnly separated hereunto on the 28th of November, 1770. Mr. Thayer continued not quite twelve years with the people, being dismissed from office August 14th, 1782.

They were destitute, after this, of a settled minister for more than three years, until September 8th, 1785, when the Rev. John Foster was ordained their third pastor; at which time the town was in a most unhappy divided state, there being but a bare majority for Mr. Foster; the other party dissenting,

dissenting, and protesting, utterly refused to hear him, and were by law exempted from contributing to his support. In this situation the people remained for three years and a half, until April, 1789, when Mr. Foster was dismissed from his pastoral relation to the people.

Mr. Foster was, in about three years after, installed at Taunton, in the county of Bristol.

After Mr. Foster's removal from Paxton the parties amicably reunited, and are in a way for the happy resettlement of the gospel ministry among them.

If the people do but continue united, they are able to support the gospel in a very honourable, generous manner: For the town, though not large, is well settled, being an excellent tract of land, and the inhabitants in general are industrious, good, and wealthy farmers. It is pleasant, although uneven, having many hills and valleys; but the soil is rich and productive: It is good for all kinds of grain, and well repays the labour bestowed upon it: It is peculiarly good for grass and pasturing, and likewise for orcharding. The high lands are moist and springy, not too rocky; and the lower lands are swamps or meadows, but easily drained. The wood which grows on the higher lands, is oak, much walnut, some chesnut; and in the lower lands, are found birch, beech, maple and ash. It is truly noticeable that the wood in this town, when cut down, never sprouts again, in consequence of which they are threatened with a scarcity of fuel.

The town is exceedingly well watered by springs from the hills; and by small streams, on which they have both corn and saw mills. From the same spring, about half a mile north of the meetinghouse, waters issue, which soon divide and take quite different and contrary directions; part runs northeasterly into the river Nashaway; part runs southwesterly into Connecticut river. There are two hills in the town of great height, and worthy of particular mention: One is called Turkey Hill, near Rutland line, this is large, and affords good farms; and especially fine pasture land: At the foot of this hill, on the west side, lies Turkey Hill Pond, large, and well stored with fish; and from this pond runs a stream which empties into Chicabee River, and from thence into Connecticut river. On the east side of the town, and in that part which was formerly Leicester, is situated what is called Asnebumskit Hill, the foot of which, on the east side, falls within the bounds of Holden. This is a large and high hill, containing several hundred acres, the land is rich and good; especially adapted for pasturage. It lies about twelve miles south of Watchusett great hill, and except that, overtops all other hills within forty or fifty miles of it. Around this hill the vapours gather so plentifully, or become so dense the evening preceding a rain, that it appears at a distance as if it rained upon its summit. To this hill many of the farmers, in the vicinity, look at evening, or a little before the setting of the sun, in the time of making hay, that they may be able to determine with a good degree

of

of certainty, what the weather will be the next day. Near the foot of this hill, is situated Asnebumskit Pond; which is a fine large pond, and well supplied with fish: From this pond there issues a stream, which runs to the northeast through Holden, and joining the stream from the foot of Watchusett Hill, helps to form the south branch of Nashaway River. From springs, on the northwesterly part of Asnebumskit Hill, a stream is formed, which running southerly, passes through Leicester, and so to French River. The above observations shew us that Paxton is situated on the height of the lands between the sea, on the east and south, and Connecticut river on the west.

In Paxton, works for making potash have lately been set up: And here a small number of cotton and wool cards are annually made.

The number of inhabitants in this town was found in 1791, to be 558.

Paxton is situated eight miles west from Worcester, and about fifty five from Boston, a little to the south of west. It is bounded on the north, by Rutland; on the east, by Holden; on the south, by Leicester and Spencer; and on the west, by Oakham and Rutland.

NORTHBOROUGH.

NORTHBOROUGH.

This was the north part of the town of Weftborough, the main part whereof was fet off from Marlborough in the year 1717. It was made the fecond precinct or parifh of Weftborough by an act of Court, on the 20th of October, 1744.

The church of Chrift was gathered in this place May 21ft, 1746, and on the fame day the Rev. John Martin was ordained their firft paftor, who continued to minifter unto them in holy things until April 30th, 1767, when after a fhort ficknefs he died in the 61ft year of his age, and the 21ft of his miniftry. In fix months and four days from his death, viz. on the 4th of November, 1767, the Rev. Peter Whitney was confecrated their fecond paftor.

Here, about thirty gentlemen have united, and eftablifhed a focial library, containing one hundred volumes at prefent; and fuch are its regulations as that it will annually increafe.

A narrative of an Hebrew inftructor at Harvard College, who died at Northborough, and his Epitaph, are thought worth preferving.

Mr. Monis, as I fuppofe, the firft Hebrew Inftructor in our Univerfity at Cambridge, was born in Italy. When he came into America I am not able to fay. He married a Mifs Marrett, of Cambridge, who died in the year 1761 ; whereupon he refigned resigned his office, and retired to Northborough, and spent the residue of his days in the family of the late Rev. John Martyn. Mrs. Monis and Mrs. Martyn were sisters. He left something very honourable and generous to the church in Northborough. He bequeathed forty six pounds thirteen shillings and four pence, to be equally divided among seven of the ministers then living in the vicinity: Also, he left about an hundred and twenty six pounds as a fund, the interest whereof was to be distributed among widows of ministers who were in indigent circumstances; and the remainder of his estate, which was considerable, he gave to the Martyn family.

The following is the inscription on his grave stone.

" Here lie buried the remains of
Rabbi Judah Monis, M. A.
Late Hebrew Instructor
At Harvard College in Cambridge;
In which office he continued 40 years.
He was, by birth and religion, a Jew,
But embraced the Christian faith,
And was publickly baptized
At Cambridge, A. D. 1722,
And departed this life
April 25th, 1764,
Aged eighty one years, two months
and twenty one days.
A native branch of Jacob see,
Which once from off its olive broke;
Regrafted from the living tree, Rom. 11. 17, 24.
Of the reviving sap partook.

From

From teeming Zion's fertile womb,   Isai. 66. 8.
As dewy drops in early morn,   Psalm. 110. 3.
Or rising bodies from the tomb,   John, 5. 28, 29.
At once be Israel's nation born.   Isai. 66. 8."

This second precinct in Westborough was incorporated February 24th, 1766, and from its local situation and bearing, was called Northborough.

There were settlers in this part of Marlborough before there were any in what is now Westborough. As early as 1700, or rather before, a few families had fixed down here. And there was a garrison kept at a house on the lower side of the town towards Marlborough, near the brook where Messrs. Bartlets now live. On August 18th, 1707, as two women belonging to the garrison were out a little way from the fort, gathering herbs, the Indians discovered and pursued them. One Mrs. Mary Fay, got safe into the fort ; the other, Mary Goodenow, a young and unmarried woman, was taken and carried over the brook into the edge of Marlborough, and there, a little south of the great road, and nigh to Sandy Hill, so called, she was killed and scalped. The enemy were pursued by some soldiers and people of Marlborough, and were overtaken the next day, in that part of Lancaster, now called Sterling,* when a most bloody battle was fought, in which two of our people, John Farrar and Richard Singletary, were killed. The Indians at length fled with great precipitation,

* See a more particular account of this battle in the history of Lancaster and Sterling.

tion, carrying off their killed and wounded, except one, whose bones were afterwards discovered; but they left behind some of their plunder, and some of their packs; in one of which our people found the scalp of the above named Mary Goodenow; and hereupon concluding she must be killed, on their return they searched for, and found her body, and there buried it; and her grave is visible to this day.

The town of Northborough lies in a kind of valley between the high lands of Marlborough on the east, and those of Shrewsbury and Boylston on the west. On its easterly side it is about four miles long, and on its westerly about five: It is on an average about three miles and an half wide from east to west, containing about 90 dwelling houses, upwards of an 100 families, and according to the late census 620 inhabitants. It would doubtless admit of 150 or more families, were the large farms (some of which contain four hundred or five hundred acres) properly divided. This is beginning to take place, and in a few years probably will be accomplished. The inhabitants are chiefly farmers, and wealthy: They have also traders in European and Westindia goods; and various tradesmen and mechanicks, especially an excellent maker of edge tools of various kinds; and considering its dimensions and number, it is doubtless one of the ablest parishes in the county. The poorest land in general appears as we travel the great road. The farms which lie off are good, and much of the land very fertile. The westerly side of of the town rifes into high land, and the north-weft angle is very high; but the land is not rocky, and the farms are excellent, and from thence the prospect is extensive. There is one beautiful hill, called *Liguor Hill*, containing towards an hundred acres of land, very good, oppofite the meetinghoufe, and not more than fixty or eighty rods from it, on the fouth fide of the poft road. This is high, and feen from all the neighbouring towns; but it is not inacceffible even to teams. Its fummit is covered with a fine growth of good wood at prefent. About one mile northeaft from the meetinghoufe is another hill, very fimilar, called Edmund Hill. Upon the river Affabet, which runs through the eafterly part of the town, are vaft bodies of rich interval and good meadow lands. And upon the other ftreams and rivulets there are large and good meadows, efpecially on that called *Cold-Harbour*, which rifes in the north part of Shrewfbury, and croffing the foutheaft angle of Boylfton, turns and runs foutherly, then turns and runs eafterly, and paffing between the poft road and meetinghoufe, foon empties itfelf into the river Affabet. On the above named ftream, in the wefterly part of the town, are a corn and faw mill, one a few rods below the other, and as there is a fmall outlet from Rocky Pond, in the eafterly part of Boylfton, which empties into this Cold Harbour ftream, fo the owner of thofe mills, by means of a fmall dam at the lower end of faid pond, furnifhes them with a rich fupply of water, although diftant a mile or more. In the north part

part of the town are a corn and saw mill together, on North Brook, which coming from a pond in Lancaster, and running through Berlin and the northeast angle of Northborough, falls into the river Assabet. A little north of the meetinghouse runs a small but lasting stream from the hills in the westerly part of the town, on which is a saw mill which performs considerable work in the spring and autumn. In the town there are two ponds; one called *Solomon's Pond*, from the circumstance of an Indian of that name being drowned therein, by falling through a raft on which he was fishing. This is in the northeasterly part of the town. It is not large; about ninety rods long, and seventy five rods wide; has plenty of fish: To this pond there is no visible inlet nor outlet.

The other is in the southeasterly part of the town, called *Little Chauncy*; this also is well furnished with fish. From *Great Chauncy* Pond, in the northeasterly part of Westborough, there is a small outlet which runs into *Little Chauncy*; and from *Little Chauncy* a brook runs northerly, and crossing the post road on the line between Marlborough and Northborough, and the boundary between the two counties of Middlesex and Worcester, empties its waters into Assabet River. On this stream are a corn and a saw mill together; and although it be small, yet by clearing it of obstructions, and a little digging in a few places, they are supplied with a large quantity of water from both

the

the ponds above named. About half a mile from the meetinghouse, on the post road, and on the river Assabet there is a mill for the fulling of cloth; and works for carrying on the clothiers' business in all its branches, where about 7000 yards of cloth are annually dressed, and the work is most acceptably performed to the honour and advantage of the town, and the interest of the community. These works are the property of two brothers, Captains Samuel and Abraham Wood; but the business is performed at present by the latter only. On the opposite side of the road and river are works for the manufacture of iron, and where many tons have been made. There is in the vicinity a great plenty of ore, especially of the bog kind. Near the forge are works for the making of potash, where large quantities are manufactured yearly. About a mile below, on this same river, is a grift mill which fails not to grind through the year. Thus there are four corn, and four saw mills within the town.

There are, in this town, curious works for the conveyance of water to a great distance, the property, contrivance, and execution of Major Holloway Taylor. I know not that there are any similar works in the county, and would therefore describe them.

From springs issuing out of ledges of rocks on rising lands, this gentleman has raised a small pond, and from thence brings fine water (about seventy rods, through bored logs, under ground, not only in low lands, but in some places higher lands,

lands, where the water repeatedly afcends and defcends) into the back part of his houfe, into a large vat, near three feet in height, by a tube, from the laſt log, entering the bottom of the vat; which is, or may be kept conſtantly full, and running over; and the fuperfluous water is conveyed from the vat, by another tube, out on to the grafs land. As the water paſſes under ground nigh the barn yard by a tube from a log, entering the bottom of a large trough, he has a rich fupply of water for a great ſtock of cattle; and fuch is the quality of the water that it has feldom ever been known to freeze in trough or vat.*

The general growth of wood in the town is chefnut, walnut, the feveral forts of oak, fome white pine, and large quantities of pitch pine, which of late years, is in great demand, as an excellent wood for fuel.

Northborough lies about thirty fix miles from the Statehoufe in Boſton, and is eight or nine degrees to the fouth of weſt; and is ten miles from the courthoufe in Worceſter, a few degrees to the north of eaſt. This town is greatly benefited by the

---

* As this account may be read by fome not much acquainted with natural philofophy, and who therefore may think it incredible that water can be made to pafs over rifing grounds, and through low lands, alternately, as in this cafe, and then rife to fuch a height in the houfe; (for thefe logs are carried along under ploughed fields and mowing lands ;) for the fake of fuch it ought to be obferved, that water may be conveyed any where, to rife exactly to the height of the fountain or pond from whence it proceeds; although it cannot be carried to a greater height in its way to the place intended.

Should any perfons wifh to convey water in this manner, they may be informed, that yellow or pitch pine logs are much beſt for the purpofe; they are harder and more durable; thofe of chefnut are too fpungy and porous.

the publick roads, which in different directions pass through it. Besides the post road from Boston to Worcester, (and so to the seat of government,) which runs through it but a few rods south of the meetinghouse; there is another from New-hampshire State, and the northern part of the county of Worcester, and coming through Lancaster or Harvard, and Bolton and Berlin, passes directly through this town, just by the meetinghouse, and crossing the post road, leads on to Mendon and Providence. The road also from Worcester and Shrewsbury, through Framingham to Boston, passes through the south part of the town into Westborough. There is also a road of much travel from Hubbardston, Princeton, Holden, Sterling, and especially Boylston, which coming in upon the northwesterly part of the town, passes directly in front of the meetinghouse, and then in the space of about fifty rods, falls into the post road.

Another great benefit the town reaps, is from the great resort of people from all the neighbouring towns to the corn and saw mills, to the fulling mill and forge, and to the blacksmiths', for their works of various kinds, as well as to the shops and stores.

Northborough is bounded on the north, by Berlin; on the east, by Marlborough and Southborough; on the south, by Westborough; and on the west, by Shrewsbury and Boylston.

HUBBARDSTON.

HUBBARDSTON.

THIS was called "the northeaſt quarter of Rutland," being wholly included in the original grant of that town, and was incorporated on the 13th day of June, 1767, and called Hubbardſton, to perpetuate the name and memory of the late Hon. Thomas Hubbard, Eſq; of Boſton, who had been ſometime ſpeaker of the houſe of Repreſentatives; after that, ſeveral years a counſellor of the then province, and for many years treaſurer, and of courſe a member, of the corporation of Harvard Univerſity in Cambridge. He was a large proprietor of lands in this place.

The congregational church in Hubbardſton was imbodied on the 13th of June, 1770, and on the ſame day the Rev. Nehemiah Parker was ordained to the work of the goſpel miniſtry in the place, and who ſtill continues in peace and love with the people, and miniſtering to them in holy things.

We proceed to a deſcription of this place. It is about ſix miles ſquare; and is bounded weſt by Barre; ſouth, by Rutland; eaſt, by Princeton; northeaſt, by Weſtminſter; and north, by Gardner, Templeton and Gerry. The town is agreeably interſperſed with hills and valleys. Perhaps about a twelfth part of it is meadow and interval. The uplands are generally, excellent for grazing and ſome conſiderable part very good for the

T growth

growth of English grafs. The land in general, is not the best for grain; though in common years a sufficiency is raised for the inhabitants. It is rather too cold for orcharding, although there are a number of flourishing orchards in the town, and some years a considerable quantity of cider is made. Hills there are several in the town, however, but two which we shall notice: The largest, in the northwesterly part of the town, extends quite through it, from Templeton to Barre; this is called Burnshirt Hill, and is most excellent land. The other is called Read's Hill, situated about one mile and an half east from the centre of the town; this is also very good land.

It is supposed this town is rich in iron ore, at least; there is a hill in the north part of it, extending into Templeton,* where a number of gentlemen from Boston and other places, wrought near fifty years ago. They dug several rods into the hill, in quest of a silver mine; but whether it answered their expectations or not, was not divulged. A war commencing put a stop to their pursuit, and it has never since been reassumed.

The town is finely watered by springs, streams and rivers; There are five rivers and streams noticeable, which pass through the town from north to south. The most easterly of these is called Pifs River, part whereof comes from Westminster, and part from the west side of Watchusett Hill in Princeton. The next is called Ware River, which heads in Hubbardston. The next is a smaller stream, called Meadow Brook, which takes its rise in

---

* See this also noticed in the account of Templeton.

HUBBARDSTON.

in the north part of the town. Further weſt is another ſtream called Conneyſtow Brook, which has its ſource in Templeton. The moſt weſterly ſtream is known by the name of *Burnſhirt River*, the principal branch of which comes from Gerry. All theſe ſtreams running a ſoutherly direction, unite in the eaſt part of Barre, where their names, as well as waters, are ſwallowed up in Ware River. *Otter River*, ſo called, which riſes in Templeton, runs in the north part of this town, and then turning, falls back into Templeton, and at length, unites with Miller's River.* On theſe rivers and ſtreams, within the town of Hubbardſton, there are eleven ſaw mills, five griſt mills, and one clothiers' works. There are alſo works for making potaſh in the town.

There are three ponds in Hubbardſton. The largeſt of theſe, known by the name of the Great Aſnaconcomick Pond, is about two miles from the centre of the town, to the eaſt : It is a mile and a half in length, from north to ſouth; the breadth is various, from half a mile to five rods, ſuppoſed to cover about three hundred acres. About half a mile further to the northeaſt, is ſituated Little Aſnaconcomick Pond, of a circular form; and what merits particular notice is this, that for a conſiderable part of the way round this pond, there is every appearance that once a ſtone wall was built, or building. In ſome places it is two feet and an half in height, as if laid up by the hands of men; and where there is not one ſtone

* See this more particularly deſcribed in the account of Templeton.

stone upon another, the appearance is as of a large stone wall thrown down. If this was the work of art, when and by whom it was performed, or wherefore, perhaps can never be ascertained. Both the Ponds before described are fed by small springs. There is a small outlet from each. Another small pond is situated about a mile northwest from the centre of the town; it is called *Natty Pond,* which has both an inlet and an outlet. The growth of wood in this place is chiefly white pine and pitch pine in great plenty, hemlock, beech, maple and oak; there is but little of any other sort.

The town is settled in general, with industrious farmers; and they are become numerous, and are increasing in wealth. There are about 150 families, and near 1000 souls in the place.

Hubbardston is situated sixty miles, nearly west, from Boston; and twenty from the courthouse in Worcester, to the northwest. A road much used, leads through the town from the south to the north, in which people pass from Rhodeisland, &c. &c. to the western part of Newhampshire, and to the State of Vermont. It is also in contemplation to open a road from the towns on Connecticut river, in the county of Hampshire, through Petersham, to Hubbardston, and so on through Princeton and Lancaster, to Boston. This undoubtedly, would be the nearest route, from Hadley and towns adjacent, to the metropolis of the Commonwealth.

NORTHBRIDGE.

NORTHBRIDGE.

THE town of Northbridge takes its name from its situation and bearing with respect to Uxbridge, from which it was chiefly taken; five or six families only being set off to it from Sutton south or first parish. It is about five miles in length, and about four in width; and is bounded, by Uxbridge, on the south; by Sutton, on the west; by Grafton, on the north; and by Mendon and Upton, on the east and northeast. It was incorporated on the 14th of July, 1772. It is not large, having, at the time of the late enumeration 83 houses, and 570 inhabitants. The congregational church here was imbodied, June the 6th, 1782, and on the 25th of June, 1783, the Rev. John Crane was ordained their pastor. Here also there is a society of Baptists of about ten families; at present destitute of any settled teacher. There are also within the town twelve families of Quakers, and two or three of the Universalists.

We shall proceed to some Topographical Description of this place.

It is uneven and somewhat rocky and rough; but the land and soil, in general, rich, strong and good. As it has alternately, high and low lands, it is well calculated for orcharding, for pasture and grass land, and bears rye, Indian corn, oats, flax, &c. Hills there are none high, or, on any account remarkable. The meetinghouse indeed, stands

stands on an eminence, and commands a good prospect for four or five miles round. As the lands in general are high, the air is salubrious, and the inhabitants have been blessed with great health from the first settlement of the place.

There are no stagnant waters or ponds in the town: But it is finely watered by springs, streams and rivers. Two of these are noticeable: Blackstone River, which originates in Sutton, and passing through the westerly part of Grafton, enters this town, and runs from north to south the whole length of the town, on the westerly side thereof. This is a large and fine river; and upon this there are great bodies of very excellent interval lands: Some of these are high, and bear corn and flax; the lower are good for grass.

There is another river, not so large, which enters this town in the southwest part from Douglass, and joins Blackstone River. On this river there is a quantity of valuable meadow: But the land adjoining the meadow is not the most fertile.

There are within the town, two corn mills, one saw mill, and one forge, where much work is performed.

The growth of wood, on the high lands is very valuable, consisting of walnut, oak and chesnut; that on the low lands is less valuable; but like that of other towns in general; the quantity of pine timber is small. The people here subsist, chiefly by farming; they have the character of an industrious and flourishing people; and it is said there is

hardly,

hardly an idle perfon, or a tavern haunter in the place.

Northbridge is fituated forty three miles from Bofton, nearly fouthweft; and from the courthoufe in Worcefter, it is twelve miles, lying about foutheaft. The road from Bofton, through Mendon and Oxford, to Connecticut, paffes through this town: And the neareft and moft direct road to Providence, from Worcefter, would pafs about half a mile weft of Northbridge meetinghoufe.

BARRE.

THIS was the northweft part of Rutland Original Grant; it was made a diftrict by act of the Legiflature in the year 1749, and called Rutland Diftrict, until June 14th, 1774, when it was made a town, and the name of *Barre* was given to it, as a token of refpect to a great and worthy friend of America, at that time a member of the Britifh Houfe of Commons. Barre is bounded on the north, by Peterfham; on the eaft, by Hubbardfton; on the foutheaft, by Rutland; on the fouth, by Oakham; on the fouthweft, by Newbraintree; and on the weft, by Hardwick.

The church of Chrift in this place, was gathered July 30th, 1753, and the Rev. Thomas Frink was installed

installed their pastor, on the last Wednesday of October following. Mr. Frink was the first minister of Rutland, and being dismissed from thence, he was installed a pastor of the third church in Plymouth, November 7th, 1743, where he continued but a little time before his removal. He continued in the ministry at Barre, but about thirteen years, being dismissed from his sacred office, by advice of an ecclesiastical council July 17th, 1766. He was succeeded in the pastoral office at Barre, by the Rev. Josiah Dana, who was consecrated hereunto October 7th, 1767. Mr. Dana continues in the work of the gospel ministry in this place, and in peace and esteem with the people of his charge.

The following sorrowful occurrence took place in this town. In March, 1780, the house of Mr. Peter Bent was consumed by fire in the night, with almost every thing contained therein, and two of his children, a son and daughter, of adult age, perished in the flames.

The town of Barre is large in extent, being rather more than six miles square. And it is one of the best townships of land in the county; the soil is exceedingly rich and strong. The land in general, is very hilly and uneven. The hills, indeed, are not so very high, but some are steep, and being somewhat rocky, the roads are not so good: But this is commonly the case in most towns where the soil is excellent, and moist: The town is well watered by numerous springs and rivulets, and the people enjoy great advantages for turning

and

and conveying the water over their grafs land. The foil is peculiarly adapted to mowing and pafturage; and here they fat great multitudes of cattle, and make the beft of beef. Here alfo they have many and large dairies; and it is fuppofed that more butter and cheefe is carried from hence into the market, annually, than from any other town of the fame extent. The foil bears Indian corn well; but it is not fo well adapted to Englifh grain as fome other places. However, they raife a fufficiency of all kinds for themfelves, and confiderable for exportation. As the town is uneven and hilly, it affords no large and commanding view of itfelf, but from the hills there is an extenfive profpect into other towns. The pleafantnefs of Barre confifts in the richnefs and fertility of the land, and the large, handfome, well finifhed buildings of all kinds; but from no one place can many of them be feen at once. The farms are large, and very productive: The people are induftrious, and they have great encouragement to labour: Their modes of hufbandry are good, and there are fure indications of wealth and opulence all over the town. And indeed it is one of the foremoft towns in the county, there being but three which pay more to a State tax. It is become numerous, having, when the late cenfus was taken, upwards of 1600 inhabitants, although but one religious fociety; and they have the largeft meetinghoufe in the county, fifty fix by feventy four feet.

The general growth of wood in the town, is large and plenty, confifting of oak of all kinds, efpecially ly an unusual proportion of white oak; considerable chesnut, some walnut; birch, beech, ash, white pine, pitch pine, some hemlock, &c. There is one large river, called Ware River, which coming from Templeton, through the westerly part of Hubbardston, passes through the easterly and southerly parts of Barre, and then runs into Hardwick. There is also a stream originating in Gerry which runs through the town on the easterly side, within a mile of the meetinghouse, called Pleasant Branch: This falls into Ware River, in the south part of the town. In the north part of the town, on the westerly side, rises another stream from springs, which is called Moose Brook, which runs into Hardwick, and there empties itself into Ware-River. On these streams there are some meadows, and very good interval lands on Ware River in the southerly part of the town. On this river, and on these streams there are four grist mills, several saw mills, and clothiers' works.

The people in Barre subsist, mainly, by farming; here are, however, all the usual tradesmen and mechanicks, and two or three dealers in European, East and West India goods; here also the pot and pearl ash works are carried on.

Barre is situated sixty six miles from Boston about west; and it is about twenty four miles from the courthouse in Worcester, about northwest.

WARD.

W A R D.

THIS place was not an original grant, but was taken from several other towns, as Worcester, Oxford, Sutton and Leicester, together with a gore of land lying between Oxford and Leicester, not previously belonging to any town. On the 23d of June, 1773, this place was erected into a poll parish, and commonly called the south parish of Worcester. The parish was limited and bounded in the following manner: It was to extend three miles into Worcester, as the roads were then trod; three into Oxford, and three into Leicester by their roads, and one mile and an half into Sutton, from the meetinghouse place. This place as above described, was incorporated and made a distinct town, and vested with all the privileges which other towns enjoy, by an act of the Legislature, April 10th, 1778, when it received the name of Ward, as a compliment to the Hon. Major General Artemas Ward, Esq; of Shrewsbury, and now Representative of this county in the Congress of the United States of America. The town is bounded northerly on Worcester; easterly, by Grafton; southeast, by Sutton; south, by Oxford; and westerly, by Leicester.

The church of Christ in Ward was imbodied on the 25th of January, 1776; and on the 3d of November,

vember, 1784, the Rev. Isaac Bailey was ordained to the pastoral care thereof, and still continues in the sacred office.

We shall now present the reader with a Geographical Description of the town of Ward.

It is considered, by good judges, as a most excellent tract of land: The soil in general is fertile, rich and strong, suitable for orcharding and all kinds of fruit; well adapted to pasturage and mowing, and produces large crops of rye, oats, wheat, barley, Indian corn, and flax. It is not very rocky; but affords stone sufficient for fencing in the farms: It is not level, but rather uneven, abounding in hills and valleys. The hills, however are not high; but the lands on them are good. Part of the hill, called Prospect Hill, to the south, lies within this town; also part of the hill, called *Boggachoag*, to the north; and part of the hill, called *Grassy Hill*, to the southeast of the meetinghouse. On and near these hills, there are very fine farms. The general growth of wood is oak of the various sorts, chesnut, walnut, on the high lands; and in the lower lands, pine, maple, cedar, &c. &c.

The town is as well watered, by springs and perennial rivulets, as perhaps any other town in the county. The course of the streams is circuitous, and so meandering as greatly to benefit the town. The principal stream is that which is called French River. There is another called Kettle Brook, which passes through the town. On these streams there are four saw mills and two grist mills, within

the

the town, alfo one clothiers' works; befides which there is a wind mill erected on *Profpect Hill*, which does confiderable work.

There are three or four fmall ponds in the town, the largeft of which covers perhaps, about thirty acres, fituated about a mile fouth of the meetinghoufe. There is an outlet from this pond, to the north, ufually called Dark Brook; and there is an inlet from the fouth, while the pond is in its natural ftate, but by an artificial raifing of this pond about four feet, the current in the inlet is reverfed, and the difcharge of water is to the fouth.

The town is not large, but it is wealthy; there are about 80 houfes; about 90 families, and when they were numbered there were 473 fouls: It is fituated fifty five miles from Bofton, a little to the fouthweft; and five miles from the courthoufe in Worcefter, almoft fouth.

MILFORD.

THIS place was the northeafterly part of the ancient town of Mendon: It was fet off from Mendon as a precinct, or parifh, in the year 1741, and was commonly known by the appellation of Mill River. It was incorporated and invefted with all diftinct town privileges, on the eleventh

enth of April, 1780. Soon after it was made a parifh, a congregational church was here gathered, viz. on the 15th of April, 1741, confifting of twenty fix male members; and on the 21ft of December, 1743, the Rev. Amariah Froft, was folemnly invefted with the paftoral office in the place. Some time after the fettlement of Mr. Froft, a feparation took place here; a Mr. Hovey preached to the difaffected, and was ordained among them. He tarried but a few years; fince his time preaching by itinerants and laymen, and meetings held occafionally on the fabbath, have been continued among them. A number, not large, believing in the falvation of all men, have kept up publick meetings, and fometimes had preaching. There are a few anabaptifts in this place, and but one family of friends or quakers. The Rev. Mr. Froft continued the worthy and faithful paftor of the congregational church in Milford, until March 14th, 1792, when he died in the feventy fecond year of his age, and the forty ninth of his miniftry.

An addition to, and a general repair of their meetinghoufe was made in 1792, and it is now a very decent and convenient building.

There has been greater candour and moderation of late between thofe of different fentiments in this town, than formerly was difcovered; and it is hoped greater unanimity will take place in the refettlement of the gofpel miniftry among them.

We proceed to a Geographical Defcription of the town of Milford.

Milford

MILFORD.

Milford is situated on the easterly side of the county; and is bounded on the north, by Hopkinton; on the east, by Holliston, in the county of Middlesex; on the southeast, by Bellingham in the county of Suffolk; on the west, and southwest, by Mendon; and on the northwest, by Upton. It is situated southwest from Boston, at the distance of thirty four miles; and from Worcester courthouse, it is southeast, distant twenty miles; and it is twenty five miles from Providence.

The town of Milford is not a level, champaign tract of land, neither yet is it very hilly and uneven; there is indeed, one large hill, a little from the centre of the town, to the southeast, called Bear Hill. This is mostly very good land. The whole of the north part of the town is high and good land; it rises by a gradual ascent; and from the highest places there is a large and variegated prospect; from these heights may be seen the Watchusetts and Monadnock mountains, as also the hills south of Boston. This northern part was a purchase from the Indians, by the proprietors of the ancient township of Mendon; and was commonly called the North Purchase. This part is the most distant from the meetinghouse in Milford; and in this quarter, the sectaries in the town have usually held their religious meetings. The northern and western parts of the town, especially, are rough and rocky; but the soil is generally strong and good; and well adapted to orcharding, grass and pasturage, and suffers but little by a dry season. They raise grain here of all kinds in sufficient quantities,

most

most commonly for themselves; but their articles of produce for market, are chiefly butter, cheese, pork, beef, &c. perhaps equal in quality to any in the county. There are but few mechanicks in the place, and seldom more than two traders in European and India goods. The people subsist mainly by the business of husbandry, and are industrious and good livers. The town is supposed to contain about as much as five miles square. There are 135 dwelling houses, and 840 inhabitants in the town, according to the late census.

There are two rivers running through this town, from north to south, nearly parallel with each other, about one mile and an half distant, in some places not so much; one on the west, the other on the east side of the town: These have their sources in the high lands beforementioned, in the borders of Hopkinton. That on the west is called Mill River, the name by which this place was designated until its incorporation, this is large, running through the easterly part of Mendon, it passes to Providence. That on the east is a principal branch of Charles's River, which soon turns and runs easterly, and falls into the sea in Boston harbour. Mill River is the outlet of a large pond, said to be a mile in length, partly in Milford, but principally in Hopkinton and Upton, called North Pond. There is another pond, a little more than a mile from the centre of the town, called Cedar Swamp Pond; this is small, though there be plenty of fish therein, as in the other; the branch of Charles's River spoken of above, runs directly through this

MILFORD.

this pond. There are very good meadows, and interval lands upon the borders of both the rivers defcribed before, as well as fmall pieces in other parts of the town, which are a fingular advantage to the farmers. The town abounds in fprings, rivulets and brooks in all parts: And on the rivers and ftreams they have four grift mills, three faw mills, one clothiers' works, and one trip hammer within the limits of Milford.

The growth of wood in this town is oak of all forts, chefnut, walnut, &c. there is very little pine or cedar at this day.

The roads in this town are not good, efpecially for carriages; but they may be made in time, much better than at prefent.

We fhall clofe our account of Milford, with mentioning, that in this place was born Alexander Scammell, Efq; who graduated at Harvard Univerfity, A. D. 1769; who was appointed a furveyor of maft timber, &c. in Maffachufetts, and province of Maine, under the Britifh government; was Brigade Major in the American army, in 1775; a Colonel in the year 1777, at the taking of Gen. Burgoyne, and Adjutant General of the army at Yorktown, where he was unfortunately wounded in reconnoitering, September 30, 1781, juft before the furrender of Lord Cornwallis, of which wound he foon after died.

STERLING.

STERLING.

THIS was for many years, the second parish in Lancaster, and was commonly called *Chockset*. It was made a separate parish in the year 1743, and remained united with Lancaster until April 25th, 1781, when it was incorporated by act of the Legislature, and received its present name, in compliment to Lord Sterling, of Newjersey, who served as a General in the American army, in the late war between Greatbritain and these United States. This is a large, populous, and wealthy town; is about seven miles in length, from north to south, and six in width from east to west. It is situated about five miles from Lancaster, a little to the south of west, on the road to Princeton. It is bounded by Holden and Princeton on the west; eight miles from Holden, and seven from Princeton, six miles from Boylston, which lies to the south of it; and from Leominster, on the north, it is seven miles.

This town is rather hilly and uneven, though there is very little broken, or waste land in it. It is not very rocky, but a most excellent, fertile soil, producing in rich abundance, to repay the husbandman for its cultivation. The high lands are excellent for all kinds of fruits, especially apples; and here are large orchards; also, for grass and grazing;

grazing; for the land is naturally moist, and by the help of the rivulets, the water may be turned over the sides of most of the hills. As the town is very uneven, there is no extended prospect. Nevertheless, the fertility of the soil, the high degree of cultivation, and the interspersion of hills and valleys, afford peculiar gratification to the eyes of observing travellers. The meetinghouse is in a valley; and on the road, in this valley, there is a large collection of tradesmen and mechanicks and they are lively, active and industrious.

But the bulk of the people are large farmers, and, as the bounteous Author of Nature has blessed them with a fruitful soil, they have great encouragement to labour. Though the town be hilly, as above observed, yet there are but two worthy of particular notice. The first is *Redstone* Hill, so called from the colour of the stones which are upon it.

This lies about a mile from the meetinghouse, on the road leading from Sterling to Lancaster.

The second is called Justice's Hill, which is situated about four miles northwest from the meetinghouse, on the road leading to Westminster.

There is but one river in the town, called *Still River*, from the slow motion of its waters; for after it enters this town, it runs in a vale for several miles, with but a small descent. The waters which form this river, are furnished from three distinct sources. The western branch issues from the foot of Mount Watchusett, in Princeton, and after various meanders, and receiving accessions by several rivulets, which originate in the eastern side of

Princeton

Princeton hills, joins the others a little north of the road leading from Sterling to Princeton. This branch bears the name of *Hartwell's River*, upon which are several valuable mills. The middle branch originates in *Gardner's Meadows*, which are in the northeastern part of Princeton; This is the largest of the three branches; and carries several mills. The eastern branch which is called *Justice's River*, has its source in the southwesterly part of Leominster; and taking its course, through Justice's Meadows, which lie on the west side of Justice's Hill, and receiving several brooks, empties itself into the main stream, or *Still River*. After the confluence of these branches the river takes a southern direction along the western side of Sterling, for several miles, until it enters Boylston, thence taking a circuitous route through the westerly and northerly parts of Boylston, loses its name in Nashaway, or Lancaster River. On the banks of this river in Sterling there is some pitch pine plain, some meadow and interval land.

There is one considerable stream in the northerly part of the town, which running an easterly course, empties itself into the north branch of Nashaway.

There are two considerable ponds in Sterling; one lies by the county road to Worcester; the other, a little to the southeast of this: These are divided by a neck of land of about forty rods, in width, at the narrowest place; through this neck a small stream runs, affording a passage for the fish from one pond to the other. From the western pond issues a considerable stream, sufficient to carry a mill, which goes from November to May, but no longer, as the mill pond would flow a large body of meadow. Thefe are called *Waufhacum Ponds*: They are very deep in fome places. Each pond, upon the moft exact computation, is about one mile, and a quarter in diameter. The eaftern is the largeft; but the weftern the moft pleafant, on feveral accounts; as it is not furrounded with hills like the eaftern; and as it has in it an ifland, containing about half an acre of land, where fifhing parties often repair to regale themfelves with fifh, which thefe ponds afford in plenty.

There are two or three things, not to be forgotten in giving the hiftory of Sterling: One is, that near the neck of land which divides Waufhacum Ponds, on the fouth fide, was formerly an Indian fort; and near this, there was a place where they buried their dead. The ruins of the fort, and the graves were very difcernible, until within a few years paft, when by ploughing the ground thofe veftiges of antiquity and barbarifm have difappeared. On this very fpot was the palace, and Royal feat of Sholan, Sachem of the Nafhaways, and proprietor of Nafhawogg.

Another thing to be mentioned is this; that about three miles northweft from the meetinghoufe, on the road leading to Weftminfter, is a place called *The Indian Fight*, in confequence of a moft bloody battle fought there between the Englifh and Indians, on Auguft 19th, 1707; the particulars of which we gave in the account of Lancafter, to which the reader is referred.

U 3 A

A third thing not to be omitted, and a moſt ſorrowful Providence indeed, is the burning of the houſe of Mr. Joſiah Wilder of this town in January 1740; in which conflagration his wife, (pregnant, and near the time for her delivery) with four ſmall children beſides, periſhed; another child, a ſon, the father plucked as a brand out of the burning, by cutting a hole through the ſide of the houſe, near where the bed was, in which this child lay, and pulled him out thereat, while the room was full of fire and ſmoke. This child was almoſt ſuffocated; but was ſoon recovered and lived many years.

The growth of wood in Sterling is moſt excellent, and of the following ſorts, oak of the ſeveral kinds, walnut, cheſnut, on the high lands; and the uſual ſorts in the low lands and ſwamps, as birch, maple, aſh, &c. The white pine timber is chiefly cut off, and there is not much pitch pine remaining, and at this day, but little of the yellow pine.

We proceed to give ſome account of the eccleſiaſtical ſtate of this town.

The church of Chriſt here, was imbodied on December 19th, 1744, and on the ſame day their firſt miniſter, the Rev. John Mellen, was ordained, who continued with them until December 14th, 1778, when his paſtoral relation to them, was diſſolved, by mutual agreement. Soon after, the Rev. Mr. Mellen was inſtalled paſtor of the church and people at Hanover, in the county of Plymouth, where he continues to great acceptance. To Mr. Mellen,

Mellen, succeeded in the sacred work of the ministry, the Rev. Reuben Holcomb, whereunto he was solemnly separated on the 2d of June, 1779, and who still continues their pastor.

In Sterling died Mr. Sebastian Smith, a native of old Spain, on the 24th of March, 1765, in an advanced age. He came young into this country and living a single life, he devoted his considerable estate to pious and charitable uses. Several years before his death he gave to the society, a folio Bible, that a portion of the holy scriptures might be read, on Lord's days, to the congregation. He gave much to the poor in his life time; and by will also: And likewise furnished the communion table, with two silver tankards; and gave one hundred pounds sterling as a fund for schooling the more indigent children and youth. As such deeds come up as a memorial before God, so they ought to be kept in remembrance among men.

Sterling is distant from Boston, about forty six miles, nearly west; and from the courthouse in Worcester, it is twelve miles a little to the northeast. At the time of taking the census in 1791, there were in the town 209 dwelling houses, and 1428 inhabitants.

BERLIN.

ON the 13th of April, 1778, an act passed the General Court, incorporating a second parish in the south part of Bolton. And on the 16th

16th of March, 1784, this precinct was erected into a diſtrict by the name of *Berlin,* at which time ſeveral families, with about five hundred acres of land, were added, from the northweſt corner of Marlborough, and annexed to the county of Worceſter. Since that time, a few families have been added to this diſtrict from the ſoutheaſt part of Lancaſter. This diſtrict is inveſted with all the immunities and privileges of a town, excepting only that of ſending a repreſentative to the General Court; but it has the liberty of joining with Bolton in the annual choice of repreſentatives. Here a church was imbodied, under the direction of an eccleſiaſtical council, by a covenant bearing date April 7th, 1779; and on September 26th, 1781, the Rev. Reuben Puffer was ordained to the paſtoral care thereof.

There is one pond in the eaſt part of the diſtrict, called *Gates's Pond,* nearly a mile in length, and from a quarter to half of a mile in width; it abounds in the uſual pond fiſh; and a good ſand is taken up near its ſhores: No brook empties into it, but at the ſouth end there is a ſmall outlet, which falls into the river *Aſſabet.* There is alſo a large ſwamp, containing many hundred acres, lying moſtly within this diſtrict: It is a low, ſunken tract of land, but bears, however, ſpruce of a great height, and in ſome parts of it, white pine timber. The moſt valuable uplands are ſeated on ſeveral hills, which afford excellent paſturage and orcharding. Wheat has been raiſed on ſome of them to great advantage. One lies near the above named

named pond, and contains a number of very fine farms. The others are a broken range of hills, which, beginning about a mile south of the meetinghouse, run westerly until they meet with Northborough hills, then stretching in a northern direction, cover, with a few interfections, all the west and north parts of the district, and thus they continue through Bolton and Harvard, to Littleton in the county of Middlesex. A few of the bluff points of these high lands have been distinguished with arbitrary names, but no name applies to the whole range. The culture of hops has lately been introduced here, and by the experiments already made, bids fair to prove a profitable branch of husbandry. On the farm of the Hon. Samuel Baker, Esq; in the northerly part of the district, is found a quarry of most valuable stone, of a light gray colour, out of which that gentleman has built a handsome, large mansion house. These stones are remarkable for an excellent quality which resisteth the effects of fire.

The principal stream, and the only one worthy of particular mention, is called *Northbrook*; it is formed of two small streams, from the southwest, and northwest which uniting about a mile and an half west of the meetinghouse, afford a convenient seat for saw and grist mills, where considerable business is performed. Taking thence a southeasterly direction, it runs upwards of two miles, through a large and rich interval, and after passing through the northeast corner of Northborough, where there are also mills, it soon falls into the river Assabet at the southeast

southeast angle of the district. Northbrook is from two to three rods in width, and of considerable depth; and formerly it yielded great quantities of the various sorts of fresh water fish, but they are of late exceedingly diminished.

The district consists of ninety two families, of which fourteen are of the sect called quakers. The latter are mostly industrious, and some of them wealthy farmers. The number of its inhabitants, by the late census, was 512. It lies thirty four miles from Boston, nearly west, and fifteen miles from the courthouse in Worcester, to the northeast. Berlin is bounded on the north, by Bolton; on the east, by Marlborough; on the south, by Northborough; and on the west, by Boylston and Lancaster.

GARDNER.

GARDNER is a town which was taken from the towns of Westminster, Templeton, Winchendon and Ashburnham, and is accordingly bounded by them, in the following manner; by Westminster, on the south and southeast; by Templeton, on the southwest and west; by Winchendon, on the north and northwest; and by Ashburnham on the northeast.

It was incorporated, and made a distinct town on the 27th of June, 1785. It is not large in extent,

tent, its contents being about 14000 acres, but yet capable of making a good and wealthy town ; having already 85 dwelling houses, and 530 inhabitants, according to the late census.

The church in Gardner was gathered on the 1st of February, 1786, and the Rev. Jonathan Osgood was ordained as pastor thereof, October 19th, 1791.

This town was called Gardner to perpetuate the name and memory of the late famous Col. Thomas Gardner of Cambridge, near Boston, who was killed in the memorable battle upon Bunker's Hill, in Charlestown, on the 17th of June 1775, gallantly fighting in defence of the liberty and rights of his country.

The general face of this town is uneven, abounding in small hills and valleys; and though the land be somewhat rocky, yet not in general, too much so.; the soil is good, rich, strong and fertile. It produces wheat, rye, Indian corn, barley, oats, flax, &c. &c. It is peculiarly adapted to grass and pasturage, being naturally moist and abounding in springs, rivulets, streams, brooks and rivers, whereby they can water the lands at pleasure.

There is one river, called *Otter River*,[*] running from the south to the north ; coming from Hubbardston, through a part of Templeton to Gardner, it is some way a boundary between Gardner and Templeton, and, in Winchendon, falls into Miller's River. There are several brooks and streams, without names, except two; these are called Pen Brook, and Spectacle Brook ; all the waters run northerly

[*] See this river more particularly described in the account of Templeton.

erly and northwesterly, and are finally emptied into Connecticut river. Upon these several streams, and the river beforenamed, there are considerable bodies of good meadow land; and a number of saw and grist mills; but no other water works at present. There are two large and fine ponds in the town, but without names; these have, each of them, small streams running from them. They have here the usual artificers and traders; and here also are potash works. The general growth of wood in this place, is similar to that of other new places of like kinds of lands, both high and low, as oak of several sorts, birch, rock maple, white and red ash, hemlock, white pine, and hacmatack. There are two county roads leading through the town; the principal one, is that which leads from Connecticut river, through Petersham, Gerry and Templeton, on to Boston. This town lies sixty miles from Boston, northwesterly; and twenty six miles from Worcester courthouse, to the north.

BOYLSTON.

THIS was included in the original grant of the township of Shrewsbury: It was made a parish, by act of the Legislature, December 17th, 1742, and was thenceforward called the second precinct,

BOYLSTON.

precinct, or north parish in Shrewsbury, until March 1st, 1786, when it was incorporated and made a distinct town, and had the name of Boylston given to it, in honour of the rich and generous family of Boylston, two of whom in succession, were great and eminent Physicians; another not long since, founded a professorship of rhetorick and oratory in Harvard University.

This town is not a very large tract of land; and it does not lie in the most regular form; it contains 14396 acres by survey, not being five miles square.

It is bounded by Shrewsbury on the south; by Worcester, on the southwest; by Holden and Sterling, on the west and northwest; by Lancaster on the north; and by Berlin and Northborough, on the east. It is situated almost west from Boston, at the distance of forty three miles; and from the courthouse in Worcester it is eight miles.

The church of Christ in this place was imbodied on the 6th day of October, 1743, and the Rev. Ebenezer Morse was invested with the pastoral office therein, on the 26th of the same month and year. He continued until the 10th of November, 1775, when he was dismissed, more especially on account of his political sentiments respecting the controversy between Greatbritain and America. The Rev. Mr. Morse, was from the first, a skilful and eminent physician, and is still employed in that business. Mr. Morse was succeeded, as pastor of the church and congregation in Boylston, by the Rev. Eleazer Fairbank, who was ordained on the 27th of March, 1777; and continued their
pastor

pastor until April 23d, 1793, when at his earnest desire and request, the church and congregation consented to his dismission, in the presence, and under the direction of a mutual council. Mr. Fairbank was installed pastor of the church and congregation of Wilmington in the State of Vermont, September 11th, 1793.

We shall now attempt some description of the town of Boylston.

It lies in general, high, descending to the north, and northeast; but the land is not so high in the middle, and round about the meetinghouse, as it is on the east, south and west. It is rather hilly, rough and uneven; although there are some considerable plains, covered with pitch pine. The hills on the east side, adjoining to Northborough, are large and high, and pretty steep where the road passes; and although there is considerable broken land in the town, yet none but what is good for, and well covered with wood, of which there is a plenty. The wood which grows on the high and hard land, is of all the sorts of oak, some walnut, plenty of chesnut, some sassafras; in the swamps and swales, grow some ash, birch, maple, spruce, juniper, some white pine and some hemlock. The prickly ash also, is a native of this place; it is a bush or shrub, seldom growing more than six or seven feet in height; though it grows in moist, yet not in cold land; it possesses some singular qualities and virtues, and its bark and seeds are highly esteemed, and much used, by Physicians.

The

The soil in this town is generally good, rich and fertile. There are good arable lands; but it is very excellent for orcharding, for pasturage and grass; and here are some of as large and good farmers, as perhaps any where in the county, who keep great stocks of cattle. The people raise all kinds of country produce, especially beef, pork, grain, butter and cheese, vastly more than they consume, and carry more into the market, than perhaps, any other town of its bigness and number. The town enjoys a fine healthy air, and the place has been famed for the longevity of its inhabitants. There are really no stagnant waters. There are two ponds, but the waters are kept in motion by a current, in consequence of inlets and outlets. Rocky Pond, so denominated from its general stony bottom, and more stony shore, is situated in the easterly part of the town from whence there is an outlet at the south end, into Cold Harbour Brook, and so into the river Assabet, in Northborough. This is a fine pond for all kinds of small fish, especially pickerel. It covers about thirty six acres of ground as appears from actual survey; and by the dam at the south end, the pond is raised so as to cover thirty acres of meadow. Sewall's Pond, so denominated from a family of that name, who owned the lands round it, lies in the southwest part of Boylston, towards Worcester. This is large, covering a hundred acres of land perhaps, or more. It is well supplied with all kinds of pond fish; there are two rivulets, from springs which run into it, from the north and northeast;

and

and at the south is the large outlet, which crossing the roads to Rutland and Worcester, in Shrewsbury, falls into Qüinsigamond, or Long Pond. There are three small brooks in the town, which originating from springs in Boylston, run northerly into the south branch of the river Nashaway. Gates's Brook empties into the river in the west part of the town, near to Major Beaman's. Muddy Brook empties in about a mile west of the meetinghouse. On this brook there is a saw mill, and a body of meadow. Mill Brook, on which there is also a saw mill, rises and falls into the river in the easterly part. The great south branch of the river Nashaway runs through Boylston from the northwest, and passing southeasterly, till it comes within about a mile of the meetinghouse, then turns and runs northeasterly, into Lancaster. This river is formed by the junction of two large streams or rivers. One comes from the east side of Watchusett mountain, and passing through the southerly part of Sterling, and called Still Water River, is, on the road at the bridge, the boundary between Sterling and Boylston, and running southeasterly about a mile in Boylston, is joined by Quinepoxet Stream, so called : This runs from a pond, called Quinepoxet on the south side of Princeton, partly in Holden, and running southeast in Holden about two miles, turns and runs northeast, until it joins Still Water, on the west side of Boylston. After the confluence of these streams, there are four large bridges, on the river within Boylston; two of them are good, handsome, strong and well constructed. On the west

MINISTERS, &c.

Towns.	Dates of Incorporation,	Ministers Settled, and Removed.		Number of Inhabitants.
Brookfield,	October 15, 1673.	Thomas Cheney, Settled,	October, 1717.	3100
		Died,	December 11, 1747.	
		Elisha Harding, Settled,	September 13, 1749.	
		Dismissed,	May 8, 1755.	
		Joseph Parsons, Settled,	November 23, 1757.	
		Died,	January 17, 1771.	
——Second parish,	March 29, 1750.	Ephraim Ward, Settled,	October 23, 1771.	
		Eli Forbes, Settled,	June 3, 1752.	
		Dismissed,	March 1, 1775.	
——Third parish,	November 8, 1754.	Joseph Appleton, Settled,	October 30, 1776.	1965
Charlton,	November 2, 1754.	Nathan Fiske, Settled,	May 24, 1758.	
		Caleb Curtis, Settled,	October 15, 1761.	
		Dismissed,	October 29, 1776.	
		Archibald Campbell, Settled,	January 8, 1783.	
		Dismissed,	April 9, 1793.	
Douglass,	1746.	William Phipps, Settled,	December 16, 1747.	1080
		Dismissed,	July 10, 1765.	
Dudley,	February 2, 1731.	Isaac Stone, Settled,	October 30, 1771.	1114
		Perley Howe, Settled,	1735.	
		Dismissed,	1743.	
		Charles Gleason, Settled,	October 31, 1744.	
		Died,	May 7, 1790.	
Fitchburg,	February 3, 1764.	Joshua Johnson, Settled,	December 1, 1790.	1151
Gardner,	June 27, 1785.	John Payson, Settled,	January 27, 1768.	530
Gerry,	October 20, 1786.	Jonathan Osgood, Settled,	October 19, 1791.	740
		Ebenezer Tucker, Settled,	November 5, 1788.	

MINISTERS, &c.

Towns.	Dates of Incorporation.	Ministers Settled, and Removed.		Number of Inhabitants.
Grafton,	April 18, 1735.	Solomon Prentice,	Settled, December 29, 1731.	880
			Dismissed, July 8, 1747.	
		Aaron Hutchinson,	Settled, June 6, 1750.	
			Dismissed, November 18, 1772.	
		Daniel Grosvenor,	Settled, October 19, 1774.	
			Dismissed, January 1, 1788.	
Hardwick,	January 10, 1738.	David White,	Settled, November 17, 1736.	1725
			Died, January 6, 1784.	
Harvard,	June 29, 1732.	Thomas Holt,	Settled, June 25, 1789.	1400
		John Seccombe,	Settled, October 10, 1733.	
			Dismissed, September 7, 1757.	
		Joseph Wheeler,	Settled, December 12, 1759.	
			Dismissed, July 28, 1768.	
		Daniel Johnson,	Settled, November 1, 1769.	
			Died, September 23, 1777.	
		Ebenezer Grosvenor,	Settled, June 19, 1782.	
			Died, May 28, 1788.	
Holden,	January 9, 1740.	William Emerson,	Settled, May 23, 1792.	1080
		Joseph Davis,	Settled, December 22, 1742.	
			Dismissed, October 18, 1772.	
		Joseph Avery,	Settled, December 21, 1774.	
Hubbardston,	June 13, 1767.	Nehemiah Parker,	Settled, June 13, 1770.	1000
Lancaster,	May 18, 1653.	Joseph Rowlandson,	Settled, 1658.	1460
			Removed, 1676.	
		John Whiting,	Settled, probably, 1691.	
			Killed by Indians, September 11, 1697.	

MINISTERS, &c.

Towns.	Dates of Incorporation.	Ministers Settled, and Removed.		Number of Inhabitants.
Lancaster,		John Prentice, Settled,	March 29, 1708.	
		Died,	January 6, 1748.	
		Timothy Harrington, Settled,	November 16, 1748.	1100
		Nathaniel Thayer, Settled,	October 9, 1793.	
Leicester,	1720, or 1721.	David Parsons, Settled,	1721.	
		Dismissed.		
		David Goddard Settled,	June 30, 1736.	
		Died,	January 19, 1754.	
		Joseph Roberts, Settled,	October 23, 1754.	
		Dismissed,	1762.	
		Benjamin Conklin, Settled,	November 23, 1763.	
Leominster,	June 23, 1740.	John Rogers, Settled,	September 14, 1743.	1190
		Dismissed,	1757.	
		Francis Gardner, Settled,	December 22, 1762.	
—Second parish,	About 1760.	John Rogers,		
Second parish dissol.		Died,	October, 1789.	
Lunenburg,	August 1, 1728.	Andrew Gardner, Settled,	May 15, 1728.	1300
		Dismissed,	February 22, 1732.	
		David Stearns, Settled,	April 18, 1733.	
		Died,	March 9, 1761.	
		Samuel Payson, Settled,	September 8, 1762.	
		Died,	February 14, 1763.	
		Zabdiel Adams, Settled,	September 5, 1764.	
Mendon,	May 15, 1667.	Joseph Emerson, Settled, probably,	1667.	1555
		Removed,	1675.	

MINISTERS, &c.

Towns.	Dates of Incorporation.	Ministers Settled, and Removed.	Number of Inhabitants.
Mendon,		Grindall Rawson, Settled, probably, 1680. Died, February 6, 1715. Joseph Dorr, Settled, 1716. Died, March 9, 1768. Joseph Willard, Settled, April 19, 1769. Dismissed, December 4, 1782. Caleb Alexander, Settled, April 12, 1786. Benjamin Balch, Settled, 1766. Removed, 1768.	
———Second parish,			
Milford, called 2d parish of Mendon,	April 11, 1780.	Amariah Frost, Settled, March 27, 1772. Died, December 21, 1743.	840
Newbraintree,	January 31, 1751.	Benjamin Ruggles, Settled, March 14, 1792. April 18, 1754. Died, May 12, 1782.	940
Northborough, or Second parish of Westborough,	February 24, 1766.	Daniel Foster, Settled, October 29, 1778. John Martyn, Settled, May 21, 1746. Died, April 30, 1767.	620
Northbridge,	October 20, 1744.	Peter Whitney, Settled, November 4, 1767.	570
Oakham,	July 14, 1772. June 7, 1762.	John Crane, Settled, June 25, 1783. John Strickland, Settled, April 1, 1768. Dismissed, June 2, 1773. Daniel Tomlinson, Settled, March 11, 1786.	772
Oxford,	May 16, 1683.	John Campbell, Settled, March 11, 1721. Died, May 25, 1761. Joseph Bowman, Settled, November 14, 1764. Dismissed, August 28, 1782. Elias Dudley, Settled, April 13, 1791.	1000

MINISTERS, &c. 333

Towns.	Dates of Incorporation.	Ministers Settled, and Removed,		Number of Inhabitants.
Paxton,	February 24, 1765.	Silas Biglow,	Settled, October 21, 1767.	558
			Died, November 16, 1769.	
		Alexander Thayer,	Settled, November 28, 1770.	
			Dismissed, August 14, 1782.	
Petersham,	April 20, 1754.	John Foster,	Settled, September 8, 1785.	1520
			Dismissed, April, 1789.	
		Aaron Whitney,	Settled, December, 1738.	
			Died, September 8, 1779.	
Princeton,	October 20, 1759.	Solomon Reed,	Settled, October 25, 1780.	1016
		Timothy Fuller,	Settled, September 9, 1767.	
			Dismissed, April 19, 1776.	
		Thomas Crafts,	Settled, June 28, 1786.	
			Dismissed, March 14, 1791.	
Royalston,	February 16, 1765.	Joseph Lee,	Settled, October 19, 1768.	1130
Rutland,	June or July, 1722.	Thomas Frink,	Settled, November 1, 1727.	1072
			Dismissed, September 8, 1740.	
		Joseph Buckminster,	Settled, September 15, 1742.	
			Died, November 3, 1792.	
Shrewsbury,	December 19, 1727.	Hezekiah Goodrich,	Settled, June 19, 1793.	963
		Job Cushing,	Settled, December 4, 1723.	
			Died, August 6, 1760.	
Southborough,	July 6, 1727.	Joseph Sumner,	Settled, June 25, 1762.	840
		Nathan Stone,	Settled, October 24, 1730.	
			Died, May 31, 1781.	
		Samuel Sumner,	Settled, June 1, 1791.	

MINISTERS, &c.

Towns.	Dates of Incorporation.	Ministers Settled, and Removed.	Number of Inhabitants.
Spencer, or Second parish of Leicester,	April 3, 1753.	Joshua Eaton, Settled, November 7, 1744. Died, April 2, 1772.	1322
Sterling, or Second parish of Lancaster,	In 1744. April 25, 1781.	Joseph Pope, Settled, October 20, 1773. John Mellen, Settled, December 19, 1744. Dismissed, December 14, 1778.	1428
Sturbridge,	1743. June 24, 1738.	Reuben Holcomb, Settled, June 2, 1779. Caleb Rice, Settled, September 29, 1736. Died, September 2, 1759.	1800
Sutton,	1718.	Joshua Paine, Settled, June 17, 1761. John MacKinstry, Settled, November 9, 1720. Dismissed, September 2, 1728.	2642
———Second parish,	October 28, 1743.	David Hall, Settled, October 15, 1729. Died, May 8, 1789. Edmund Mills, Settled, June 23, 1790. James Welman, Settled, October 7, 1747. Dismissed, July 22, 1760.	
Templeton,	March 6, 1762.	Ebenezer Chaplain, Settled, November 14, 1764. Daniel Pond, Settled, December 10, 1755. Dismissed, August 2, 1759.	950
Upton,	June 14, 1735.	Ebenezer Sparhawk, Settled, November 18, 1761. Thomas Weld, Settled, Dismissed,	900
Uxbridge,	June 27, 1727.	Elisha Fish, Settled, June 5, 1751. Nathan Webb, Settled, February 8, 1731. Died, March 14, 1772.	1310

MINISTERS, &c.

Towns.	Dates of Incorporation.	Ministers Settled, and Removed.	Number of Inhabitants.
Uxbridge,		Hezekiah Chapman, Settled, January 27, 1774.	
		Dismissed, April 5, 1781.	
		Josiah Spalding, Settled, September 11, 1783.	
		Dismissed, October 23, 1787.	
		Samuel Judson, Settled, October 17, 1792.	
Ward,	April 10, 1778.	Isaac Bailey, Settled, November 3, 1784.	473
Westborough,	November 18, 1717.	Ebenezer Parkman, Settled, October 28, 1724.	934
		Died, December 9, 1782.	
		John Robinson, Settled, January 14, 1789.	
Western,	January, 16, 1741.	Isaac Jones, Settled, January 31, 1744.	900
		Died, July, 1784.	
		Stephen Baxter, Settled, March 9, 1791.	
Westminster,	October 20, 1759.	Elisha Marsh, Settled, October 20, 1742.	1176
		Dismissed, 1757.	
		Asaph Rice, Settled, October, 1765.	
Winchendon,	June 14, 1764.	Daniel Stimpson, Settled, December 15, 1762.	950
		Died, July 20, 1768.	
		Joseph Brown, Settled, May 24, 1769.	
Worcester,	October 15, 1684.	Andrew Gardner, Settled, in Autumn, 1719.	2100
		Dismissed, October, 1722.	
		Isaac Burr, Settled, October 25, 1725.	
		Dismissed, November, 1744.	
		Thaddeus Maccarty, Settled, June 10, 1747.	
		Died, July 20, 1784.	
		Samuel Austin, Settled, September 29, 1790.	
——Second parish,	November 13, 1787.	Aaron Bancroft, Settled, February 1, 1786.	

VALUATION LISTS.

The history of the County shall be closed with presenting the five last Valuations, whereby the reader may behold each town in a comparative view. The towns are arranged according to the proportion they paid to a tax of a thousand pounds upon the whole State.

VALUATION for 1772.

Towns.	On the thouf. £. s. d. q.	Towns.	On the thouf. £. s. d. q.
Lancaster,	7 19 2 1	Western,	2 13 8 3
Brookfield,	7 13 1 3	Newbraintree,	2 10 9 1
Sutton,	7 12 1 3	Dudley,	2 9 8 3
Worcester,	6 7 8 3	Westminster,	2 9 1 0
Mendon,	5 18 1 3	Spencer,	2 8 10 1
Shrewsbury,	5 7 10 1	Holden,	2 0 7 0
Hardwick,	4 5 1 1	Northborough,	1 19 3 0
Lunenburg,	3 18 9 3	Templeton,	1 18 9 0
Harvard,	3 17 4 1	Princeton,	1 16 4 0
Uxbridge,	3 16 6 3	Douglass,	1 13 5 3
Bolton,	3 14 2 0	Paxton,	1 12 2 3
Rutland,	3 13 7 3	Athol,	1 11 8 1
Sturbridge,	3 9 4 3	Upton,	1 10 5 0
Barre,	3 4 7 3	Fitchburg,	1 6 10 3
Leominster,	2 18 3 0	Oakham,	1 2 3 0
Westborough,	2 18 1 1	Ashburnham,	0 17 5 1
Petersham,	2 17 9 1	Winchendon,	0 14 4 1
Grafton,	2 17 3 0	Hubbardston,	0 12 9 3
Southborough,	2 16 11 0	Royalston,	0 12 4 3
Leicester,	2 16 2 1		
Charlton,	2 15 6 3	41 Towns. Total fum. £.125 14 2 1	
Oxford,	2 15 2 1		

VALUATION

VALUATION LISTS.

VALUATION for 1778.

Towns.	On the thouf. £ s. d.	Towns.	On the thouf. £ s. d.
Brookfield,	7 15 0	Templeton,	2 13 6
Lancaster,	7 8 4	Western,	2 11 0
Worcester,	7 7 0	Oxford,	2 8 0
Sutton,	7 6 0	Dudley,	2 8 0
Mendon,	5 17 0	Athol,	2 3 0
Shrewsbury,	5 5 0	Princeton,	2 1 0
Barre,	4 3 0	Holden,	2 0 0
Hardwick,	4 0 0	Fitchburg,	2 0 0
Harvard,	3 14 6	Paxton,	2 0 0
Charlton,	3 13 6	Leicester,	1 18 0
Bolton,	3 10 6	Northborough,	1 17 0
Lunenburg,	3 10 0	Royalston,	1 16 1
Rutland,	3 9 0	Upton,	1 11 0
Sturbridge,	3 9 0	Douglass,	1 10 6
Uxbridge,	3 6 6	Winchendon,	1 9 0
Petersham,	3 2 0	Oakham,	1 8 6
Leominster,	3 0 0	Hubbardston,	1 8 6
Spencer,	3 0 0	Ashburnham,	1 6 0
Westborough,	2 16 7	Ward,	1 3 5
Grafton,	2 15 3	Northbridge,	1 0 0
Newbraintree,	2 15 0		
Southborough,	2 14 0	43 Towns. Total Sum.	£133 13 2
Westminster,	2 13 6		

VALUATION for 1782.

Towns.	On the thouf. £ s. d.	Towns.	On the thouf. £ s. d.
Brookfield,	8 5 0	Westminster,	3 4 6
Sutton,	7 19 0	Templeton,	3 0 0
Shrewsbury,	6 5 6	Westborough,	2 19 9
Worcester,	5 13 10	Leicester,	2 17 0
Hardwick,	4 19 0	Leominster,	2 17 0
Barre,	4 18 1	Western,	2 15 0
Petersham,	4 1 10	Princeton,	2 15 0
Sturbridge,	4 0 0	Southborough,	2 14 0
Lancaster,	3 17 11	Athol,	2 13 4
Sterling,	3 17 9	Dudley,	2 13 0
Charlton,	3 16 4	Milford,	2 13 0
Harvard,	3 15 1	Holden,	2 12 4
Rutland,	3 14 6	Oxford,	2 12 3
Bolton,	3 14 2	Grafton,	2 10 5
Spencer,	3 13 10	Fitchburg,	2 7 5
Mendon,	3 12 6	Newbraintree,	2 6 5
Uxbridge,	3 7 5	Upton,	2 6 0
Lunenburg,	3 6 0	Douglass,	2 1 0
		Northborough,	

VALUATION LISTS.

Towns.	On the thouſ. £ s. d.	Towns.	On the thouſ. £ s. d.
Northborough,	2 0 0	Aſhburnham,	1 10 0
Paxton,	1 18 7	Oakham,	1 8 0
Hubbardſton,	1 16 0	Northbridge,	1 8 0
Ward,	1 16 0		
Royalſton,	1 15 5	45 Towns. Total Sum.	£146 4 9
Winchendon,	1 12 6		

VALUATION for 1786.

Towns.	On the thouſ. £ s. d. q.	Towns.	On the thouſ. £ s. d. q.
Brookfield,	7 17 5 1	Weſtern,	2 9 2 0
Sutton,	7 2 9 0	Bolton,	2 8 5 3
Worceſter,	5 15 6 0	Milford,	2 8 5 0
Shrewſbury,	5 14 9 0	Holden,	2 8 0 0
Barre,	4 13 8 3	Dudley,	2 7 10 0
Hardwick,	4 7 7 0	Southborough,	2 5 2 0
Sterling,	3 16 8 3	Oxford,	2 4 11 0
Charlton,	3 15 5 0	Newbraintree,	2 4 7 0
Peterſham,	3 14 3 0	Fitchburg,	2 4 5 1
Lancaſter,	3 13 3 0	Athol,	2 2 8 0
Sturbridge,	3 12 11 0	Winchendon,	2 1 0 0
Rutland,	3 11 9 0	Upton,	2 0 6 1
Mendon,	3 11 8 0	Douglaſs,	1 19 0 0
Spencer,	3 8 2 0	Northborough,	1 15 9 0
Lunenburg,	3 6 4 1	Royalſton,	1 15 0 0
Harvard,	3 6 1 3	Paxton,	1 14 11 0
Uxbridge,	3 5 6 0	Hubbardſton,	1 14 3 1
Weſtminſter,	3 4 0 0	Aſhburnham,	1 13 1 0
Leiceſter,	2 19 10 0	Oakham,	1 13 0 0
Templeton,	2 18 3 0	Ward,	1 8 1 0
Weſtborough,	2 13 11 1	Berlin,	1 5 2 3
Leominſter,	2 12 9 2	Northbridge,	1 2 0 0
Grafton,	2 12 6 0		
Princeton,	2 11 6 0	46 Towns. Total Sum.	£138 0 0 2

VALUATION for 1793.

Towns.	Polls.	On the tho. £ s. d. q.	Towns.	Polls.	On the tho. £ s. d. q.
Brookfield,	675	6 13 4 3	Lancaſter,	356	3 3 5 0
Worceſter,	540	6 8 3 2	Rutland,	298	3 2 3 1
Sutton,	660	5 18 6 3	Mendon,	318	3 2 2 0
Barre,	466	4 9 7 1	Harvard,	359	3 1 9 3
Peterſham,	390	3 16 0 0	Spencer,	349	3 1 7 1
Sturbridge,	454	3 15 10 2	Uxbridge,	306	3 0 2 0
Charlton,	385	3 13 4 3	Weſtminſter,	318	2 14 8 1
Hardwick,	399	3 9 3 3	Leiceſter,	262	2 11 11 1
Sterling,	364	3 6 6 1	Shrewſbury,	252	2 11 10 3
Princeton,	245	3 4 1 3	Lunenburg,	273	2 10 10 0
			Leominſter,		

VALUATION LISTS.

Towns.	Polls.	On the tho. £. s. d. q.	Towns.	Polls.	On the tho. £. s. d. q.
Leominster,	313	2 10 10 1	Southborough,	184	1 16 7 0
Westborough,	225	2 9 2 0	Douglass,	248	1 15 9 0
Grafton,	237	2 8 3 3	Athol,	206	1 14 7 0
Holden,	254	2 7 8 2	Upton,	211	1 13 9 2
Boylston,	219	2 4 5 3	Northborough,	156	1 12 6 2
Western,	229	2 4 2 3	Gerry,	177	1 12 5 3
Newbraintree,	129	2 4 0 2	Paxton,	133	1 9 2 2
Templeton,	241	2 3 5 2	Ashburnham,	226	1 9 0 0
Bolton,	220	2 1 4 1	Oakham,	204	1 8 5 3
Dudley,	248	2 0 5 0	Ward,	119	1 6 8 0
Fitchburg,	268	2 0 2 1	Gardner,	135	1 2 8 0
Winchendon,	234	1 19 11 2	Berlin,	127	1 2 6 3
Oxford,	265	1 19 11 1	Northbridge,	113	0 18 5 0
Milford,	180	1 17 11 1			
Hubbardston,	219	1 17 4 0	49 Towns.	13762	£127 5 0 2
Royalston,	263	1 16 9 0			

www.ingramcontent.com/pod-product-compliance
Lightning Source LLC
Chambersburg PA
CBHW030738230426
43667CB00007B/755